Help Me!

Guide to the Samsung Galaxy Note 3

By Charles Hughes

Table of Contents

Getting Started

Table of Contents

1. Button Layout

The Galaxy Note 3 has three hard buttons and two soft buttons, a microUSB port, and a headphone jack, which perform the following functions:

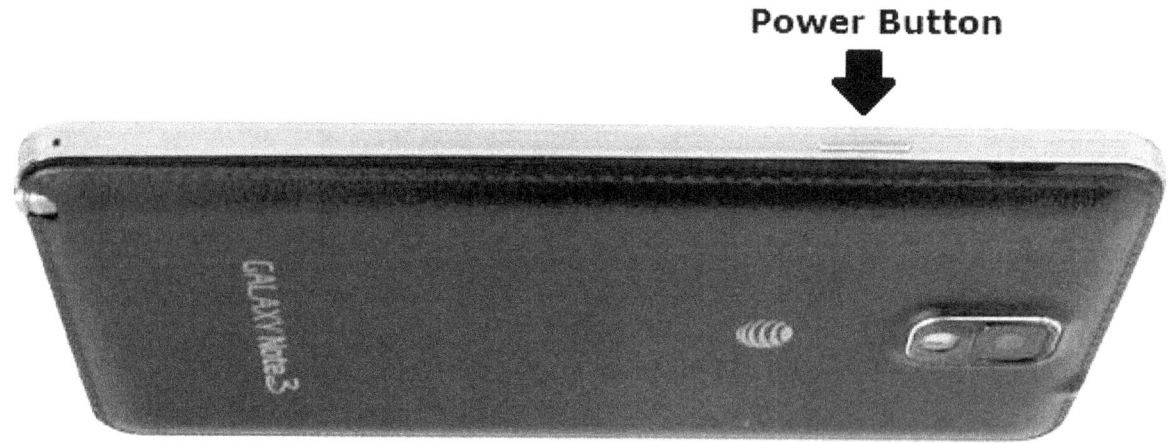

Figure 1: Right Side View

Power Button - Turns the phone on and off. Locks and unlocks the phone.

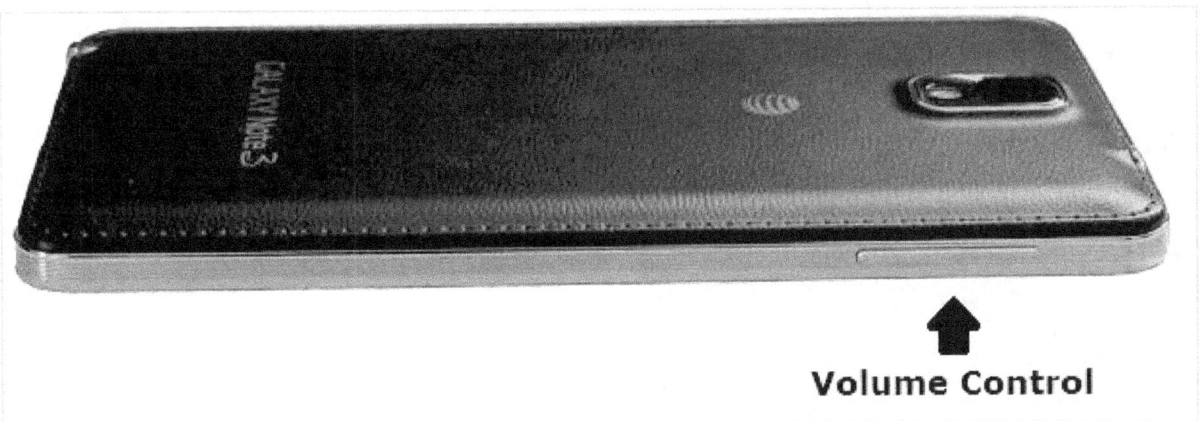

Volume Control

Figure 2: Left Side View

Volume Control - Controls the volume of the ear piece, speaker phone, and music. The soft keys only appear when the screen is turned on. Touch each button to perform the corresponding action:

Figure 3: Front View

Back Key - Returns the phone to the previous screen or menu.

Menu Key - Opens a context menu, which gives you a list of options or settings based on the application that you are currently using.

Home Button (not a soft key) - Returns the phone to the Home screen.

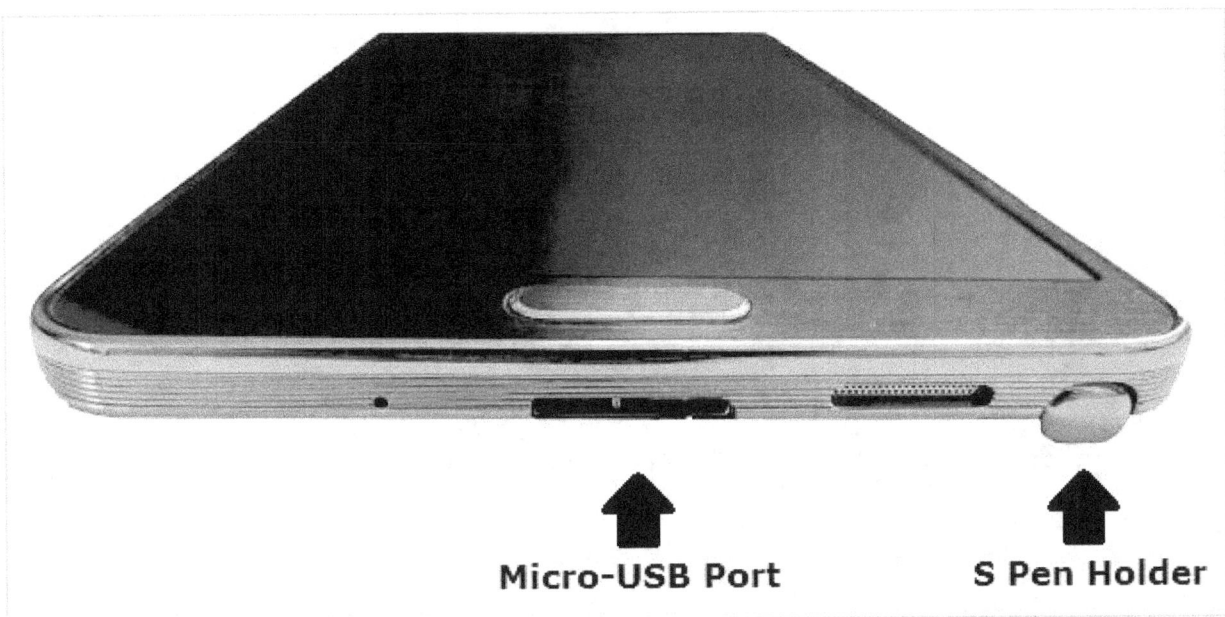

Figure 4: Bottom View

MicroUSB Port - Connects the phone to a computer in order to transfer data. Although your Note 3 comes with a MicroUSB 3.0 cable, you may also use an older microUSB 2.0 cable by plugging it into the right side of port.

S Pen Holder - Holds the S Pen while you are not using it.

Figure 5: Top View

Headphone Jack - Allows headphones or an AUX cable to be plugged in to the phone.

2. Charging the Galaxy Note 3

In order to charge the Galaxy Note 3, plug it in using the included charging adapter. While the phone is charging, "Charging" appears on the Lock screen below the date, as shown in **Figure 6**. When the phone is fully charged, "Charged" appears on the Lock screen below the date. In order to get the most out of your battery, it is recommended to discharge it below 20%, and then charge it back to 100% at least once a month.

Figure 6: Charging Screen

3. Turning the Galaxy Note 3 On and Off / Restarting the Phone

To turn the Galaxy Note 3 on, press and hold the **Power** button for three seconds. "Samsung Galaxy Note 3" appears and the phone starts up.

To turn the phone off, press and hold the **Power** button until the Device Options menu appears, as shown in **Figure 7**. Touch **Power off**. A confirmation dialog appears. Touch **OK**. The Galaxy Note 3 shuts down. You can also touch **Restart** in the Device Options menu to restart the Galaxy Note 3.

Figure 7: Device Options Menu

4. Navigating the Screens

There are many ways to navigate the screens of the Galaxy Note 3. Use the following tips:
- Press the **Home** button to return to the Home screen at any time. The last viewed Home screen will appear. Press the **Home** button again to view the main Home screen. Any application or tool that is currently in use will be in the same state when it is re-opened.
- Press and hold the **Home** button to view a list of all open applications. Touch an application to open it.
- Slide your finger to the left or right to access additional Home screens from your main Home screen.

- Touch the ⬑ key at any time to return to the previous screen, menu, or application. Once you are at the main Home screen, the ⬑ button has no function.
- Touch the top of the screen and move your finger down to view all notifications.

5. Types of Home Screen Objects

Each Home screen on the Galaxy Note 3 is fully customizable. Refer to *"Organizing Home Screen Objects"* on page 17 to learn how to customize the Home screens. Each screen can hold one or more of the following items:

- **Widget** - A tool that can be used directly from the Home screen without having to open it first like an application. Widgets usually take up the whole screen or a fraction of it, while applications are added as icons. The Calendar widget is shown in **Figure 8**.

- **Application** - A program that opens in a new window, such as a game. Applications are added to the Home screen as icons.

- **Folder** - A folder containing application icons. Please note that a folder cannot store widgets. Refer to *"Organizing Application Icons into Folders"* on page 209 to learn more.

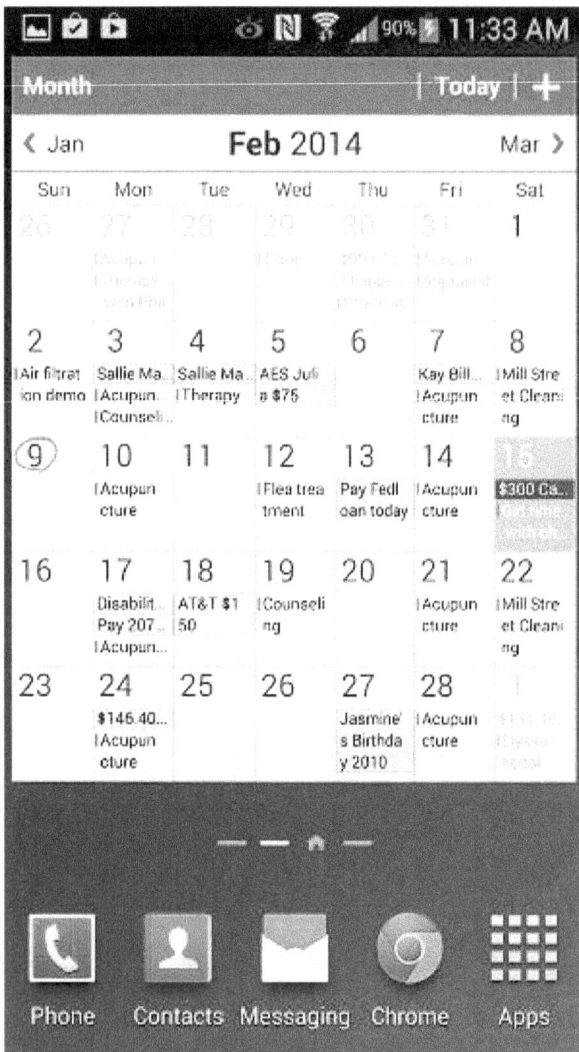

Figure 8: Calendar Widget

6. Organizing Home Screen Objects

Customize a Home screen by adding, deleting, or moving around application icons and widgets. The Galaxy Note 3 allows you to customize seven Home screens. Refer to *"Types of Home Screen Objects"* on page 15 to learn more about them.

To add an application icon or widget to a Home screen:

1. Touch the ▦ icon in the lower right-hand corner of the Home screen. The Apps screen appears, as shown in **Figure 9**.
2. Touch the screen and move your finger to the left or right to browse the applications and widgets that are installed on your phone. The applications and widgets appear.
3. Touch and hold an application or widget icon. The Home screen appears, as shown in **Figure 10**. Do not release the screen.
4. Drag the icon to the desired location. If there is no room on the current screen, drag the icon to the left or right edge of the screen or on top of a Home screen thumbnail. The adjacent Home screen appears.
5. Release the screen. The application or widget icon is placed.

To delete an application or widget icon from a Home screen:

1. Touch and hold an application icon or widget. The phone briefly vibrates and "Remove" appears at the top of the screen, as shown in **Figure 11**. Do not release the screen.
2. Drag the icon over 'Remove'. The object turns red.
3. Release the screen. The application icon or widget is deleted from the Home screen.

Note: To move an object to another location on the Home screen, touch and hold the object until the phone briefly vibrates and "Remove" appears at the top of the screen. Move the object to the desired location and release the screen. The object is placed in the new location. You cannot place an object on a page that is full or on top of another object, unless it is a folder.

Figure 9: Application Screen

Figure 10: Home Screen (while adding objects)

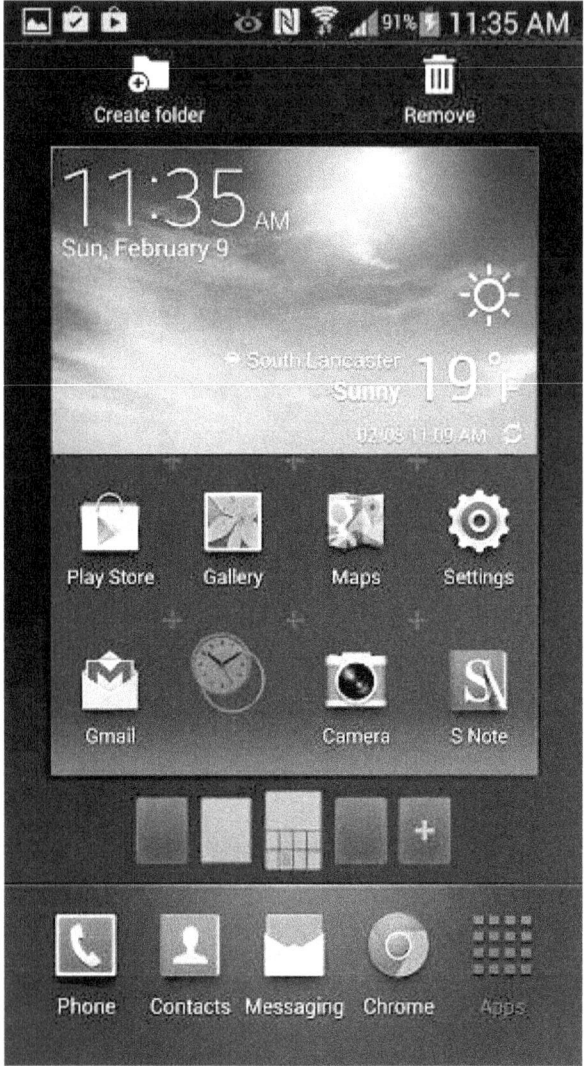

Figure 11: Home Screen (while moving or deleting objects)

7. Transferring Files to the Galaxy Note 3 Using a PC or Mac

Media files that you have obtained elsewhere can be imported to the Galaxy Note 3. To import media:

1. Connect the Galaxy Note 3 to your PC or Mac using the provided USB cable. "Connected as a media device" appears in the status bar of the phone. The PC automatically recognizes the Galaxy Note 3, but the Mac needs an additional application in order to transfer files to the phone. If you are using a Mac, download the Android File Transfer application at **www.android.com/filetransfer/** before proceeding.
2. Open **My Computer** (or **Computer** on Windows Vista or later) on a PC, and double-click the 'Galaxy Note 3' portable device. On a Mac, open the Android File Transfer program. The Galaxy Note 3 folder opens.
3. Double-click the **Phone** folder or **Card** folder (if using a microSD card), if you are using a PC. The Galaxy Note 3 Folders appear on a PC, as shown in **Figure 12**, or on a Mac, as shown in **Figure 13**.
4. Double-click a folder. The folder opens.
5. Drag and drop a file into the open folder. The file is copied and will appear in the corresponding library.

Note: When copying eBooks to the Galaxy Note 3, drag and drop the files into the corresponding folder. For instance, eBooks you wish to read using the Kindle Reader for Android should be copied to the 'kindle' folder.

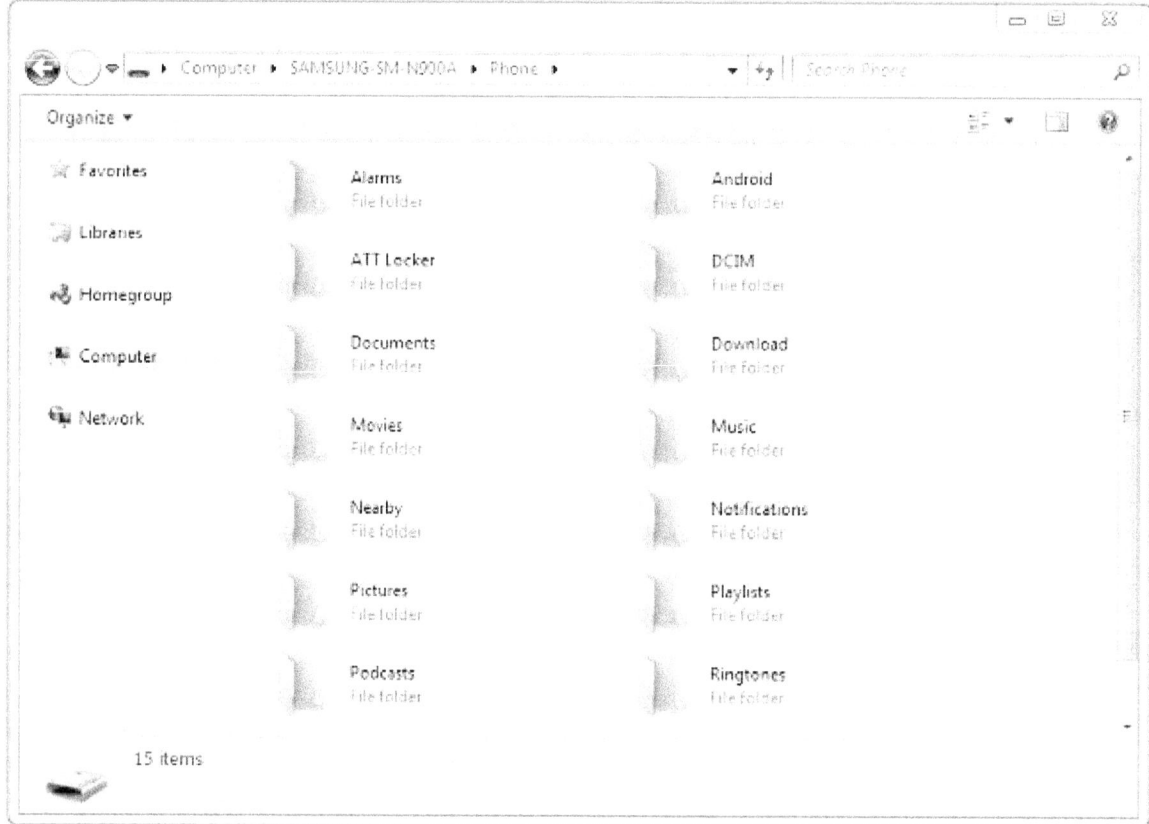

Figure 12 : Galaxy Note 3 Folders on a PC

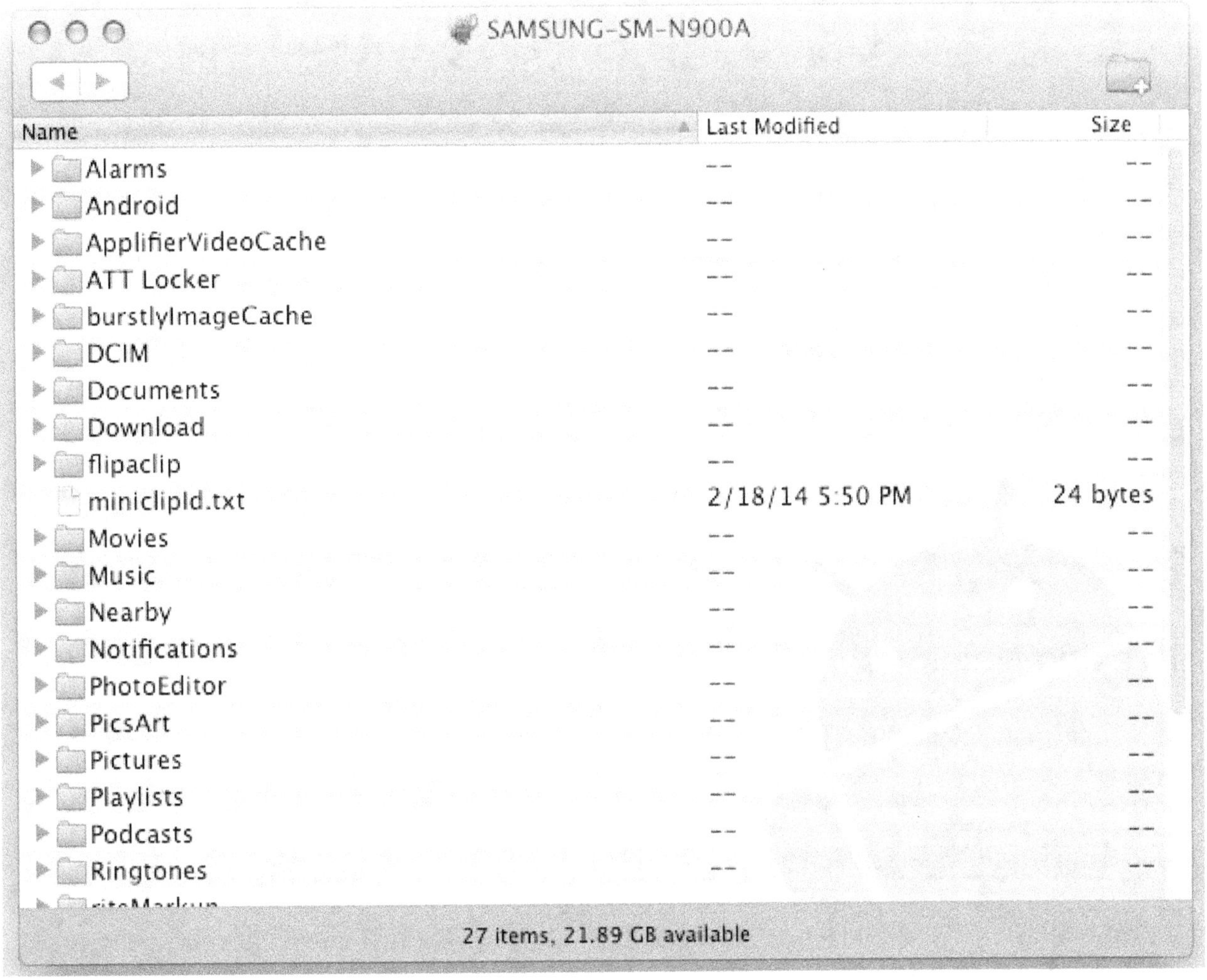

Name	Last Modified	Size
▶ Alarms	--	--
▶ Android	--	--
▶ ApplifierVideoCache	--	--
▶ ATT Locker	--	--
▶ burstlyImageCache	--	--
▶ DCIM	--	--
▶ Documents	--	--
▶ Download	--	--
▶ flipaclip	--	--
miniclipId.txt	2/18/14 5:50 PM	24 bytes
▶ Movies	--	--
▶ Music	--	--
▶ Nearby	--	--
▶ Notifications	--	--
▶ PhotoEditor	--	--
▶ PicsArt	--	--
▶ Pictures	--	--
▶ Playlists	--	--
▶ Podcasts	--	--
▶ Ringtones	--	--

SAMSUNG-SM-N900A

27 items, 21.89 GB available

Figure 13: Galaxy Note 3 Folders on a Mac

Using the S Pen Stylus

Table of Contents

1. Taking Notes Using S Note

The S Note application allows you to write memos on your Note 3. To create a new note using S Note:

1. Touch the [icon] icon. The Application Screen appears, as shown in **Figure 1**.

2. Scroll over to the right, and then touch the [icon] icon. The S Note application opens, as shown in **Figure 2**.

3. Take out the S Pen, and touch the [icon] icon. A new S Note is created, as shown in **Figure 3**.

4. Write a note, using the tools at the top of the screen to help you, as follows. Touch the ✓ icon to save the note.

[icon] - Allows you to enter typed text instead of writing with the S Pen. Touch the [icon] icon again while typing text to edit the text settings, such as the font size, style, and color. Touch anywhere outside of the typed text box to resume writing with the S Pen.

[icon] - Allows you to erase any text that was written using the S Pen. You cannot erase typed text with this tool.

[icon] - Allows you to select something that you have written or drawn, and turn it into a shape, typed text, or an algebraic formula. You may also cut, copy, or delete typed text using this tool.

[icon] - Allows you to undo the previous action.

- Allows you to redo the action that you have just undone.

- Hides the text tools.

Figure 1: Application Screen

Figure 2: S Note Application Opens

Figure 3: New S Note Screen

2. Jotting Down a Quick Note

You may jot down a note if you are in a hurry using the Action Memo feature of the S Pen. To jot down a quick note without opening S Note first:

1. Take out the S Pen. The Air Command menu appears in the lower right-hand corner of the screen, as shown in **Figure 4**.

2. Touch the ![icon] icon. A new action memo appears, as shown in **Figure 5**.

3. Write your note, and then touch the ✓ icon. The action memo is saved. To view all saved Action Memos, touch the ▦ icon, and then touch the 〰 icon.

Figure 4: Air Command Menu

Figure 5: New Action Memo

3. Using Scrapbooker

While reading a news story or watching a video online, you may capture the media and put it in a scrapbook. You can then refer to it later to read the story or watch the video. To use the Scrapbooker:

1. Take out the S Pen. The Air Command menu appears in the lower right-hand corner of the screen.

2. Touch the ![icon] icon. The ![icon] icon appears on the screen when you hold the S Pen close to the screen.
3. Circle the clipping that you would like to save. The New Clipping window appears, as shown in **Figure 6**.
4. Touch the ✓ icon. The clipping is saved in your scrapbook. To view your scrapbook, touch the ![icon] icon, and then touch the ![icon] icon.

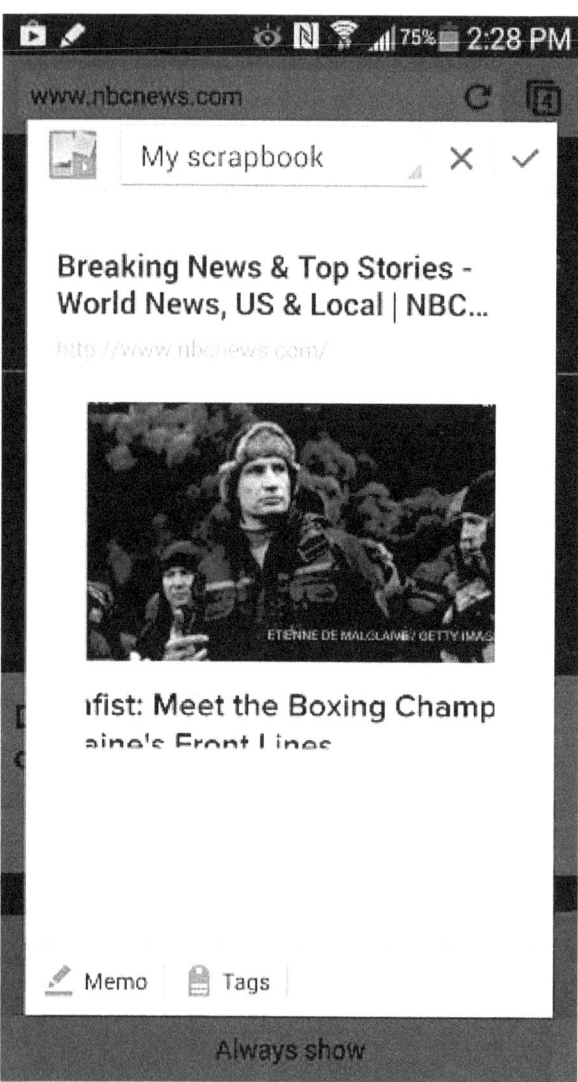

Figure 6: New Clipping Window

4. Marking Up a Screenshot

Sometimes it may be convenient to mark up a screenshot, such as marking a location on a map. To mark up a screenshot:

1. Take out the S Pen. The Air Command menu appears in the lower right-hand corner of the screen.
2. Navigate to the screen that you would like to capture.
3. Touch the ⬜ icon. A screenshot is captured and the Screenshot Markup window appears, as shown in **Figure 7**.
4. Use the S Pen to mark up the screenshot, and touch the ✓ icon in the upper right-hand corner of the screen. The marked up screenshot is saved in the 'Screenshots' album in the gallery.

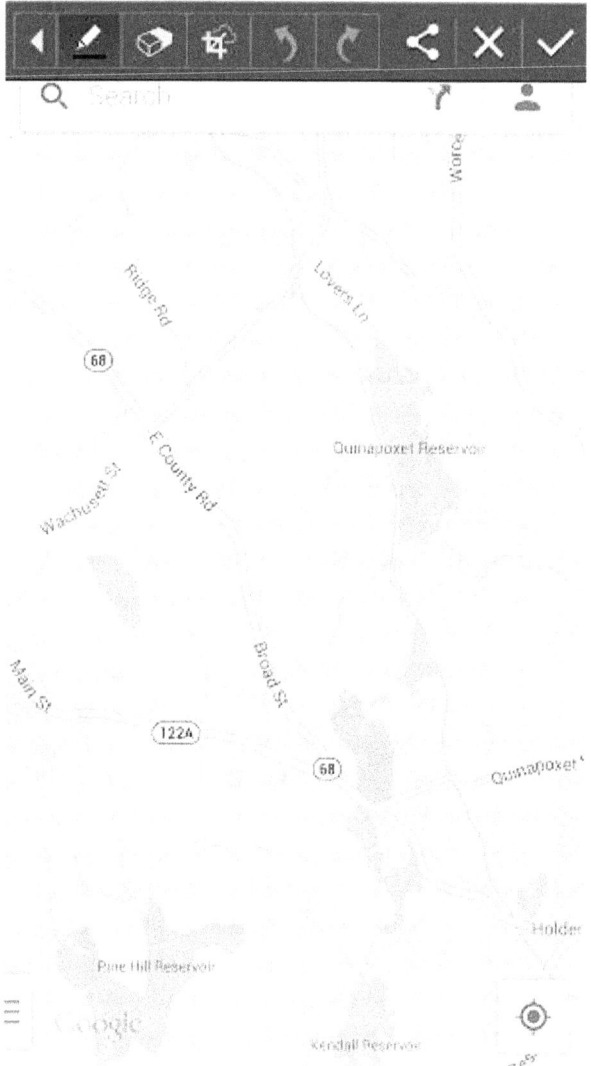

Figure 7: Screenshot Markup Window

5. Using S Finder to Search Your Note 3 and the Web

If you are ever looking for something on your phone, but don't quite remember where you saw it, try using the S Finder. If it's not on your phone, it might be something that you saw online. To use the S Finder:

1. Take out the S Pen. The Air Command menu appears in the lower right-hand corner of the screen.

2. Touch the 🔍 icon. The S Finder screen appears, as shown in **Figure 8**.

3. Hover the S Pen over 'Search' at the top of the screen, and then touch the  icon. The writing window appears, as shown in **Figure 9**.
4. Write the search terms, entering one word at a time. The S Finder recognizes your handwriting and converts your written text into typed text.

5. Touch the icon. The S Finder searches your phone and the web. Touch a result in the list to open it or navigate to it.

Figure 8: S Finder Screen

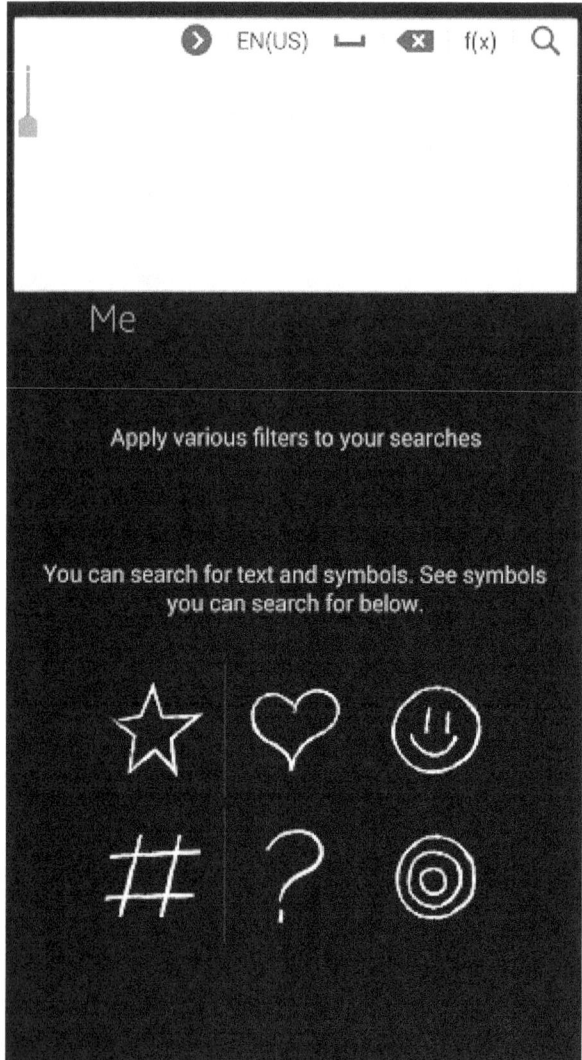

Figure 9: Writing Window

6. Multitasking Using the Pen Window

The Note 3 allows you to open two applications at once by drawing a window on the screen using the S Pen and selecting an application to open. This feature is known as the Pen Window. To use the Pen Window:

1. Take out the S Pen. The Air Command menu appears in the lower right-hand corner of the screen.
2. Touch the ![icon] icon. The first time that you do this, an informational pop-up appears. Touch **OK** to hide it. You may now draw a window on the screen. The Application selection window appears, as shown in **Figure 10**. Unfortunately, you are limited to the eight default applications in the list.
3. Touch an application in the list. The Pen Window opens with the selected application inside of it, as shown in **Figure 11**.
4. Touch one of the following icons to manage the Pen Window:

![icon] - Collapses the pen window to a small icon that resembles the application that is currently open inside of it. You may move this icon to any location on the screen. Touch the icon to re-open the Pen Window.

![icon] - Opens the application in full-screen. Once the application is in full-screen, you cannot return it to the Pen Window.

![icon] - Closes the Pen Window.

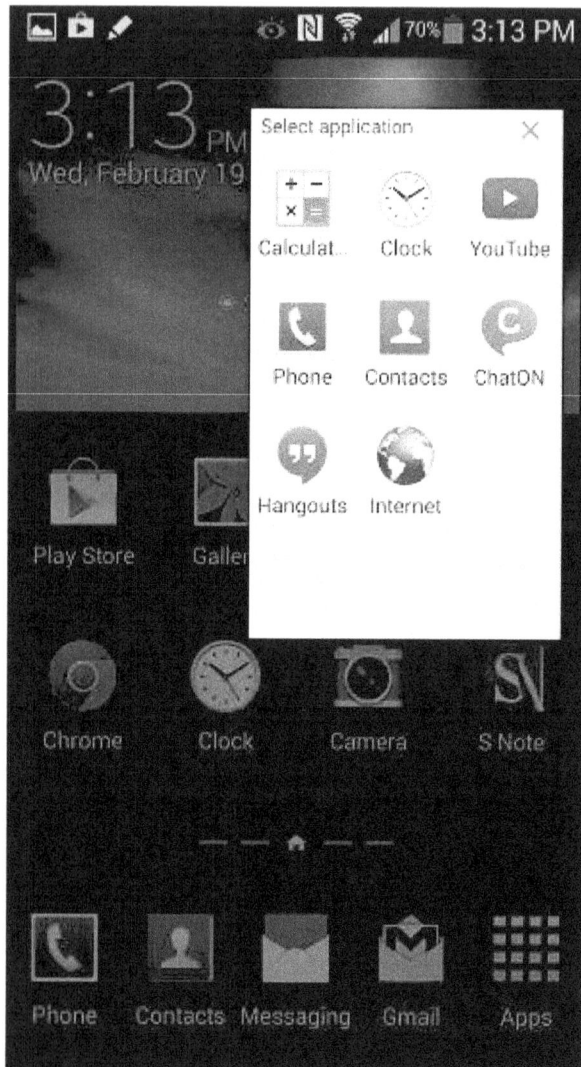

Figure 10: Application Selection Window

Figure 11: Pen Window

7. Writing Text in Messages and Emails

When you are composing a text message or email, you may enter text using the S Pen. Hover the S Pen over the text field, and then touch the ![icon] icon. The Message Writing window appears, as shown in **Figure 12**. Write your message one word at a time. The Note 3 recognizes your handwriting and enters the appropriate text. Use the following icons in the Message Writing window to edit your text:

EN(US) - Change the input language. Other options will appear only if you have installed and enabled additional languages. Refer to *"Adding an Input Language"* on page 313 to learn more.

⊔ - Adds a space after the previous character.

⊠ - Deletes the previous character.

↵ - Moves the cursor to the next line.

✎ (only available when composing a text message) - Allows you to draw a picture and attach it to the text message.

Done - Closes the message writing window.

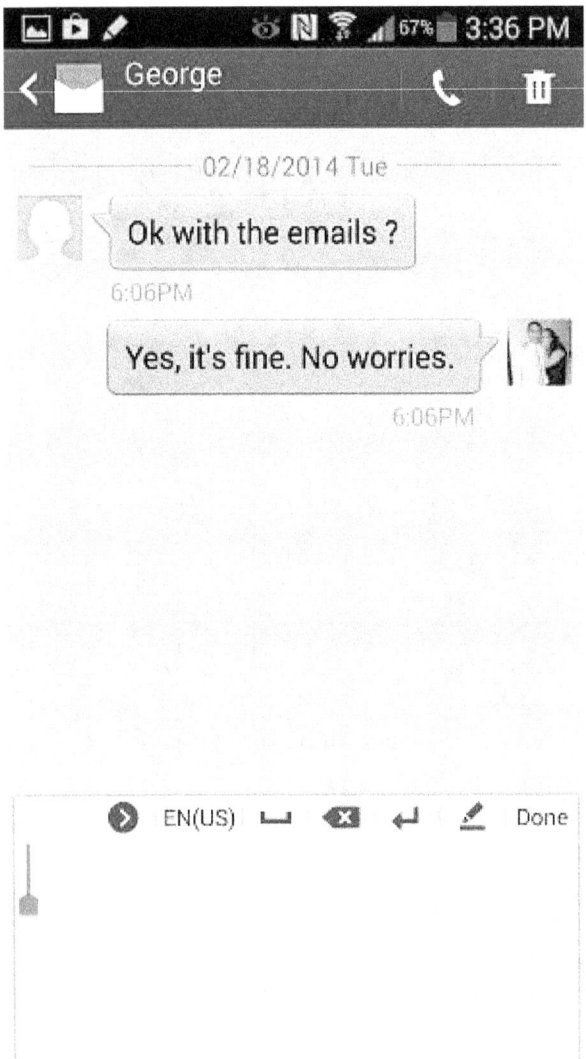

Figure 12: Message Writing Window

Making Calls

Table of Contents

1. Dialing a Number

Numbers that are not in your phonebook can be dialed on the keypad. To manually dial a phone number, touch the icon at the bottom of the screen. The keypad appears, as shown in **Figure 1**. If you see a different screen, touch the icon in the upper left-hand corner of the screen. Enter a phone number and touch the button at the bottom of the screen. The phone calls the number.

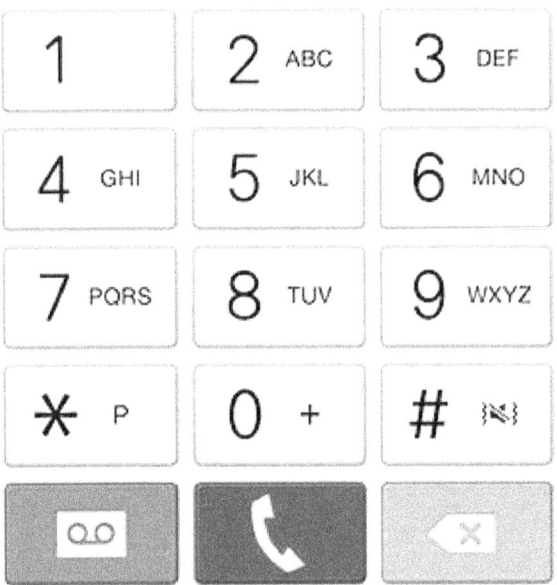

Figure 1: Phone Keypad

2. Calling a Contact

If a number is stored in your Phonebook, you may touch the name of a contact to dial it. Refer to *"Adding a New Contact"* on page 55 to learn how to add a contact to the Phonebook. To call a contact already stored in your Phonebook:

1. Touch the ![icon] icon at the bottom of the Home screen. The Phonebook appears, as shown in **Figure 2**.
2. Touch a contact's name. The Contact Information screen appears, as shown in **Figure 3**.
3. Touch the number that you wish to call. The Galaxy Note 3 dials the number.

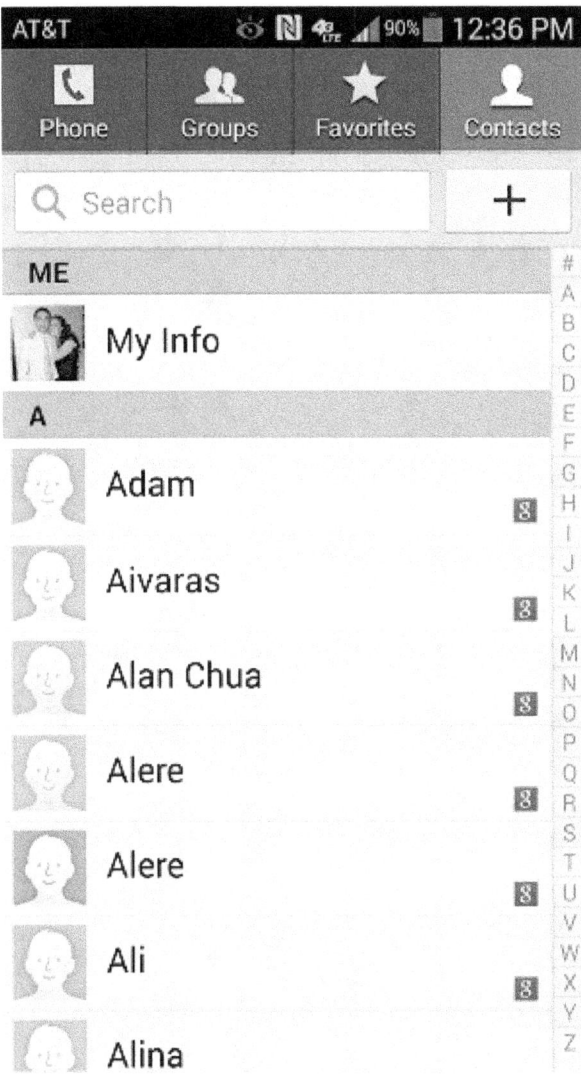

Figure 2: Phonebook

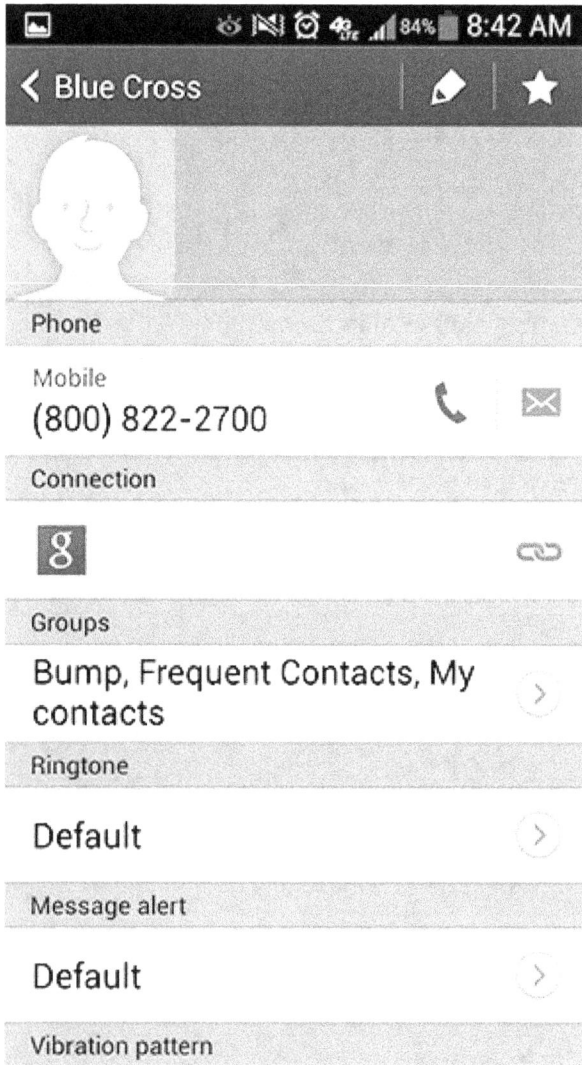

Figure 3: Contact Information Screen

3. Calling a Frequently Dialed Number

You can add a Direct Dial shortcut to the Home screen, which immediately dials a number stored in your phonebook when you touch it. To add and use a Direct Dial shortcut:

1. Touch the ▦ icon at the bottom right of the screen. The Application screen appears, as shown in **Figure 4**.
2. Touch **Widgets** at the top of the screen. The Widgets screen appears, as shown in **Figure 5**.
3. Touch the screen and move your finger to the left. Additional widgets appear.

4. Touch and hold the Dial icon. The main Home screen and a group of thumbnails representing the other Home screens appear, as shown in **Figure 6**. Do not release the screen.

5. Drag the Dial icon to the desired location and release the screen. If you wish to place the Direct Dial icon on an alternate home screen, hold the icon over one of the Home Screen thumbnails shown in **Figure 6**. The Dial icon is placed and the Phonebook appears.
6. Touch the name of a contact. The Direct Dial shortcut is set and appears on the Home screen, provided that there is only one number assigned to the contact. Otherwise, a list of phone numbers appears. Touch a phone number in the list to assign it to the Direct Dial.
7. Touch the **Direct Dial** icon. The number is dialed.

Figure 4: Application Screen

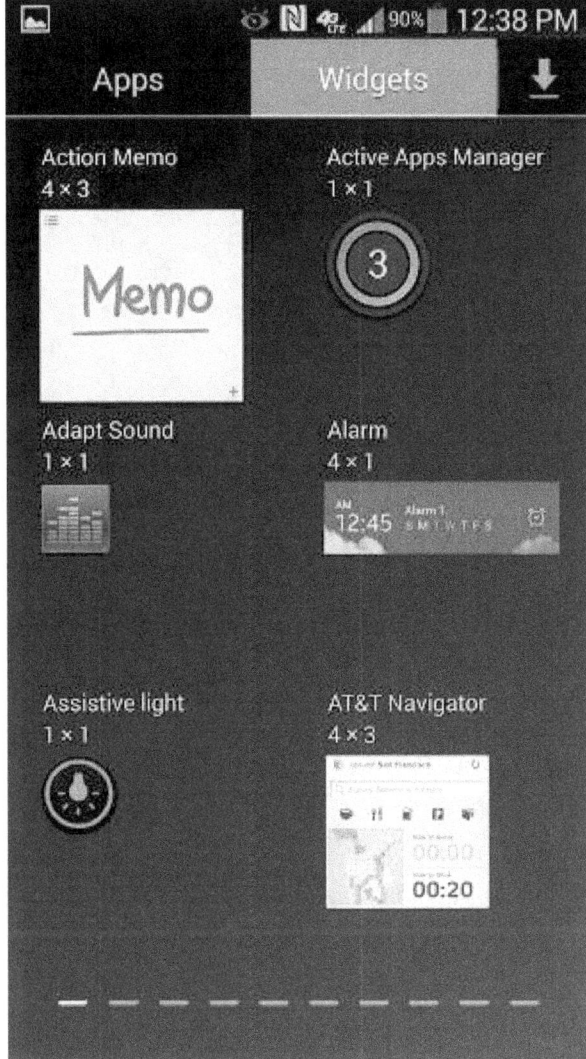

Figure 5: Widgets Screen

Figure 6: Main Home Screen and Group of Home Screen Thumbnails

4. Returning a Recent Phone Call

After you miss a call, the Galaxy Note 3 will notify you of who called and at what time. The phone also shows a history of all recent calls. To view and return a missed call or redial a recently entered number:

1. Touch the ![phone icon] icon at the bottom of the screen. The keypad appears. If you see a different screen, touch the ![keypad icon] (Keypad) at the top of the screen.

2. Touch the (Logs) icon at the top of the screen. A list of recent calls appears, as shown in **Figure 7**.
3. Touch the name of a contact and slide your finger to the right. The phone calls the selected contact.

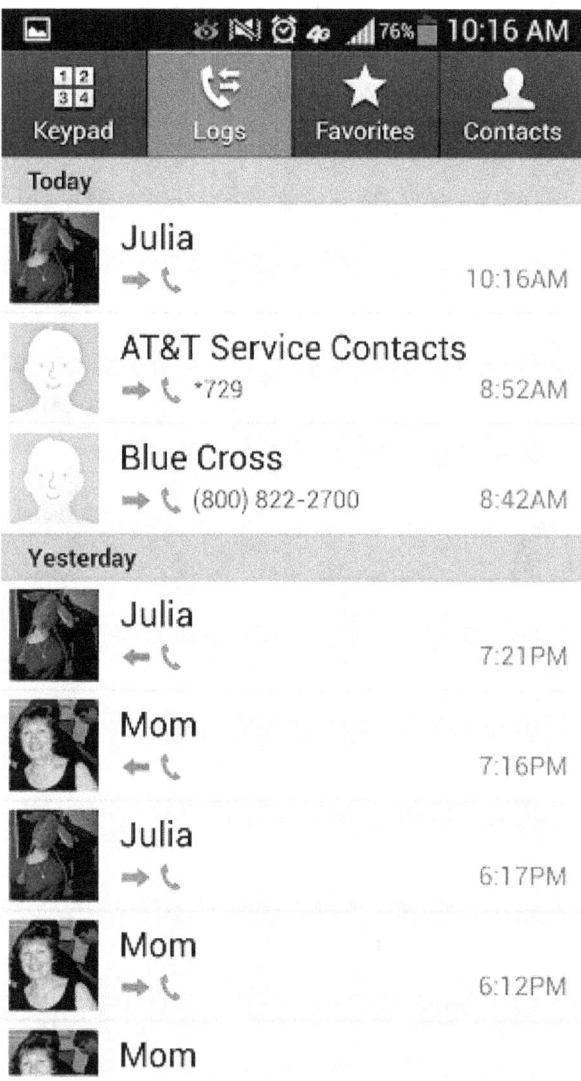

Figure 7: Full List of Recent Calls

5. Receiving a Voice Call

When receiving a voice call, the Incoming Call screen appears, as shown in **Figure 8**. To answer the call, touch the icon and drag it to the right side of the screen. The call is connected. To decline the call, touch the icon and drag it to the left side of the screen. The call is sent to voicemail.

Note: The screen shown during an incoming call when the phone is locked is the same as it is when the phone is unlocked.

Drag outside the circle to answer or reject

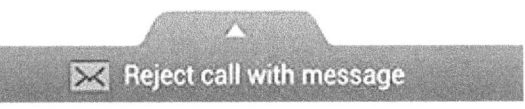

Figure 8: Incoming Call Screen

6. Using the Speakerphone during a Voice Call

The Galaxy Note 3 has a built-in Speakerphone, which is useful when calling from a car or when several people need to participate in a conversation. To use the Speakerphone during a phone call:

1. Place a phone call. The Calling Screen appears, as shown in **Figure 9**.

2. Touch the 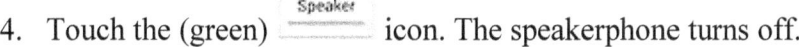 icon at the bottom of the screen. The speakerphone turns on.
3. Adjust the volume of the Speakerphone using the Volume Controls. Refer to *"Button Layout"* on page 8 to locate the Volume Controls.

4. Touch the (green) icon. The speakerphone turns off.

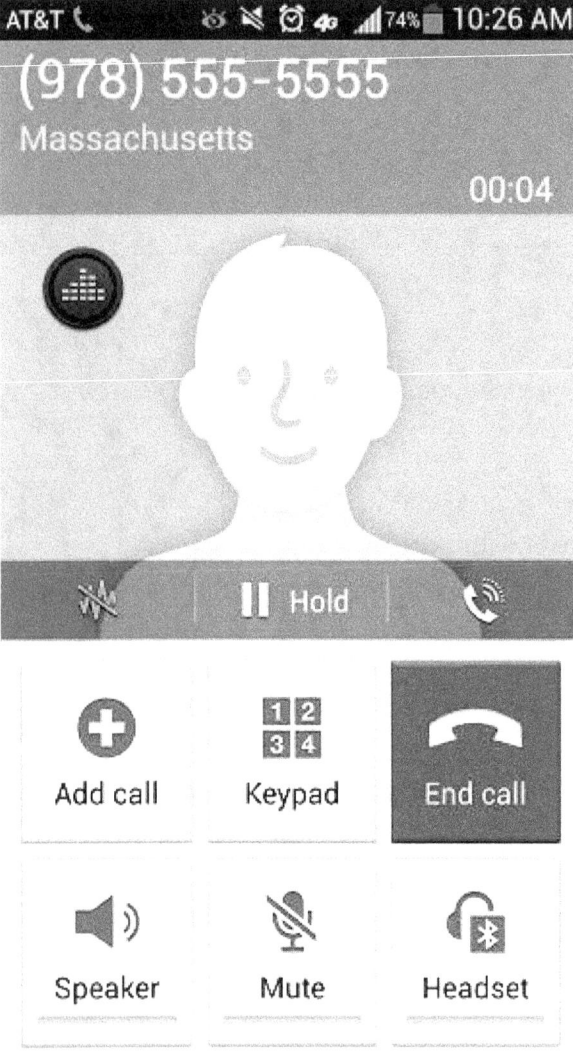

Figure 9: Calling Screen

7. Using the Keypad during a Voice Call

You may wish to use the keypad while on a call in order to input numbers in an automated menu or to enter an account number. To use the keypad during a voice call, place the call and touch

the [Keypad] icon. The keypad appears, as shown in **Figure 10**. To hide the keypad, touch

the [Hide] icon.

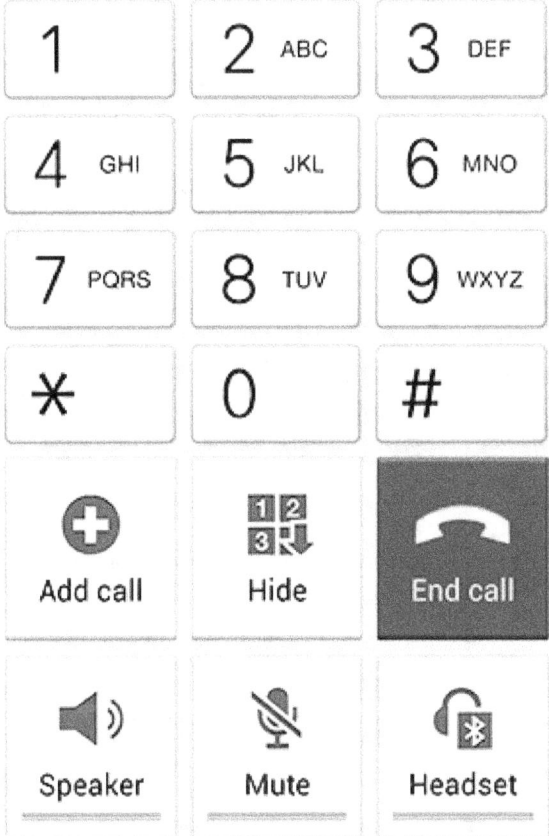

Figure 10: Phone Keypad While on a Call

8. Using the Mute Function during a Voice Call

During a voice call, you may wish to mute your side of the conversation. When mute is turned on, the person on the other end of the line will not hear anything on your side. To use Mute during a

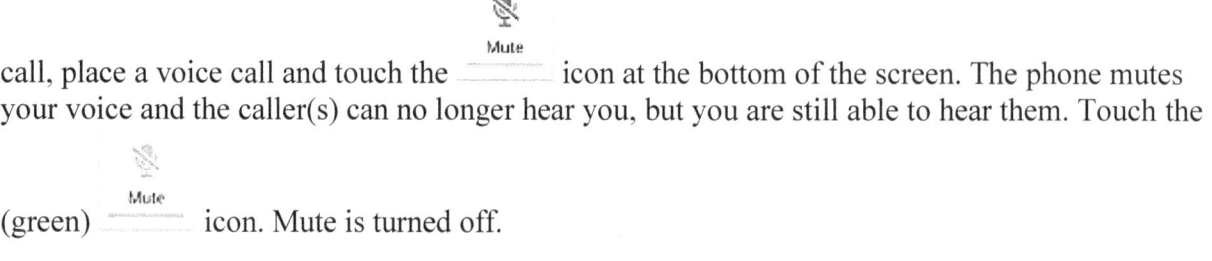

call, place a voice call and touch the _____ icon at the bottom of the screen. The phone mutes your voice and the caller(s) can no longer hear you, but you are still able to hear them. Touch the

(green) _____ icon. Mute is turned off.

9. Switching to a Bluetooth Headset during a Voice Call

While on a call, you can switch to your paired Bluetooth headset at any time. Refer to *"Setting Up*

Bluetooth" on page 254 to learn how to set up your headset. Touch the _____ icon. If the headset is already connected, you can now use it on the voice call. If the headset is not connected, the

Select Device screen appears, as shown in **Figure 11**. Touch the (green) _____ icon to disconnect from the headset.

Note: If you do not already have a Bluetooth headset connected, the phone will prompt you to turn on Bluetooth and connect a headset.

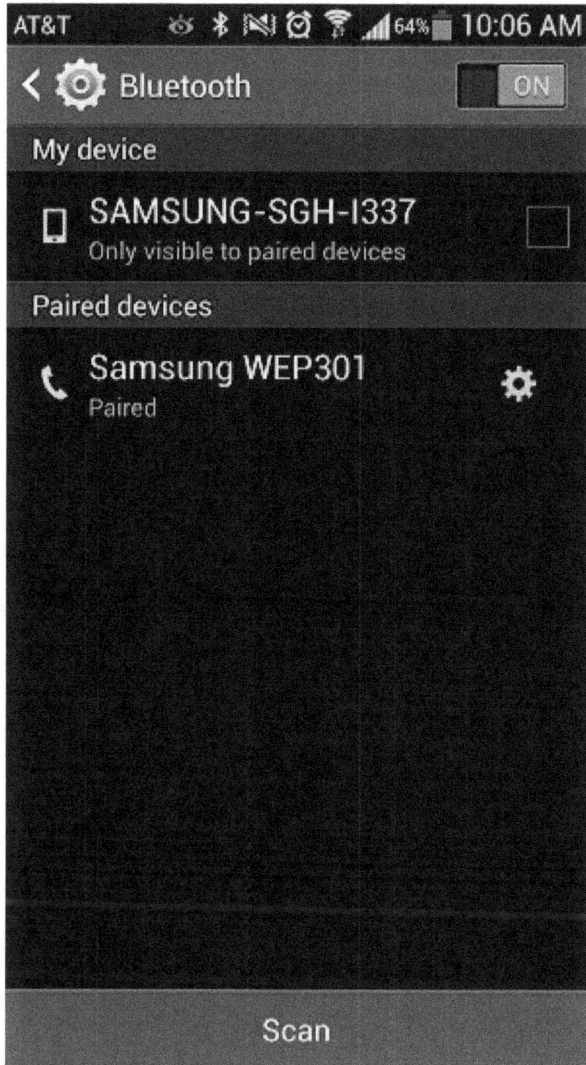

Figure 11: Select Device Screen

10. Starting a Conference Call (Adding a Call)

To talk to more than one person at a time, place a new call without ending the current one. To add a call:

1. Place a call. The call is connected and the Calling screen appears.

2. Touch the  icon at the bottom of the screen. The keypad appears.

3. Dial a number and touch the 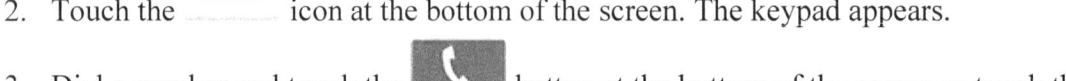 button at the bottom of the screen or touch the icon at the top of the screen and touch a number in your phonebook. The phone dials the second number.

4. Touch 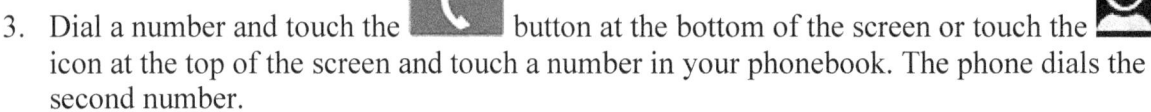 once connected. The calls are merged and a three-person conference call is started. You may add additional people to the call by repeating steps 1-4.

Managing Contacts

Table of Contents

1. Adding a New Contact

The Galaxy Note 3 can store phone numbers, email addresses, and other contact information in its Phonebook. To add a new contact to the Phonebook:

1. Touch the ![icon] icon at the bottom of the screen. The Phonebook appears, as shown in **Figure 1**.

2. Touch the ![+ icon] icon in the upper right-hand corner of the screen. The Contact Saving options appear the first time that you try to add a contact. Touch **Google** (recommended), as this will automatically back up the contact's information to your Google account, both when you create and update it. The New Contact screen appears, as shown in **Figure 2**. Alternatively, touch **Device** or **SIM** to save the contact's information to the corresponding location. If you would like to change this option in the future, touch **Google contact** on the New Contact screen.

3. Touch each field to edit it. Enter the contact's information in each field. You can also touch the ![+ button] or ![- button] buttons to add or remove a field, respectively.

4. Touch **Save** in the upper right-hand corner of the screen when you are finished. The contact's information is stored in the Phonebook.

Note: To hide the keyboard at any moment, touch the 🔙 *key. Refer to* "Tips and Tricks" *on page* 318 *to learn more about adding a new contact, including a tip on adding an extension to a phone number.*

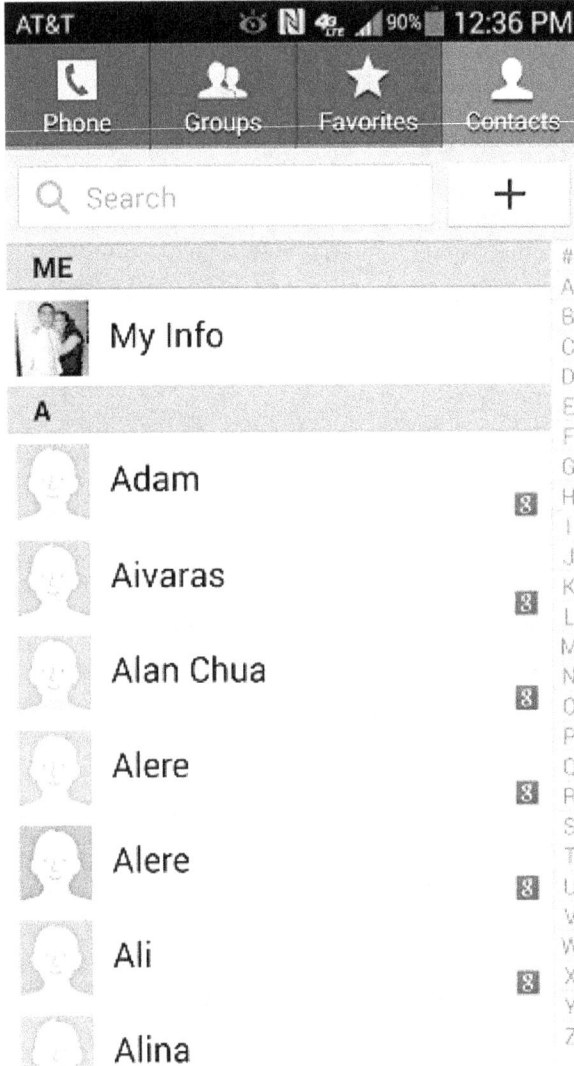

Figure 1: Phonebook

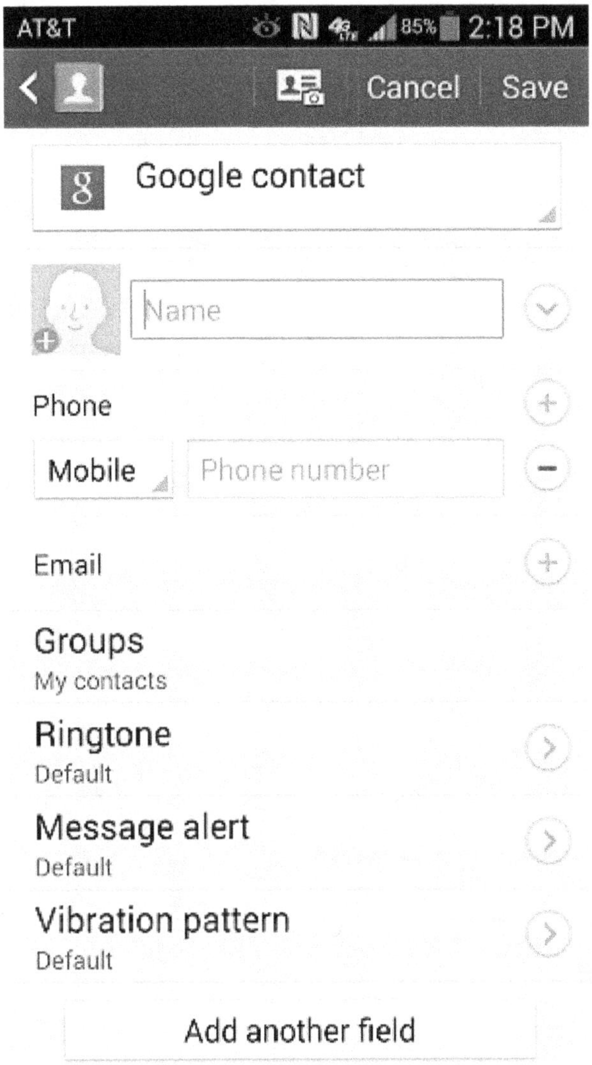

Figure 2: New Contact Screen

2. Finding a Contact

After adding a contact to your phonebook, you may search for it. To find a stored contact:

1. Touch the ![icon] icon at the bottom of the Home screen. The Phonebook appears.
2. Touch **Search** at the top of the screen. The keyboard appears.
3. Start typing the name of the contact that you wish to find. The Galaxy Note 3 searches as you type and the possible contact matches appear, as shown in **Figure 3**.

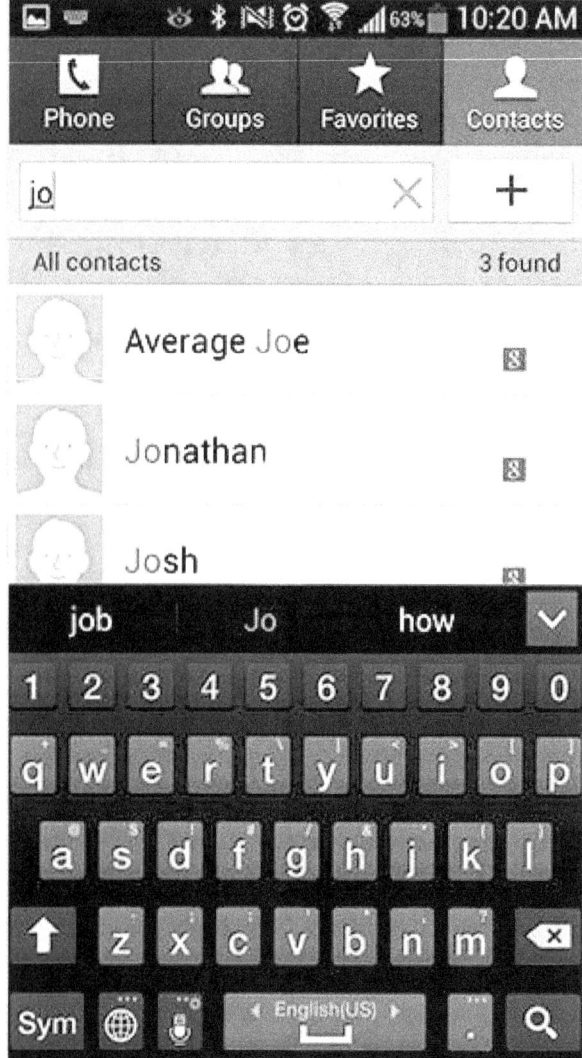

Figure 3: Possible Contact Matches

3. Editing Contact Information

After adding contacts to the Phonebook, you may edit them at any time. To edit an existing contact's information:

1. Touch the 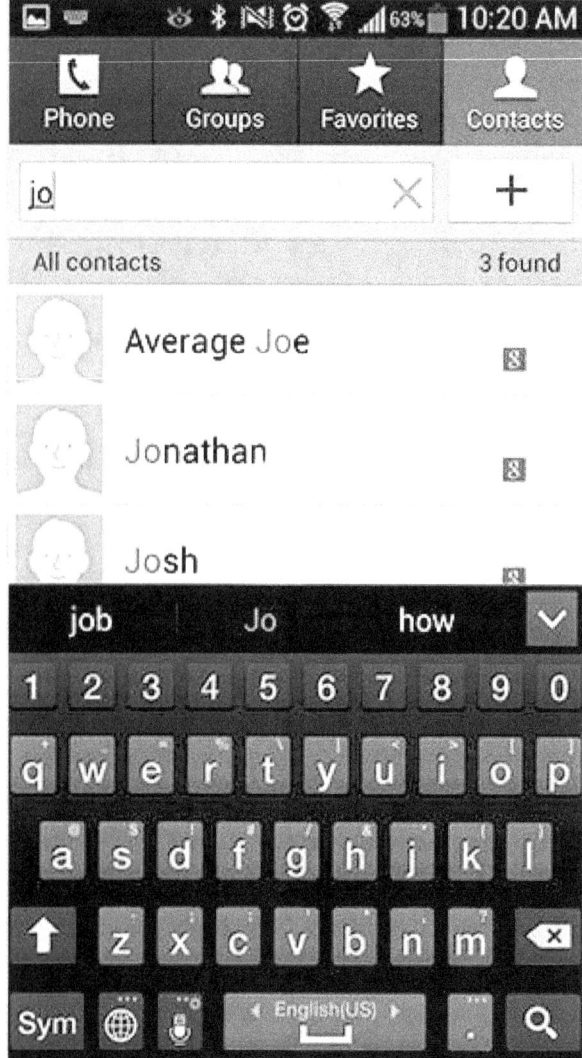 icon. The Phonebook appears.
2. Touch the name of the contact that you wish to edit. The Contact Information screen appears, as shown in **Figure 4**.

3. Touch the 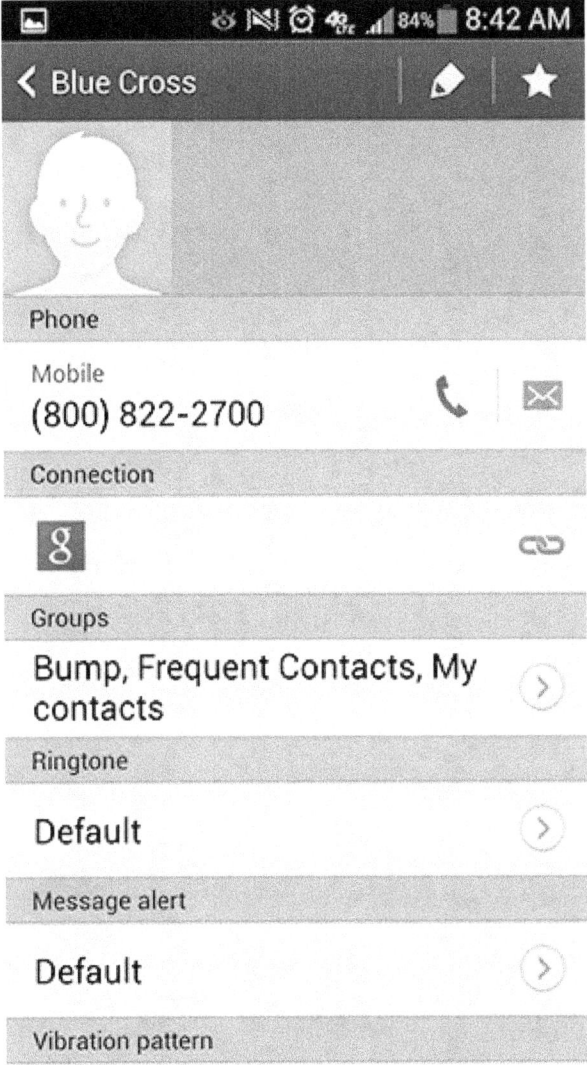 icon in the upper right-hand corner of the screen. The Contact Editing screen appears, as shown in **Figure 5**.
4. Touch a field to edit it. Enter the contact's information into each field.
5. Touch **Save** in the upper right-hand corner of the screen. The contact's information is updated.

Note: To hide the keyboard at any time, touch the ↩ *key.*

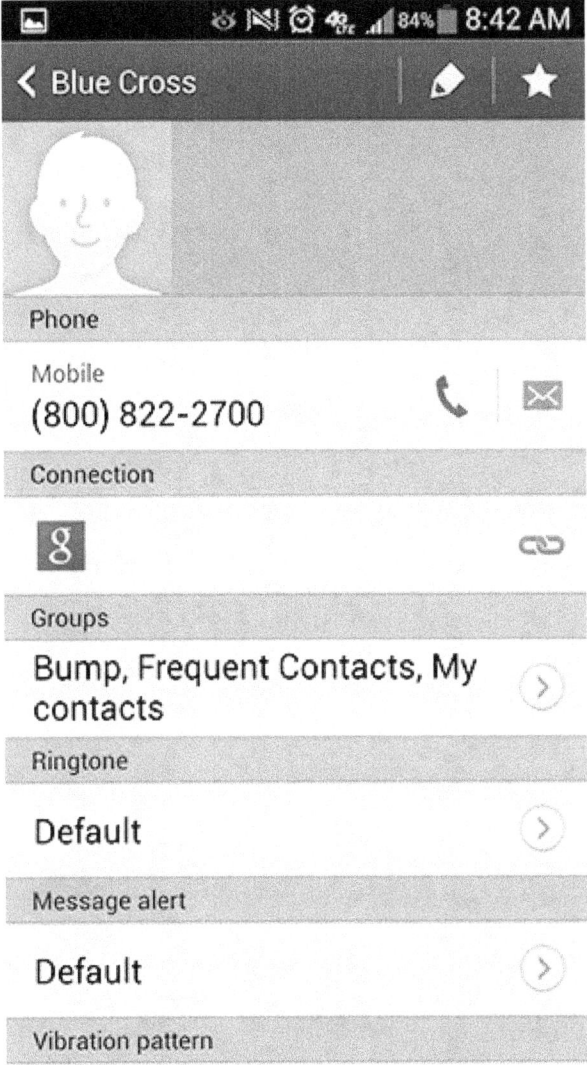

Figure 4: Contact Information Screen

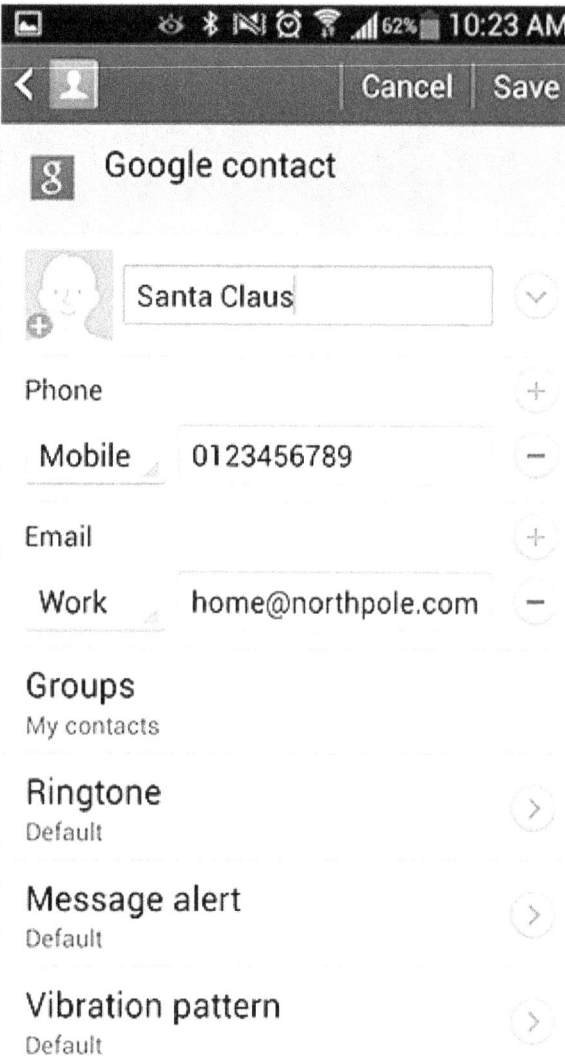

Figure 5: Contact Editing Screen

4. Deleting a Contact

You may delete a contact's information from the Phonebook in order to free up space or for organizational purposes. To delete unwanted contact information:

1. Touch the ![icon] icon. The Phonebook appears.
2. Touch the contact's name. The Contact Information screen appears.
3. Touch and hold the name of the contact that you wish to delete. The Contact Menu appears, as shown in **Figure 6**.

4. Touch **Delete**. A confirmation dialog appears.
5. Touch **OK**. The contact's information is deleted.

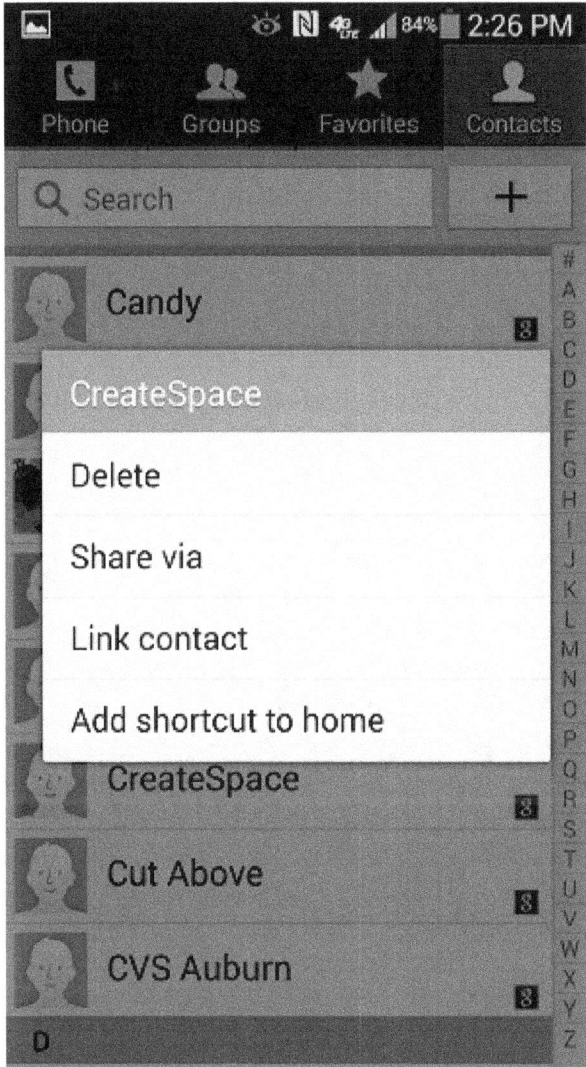

Figure 6: Contact Menu

5. Assigning a Photo to a Contact

You can assign a personal photo to a contact, which will appear next to the contact's name in the phonebook and when the contact calls. An existing photo can be assigned from the Gallery or a picture may be taken and assigned. To assign a photo from the Gallery to a contact:

1. Touch the ![icon] icon. The Phonebook appears.
2. Touch the contact's name. The Contact Information screen appears.
3. Touch the ![icon] icon in the upper right-hand corner of the screen. The Contact Editing screen appears.
4. Touch the ![icon] icon next to the contact's name. The Assign Photo menu appears, as shown in **Figure 7**.
5. Touch **Image**. The Gallery opens.
6. Touch an album. The album opens.
7. Touch a photo thumbnail. The Crop screen appears, as shown in **Figure 8**.
8. Touch the ![icon] icons and drag them in any direction to resize the crop. Touch the center of the photo and drag your finger to select the desired section of the photo. Touch **Done** in the upper right-hand corner of the screen. The photo is assigned to the contact.

To take a picture and assign it to a contact:

1. Follow steps 1-4 above. The Assign Photo menu appears.
2. Touch **Take picture**. The camera turns on. Touch the ![icon] icon if you wish to switch between the front and rear cameras.
3. Touch the ![icon] button at the bottom of the screen. The camera takes a picture and a preview of it appears.
4. Touch **Save** to use the picture, or touch **Discard** to retake it. If you touch 'Save', the Crop screen appears.
5. Touch the ![icon] icons and drag them in any direction to resize the crop. Touch the center of the photo and drag your finger to select the desired section of the photo. Touch **Done** in the upper right-hand corner of the screen. The photo that you captured is assigned to the contact.

Note: Touch the contact's photo and then touch **Remove** *to remove the assigned photo. You must be in the Contact Editing screen to remove an assigned photo.*

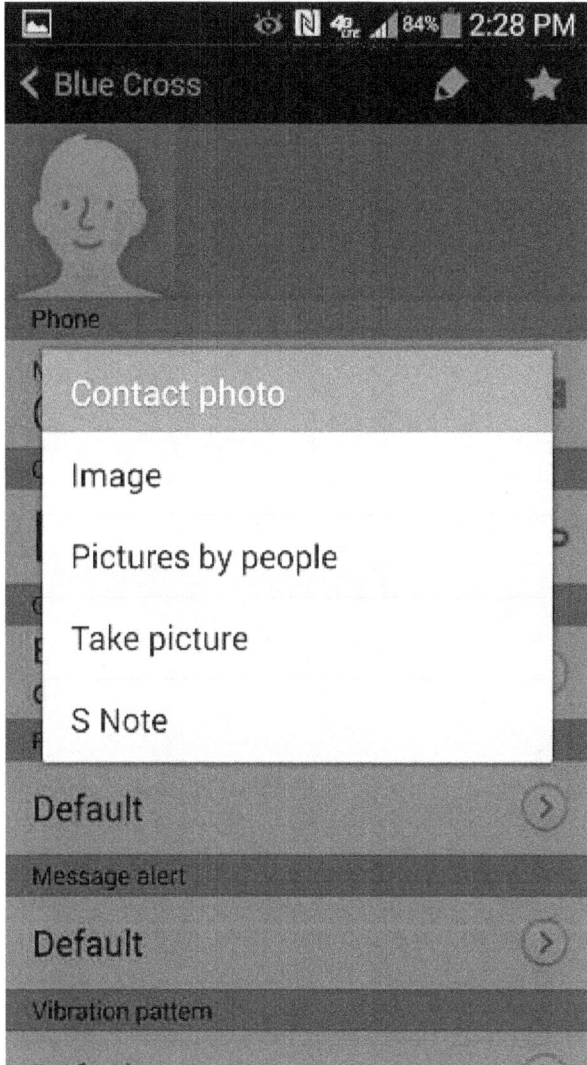

Figure 7: Assign Photo Menu

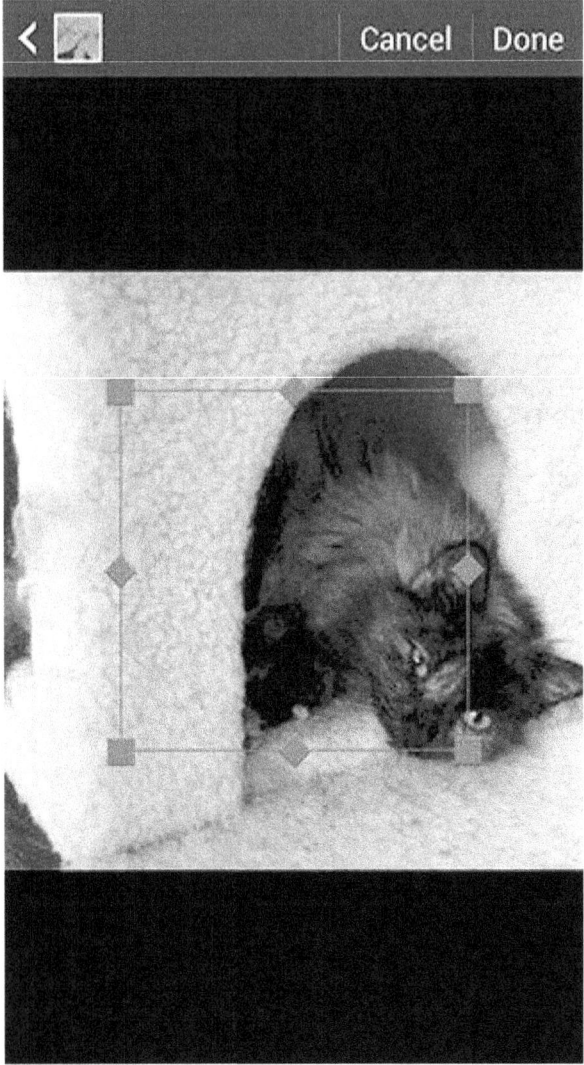

Figure 8: Crop Screen

6. Sharing a Contact's Information

When a contact is stored in the phonebook, all of the information for that contact can be shared. To share a contact's information:

1. Touch the ![icon] icon. The phonebook appears.
2. Touch the contact's name. The Contact Information screen appears.
3. Touch and hold the name of the contact that you wish to share. The Contact Menu appears.
4. Touch **Share via**. The Sharing Method menu appears, as shown in **Figure 9**.

5. Touch **Gmail**. The New Email screen appears with the contact's information attached, as shown in **Figure 10**. You can also touch **Messaging**, in which case the New Message screen appears with the contact's information attached, as shown in **Figure 11**.
6. Type the recipient's email address. The email address is entered.
7. Touch the **Subject** and **Compose** fields to enter a topic for the email and a message, respectively.
8. Touch the ▶ button in the upper right-hand corner of the screen. The contact's information is sent to the selected recipient.

Note: Sending contact information via Bluetooth is possible but is only for advanced users, and is not discussed in this basic guide.

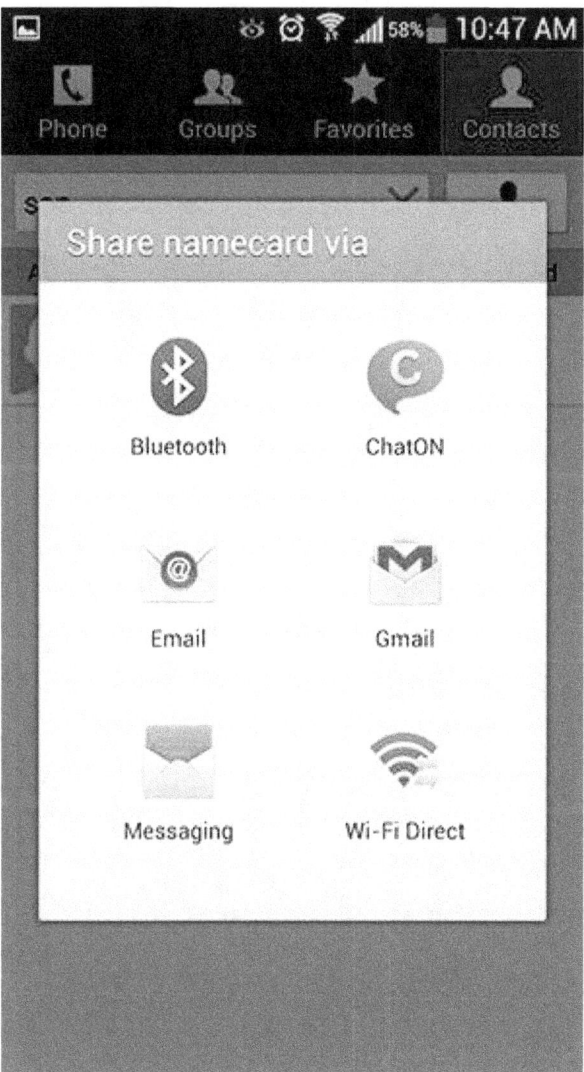

Figure 9: Sharing Method Menu

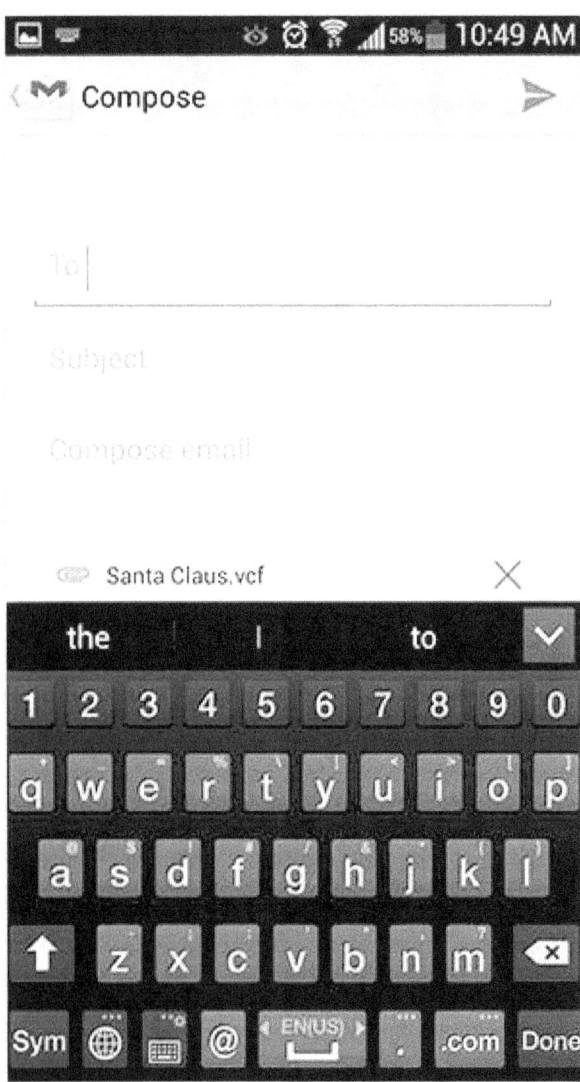

Figure 10: New Email Screen

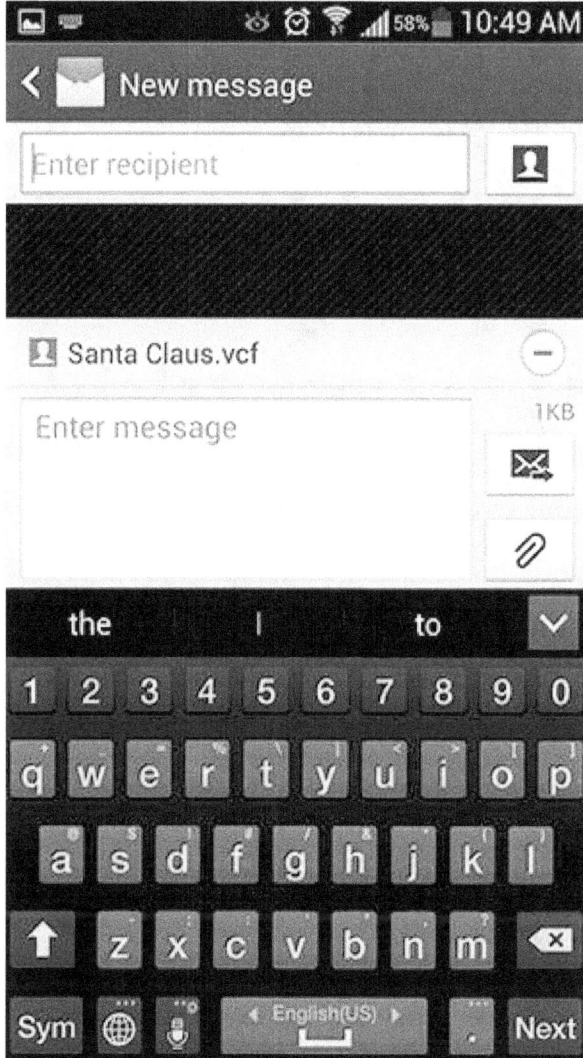

Figure 11: New Message Screen

7. Backing Up Contacts

There is no need to manually back up contacts on your Galaxy Note 3. When you log in to a Google account, the contacts are automatically backed up on Google's servers and made accessible from any device registered under the same account. If you do not have a Google account, please register at **https://accounts.google.com/signup**.

8. Adding a Contact to a Group

It can be useful to create contact groups, such as 'Family' or 'Co-workers', in order to quickly send text messages or emails to multiple people. To add a contact to a group:

1. Touch the ![icon] icon. The Phonebook appears.
2. Touch the name of the contact that you wish to edit. The Contact Information screen appears.
3. Touch the group names under 'Groups'. A list of groups appears, as shown in **Figure 12**.
4. Touch as many group names as you wish. A ✓ mark appears next to each selected group. You can also touch **Create group** to create a new group.
5. Touch **Save** in the upper right-hand corner of the screen. The contact is added to the selected groups.

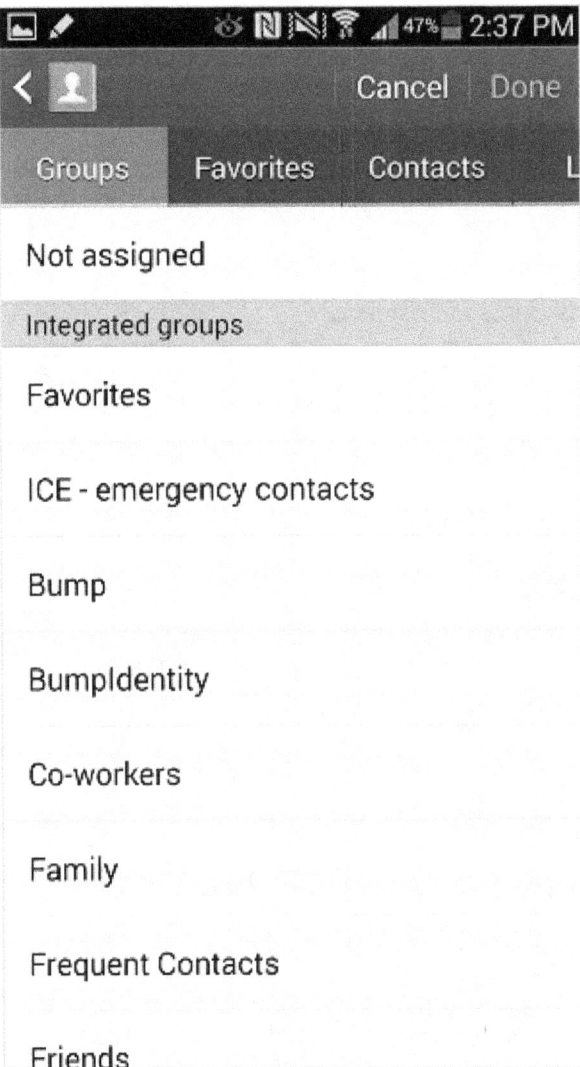

Figure 12: List of Groups

9. Adding a Contact to Favorites

In order to find your most frequently used contacts more quickly, you may wish to add them to your Favorites. To add a contact to Favorites:

1. Touch the [ ] icon. The Phonebook appears.
2. Touch the contact's name. The Contact Information screen appears.
3. Touch the [ ] icon in the upper right-hand corner of the screen. The contact is added to your Favorites. Touch **Favorites** at the top of the screen while viewing your phonebook to view your Favorites.

10. Adding a Contact to the Reject List

You may wish to block incoming calls from certain unwelcome callers, and send them directly to Voicemail. To add a contact to the Reject list:

1. Touch the [ ] icon. The Phonebook appears.
2. Touch the contact's name. The Contact Information screen appears.
3. Touch the [ ] key. The Contact Info menu appears, as shown in **Figure 13**.
4. Touch **Add to reject list**. Calls received from the selected contact will now be automatically rejected.

To remove the number from the reject list, touch the key again, and then touch **Remove from reject list**. Calls received from the selected contact will come through normally.

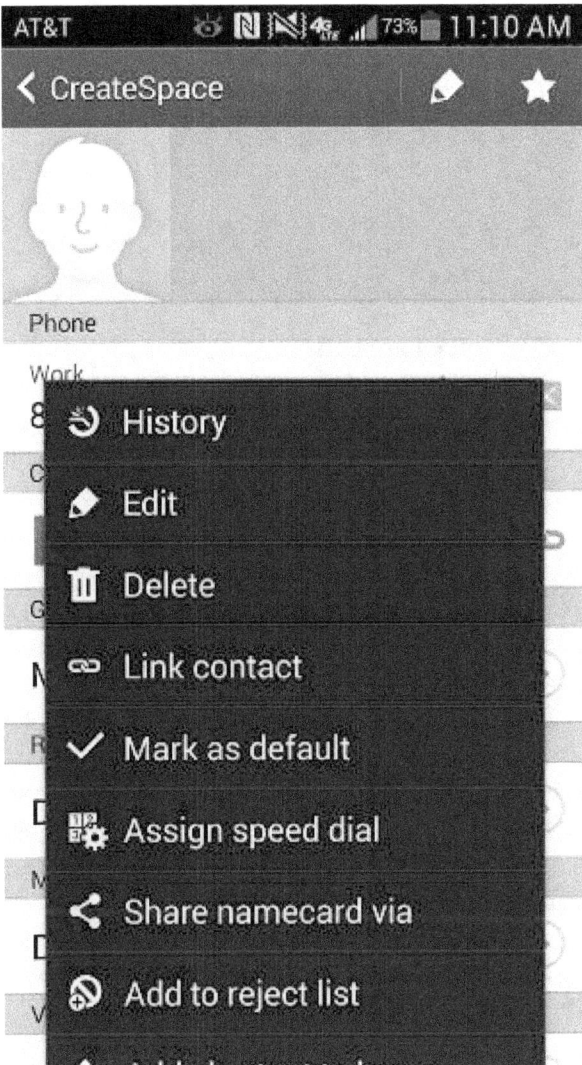

Figure 13: Contact Info Menu

11. Adding a Contact Shortcut to the Home Screen

In order to call, text, or email a person that you frequently contact, you may wish to add a contact shortcut to the Home screen. To add a contact shortcut:

1. Touch the ![icon] icon. The Phonebook appears.

2. Touch the contact's name. The Contact Information screen appears.
3. Touch and hold the name of the contact. The Contact menu appears.
4. Touch **Add shortcut to home**. A shortcut to the contact's information is added to the Home screen.

12. Importing and Exporting Contacts

If you have contacts stored on an SD card or in your Internal Storage, you can import them to your Phonebook. You can also export contacts from your Phonebook to an SD card or Internal Storage. To import or export contacts:

1. Touch the ![icon] icon. The Phonebook appears.
2. Touch the ![key] key. The Phonebook menu appears, as shown in **Figure 14**.
3. Touch **Import/Export**. The Import/Export Contacts menu appears, as shown in **Figure 15**.
4. Touch one of the options to perform the corresponding action. The Galaxy Note 3 searches for contacts stored in the selected location and imports or exports them.

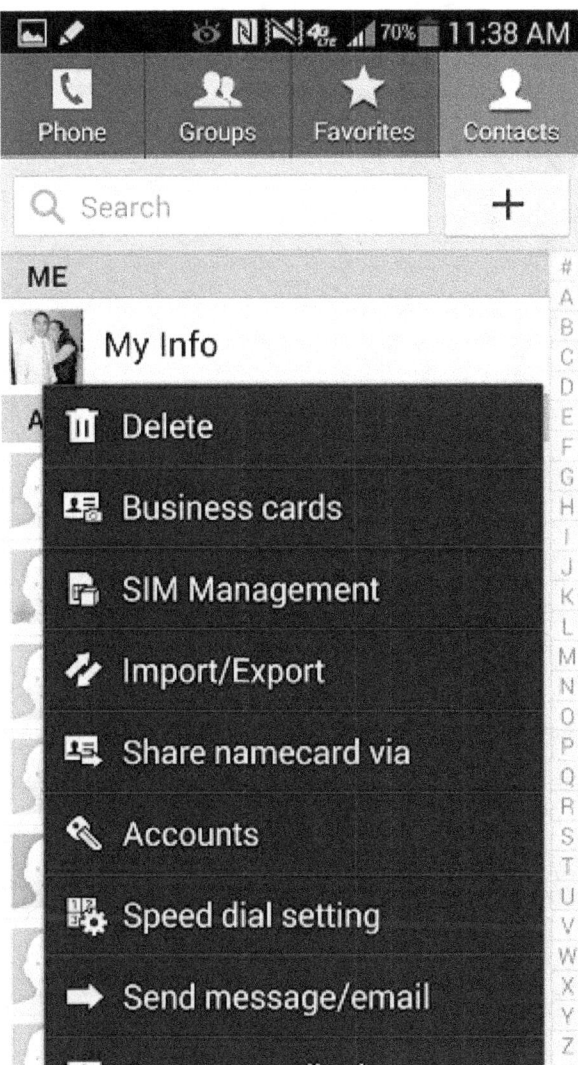

Figure 14: Phonebook Menu

Figure 15: Import/Export Contacts Menu

13. Joining or Separating Contact Information of Two Contacts

Sometimes, you may accidentally add contact information for the same person in two separate entries in the Phonebook. Instead of re-entering the information into a single entry, you may join the contacts. To join contact information:

1. Touch the ![icon] icon. The Phonebook appears.
2. Touch and hold the contact. The Contact menu appears.
3. Touch **Link contact**. The Phonebook appears.
4. Touch the contact that you wish to join with the one you selected in step 2. The two contacts are joined and their joint information will appear under the entry of the one that you selected in step 2.

To separate contact information:

1. Touch the ![icon] icon. The Phonebook appears.
2. Touch the name of the contact. The Contact Information screen appears.
3. Touch the ![key] key. The Contact Info menu appears.
4. Touch **Separate contact**. The Separate Contact screen appears, as shown in **Figure 16**.
5. Touch the ![icon] icon on the right-hand side of the screen. A confirmation dialog appears.
6. Touch **OK**. The selected contact is separated from the contact information that you are viewing. You may now view the separated contact's information under his or her name in the Phonebook.

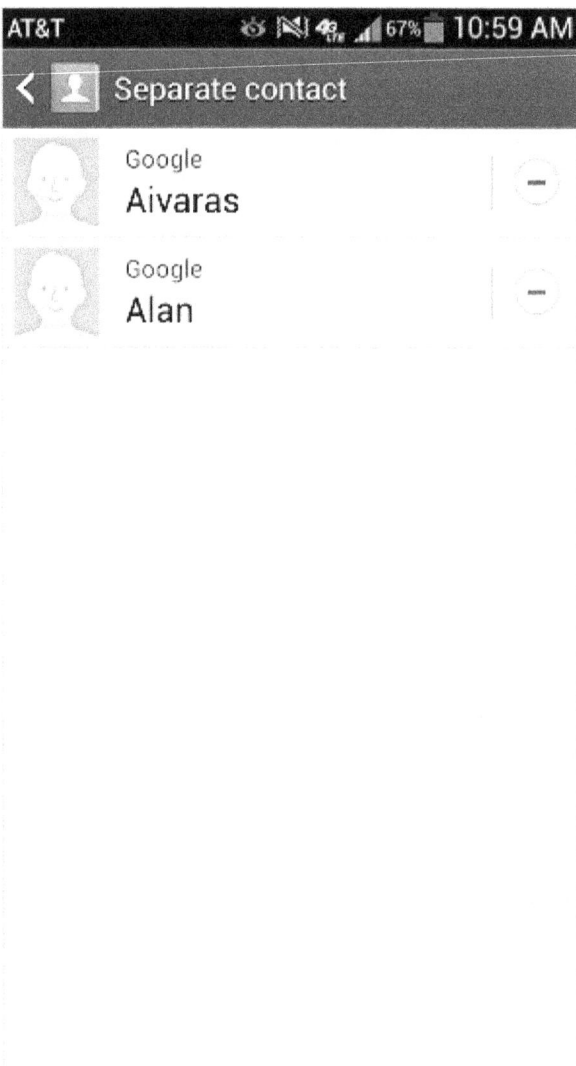

Figure 16: Separate Contact Screen

Text Messaging

Table of Contents

1. Composing a New Text Message

The Galaxy Note 3 can send text messages to other mobile phones. To compose a new text message:

1. Touch the ▬ icon at the bottom of the Home screen. The Messaging screen appears, as shown in **Figure 1**.

2. Touch the ✎ icon in the upper right-hand corner of the screen. The New Message screen appears, as shown in **Figure 2**.

3. Type the name of a contact or enter a phone number. Suggestions appear while typing. The addressee or phone number is entered.
4. Touch **Enter message** to enter a message.

5. Touch the 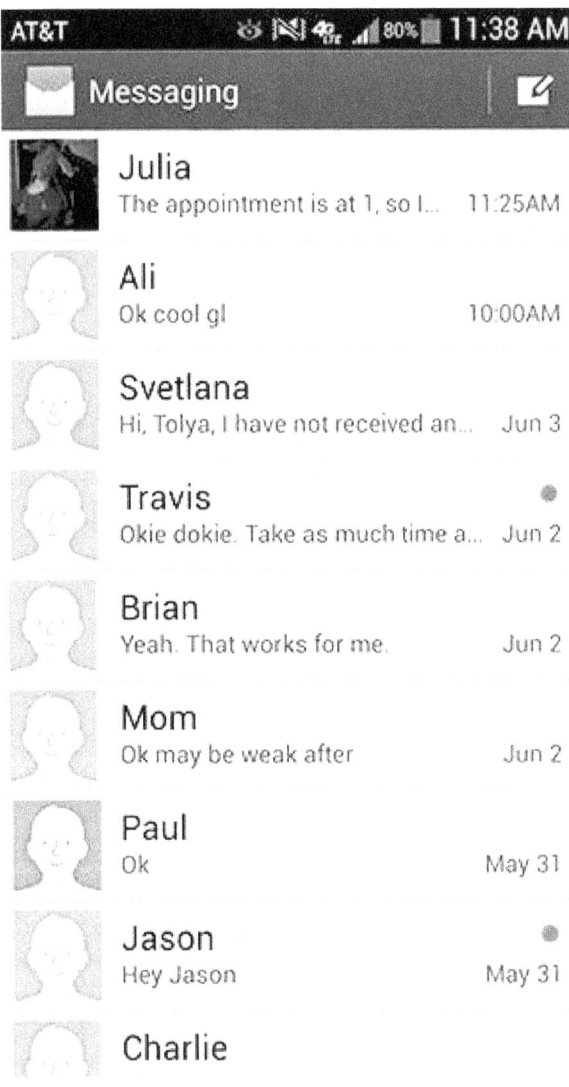 button. The message is sent and appears as a conversation, sorted by send date, as shown in **Figure 3**.

Note: Refer to "Tips and Tricks" *on page 318 to learn how to schedule a text message to be sent at a later time.*

Figure 1: Messaging Screen

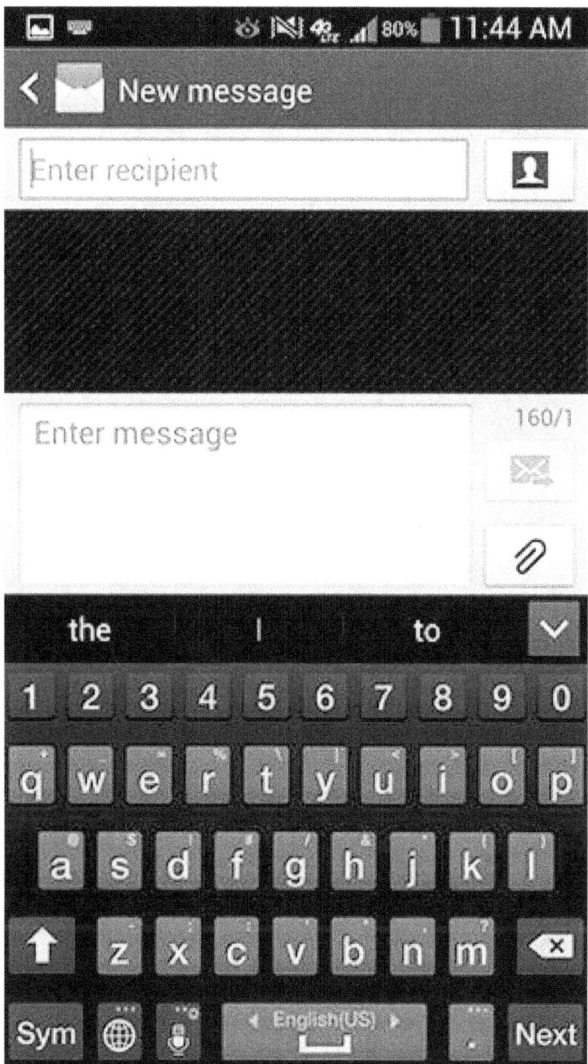

Figure 2: New Message Screen

Figure 3: Text Conversation

2. Copying, Cutting, and Pasting Text

The Galaxy Note 3 allows you to copy or cut text from one location and paste it to another. Copying leaves the text in its current location and allows you to paste it elsewhere. Cutting deletes the text from its current location and allows you to paste it elsewhere. To cut, copy, and paste text:

1. Touch and hold text on the screen. The Text options appear, as outlined in **Figure 4**. To learn how to compose a message, refer to *"Composing a New Text Message"* on page 77.
2. Touch one of the following options to perform the associated action:

- **Select All** - Selects all of the text in the field.
- **Cut** - Removes the text while copying it to the clipboard. Touch and hold any white field, even in an outside application, and touch **Paste** to enter the cut text.
- **Copy** - Leaves the text in the field while copying it to the clipboard. Touch and hold any white field, even in an outside application, and touch **Paste** to enter the copied text.

Note: The 'cut' and 'copy' options only become available when text is selected.

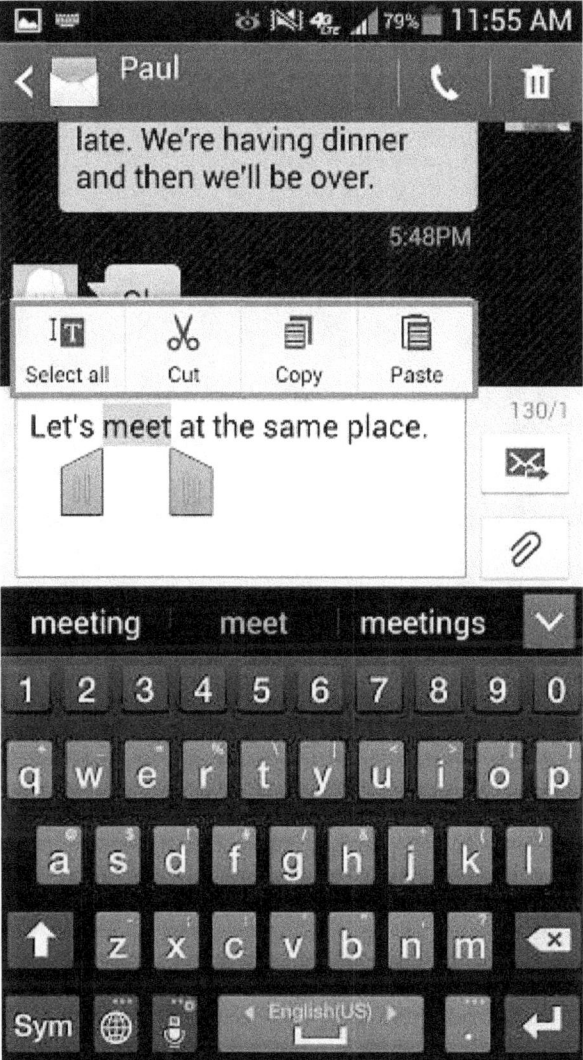

Figure 4: Text Options

3. Using the Auto-Complete Feature

While typing a text message, the Galaxy Note 3 automatically makes suggestions to auto-complete words, which appear in blue above the virtual keyboard, as outlined in **Figure 5**. This is especially useful when a word is very long. To accept a suggestion, touch the word. The word is inserted into the current message.

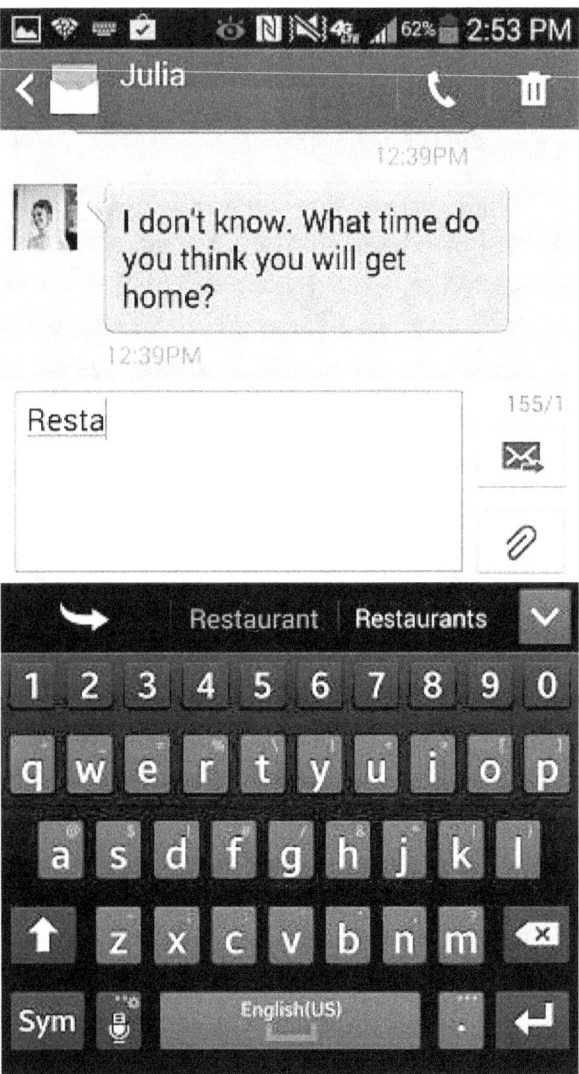

Figure 5: Auto Suggestions

4. Switching to another Language

While entering a text message, you can switch your keyboard to display a non-English keyboard. Before switching to another keyboard, you must add it via the Keyboard Settings screen. Refer to *"Adding an Input Language"* on page 313 to learn how. To switch to another language, touch the spacebar and slide your finger to the left or right. The alternate keyboard appears.

5. Receiving Text Messages

The phone can receive text messages from any other mobile phone, including non-smartphones. When receiving a text, the phone vibrates once, plays a sound, or both, depending on the settings. Refer to *"Setting the Ringtone, Media, and Alarm Volume"* on page 266 to learn how to set text message notifications.

If the screen is locked, the text message appears on the screen, as shown in **Figure 6**. Touch the text message and release the screen. Touch the center of the screen and slide your finger in any direction to unlock the phone and immediately open the text message.

If the screen is unlocked, touch the ✉ icon in the upper left-hand corner of the screen and slide your finger down. To open a newly received text message, touch the status bar at the top of the screen and drag it down (the bar where the time, battery, and signal bars are located). The Notifications screen appears, as shown in **Figure 7**. Touch the message with the ✉ icon next to it. The new text message opens.

Figure 6: Text Message on the Lock Screen

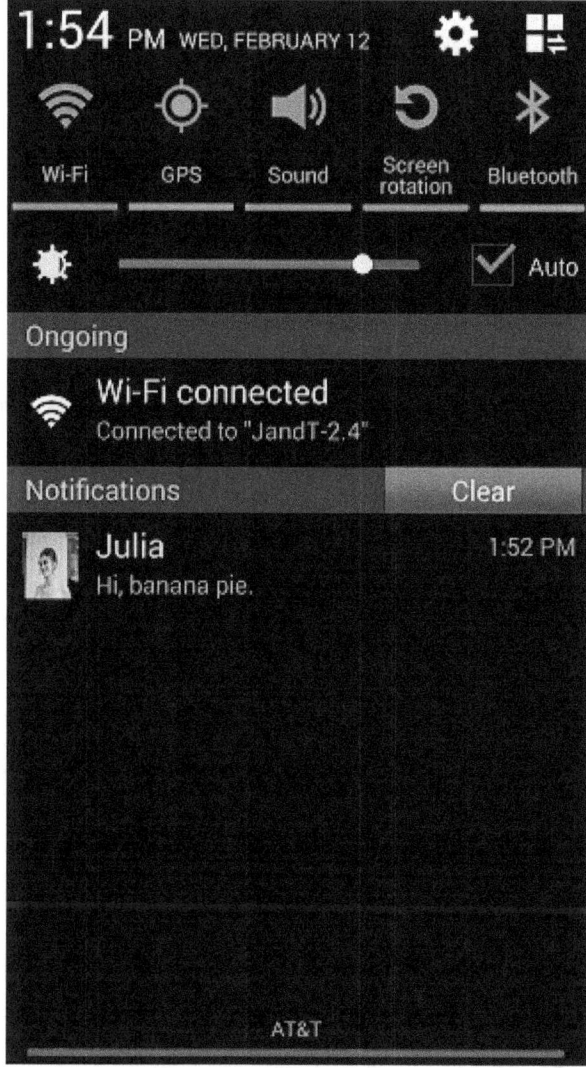

Figure 7: Notifications Screen

6. Reading Text Messages

You may read any text messages that you have received, provided that you have not deleted them.

To read stored text messages, touch the icon. The Messaging screen appears. Touch a conversation. The conversation opens.

7. Forwarding Text Messages

The forwarding feature on the phone allows a text message to be copied in full and sent to other recipients. To forward a text message:

1. Touch the   icon. The Messaging screen appears.
2. Touch a conversation. The Conversation opens.
3. Touch and hold a text message. The Message options appear, as shown in **Figure 8**.
4. Touch **Forward**. The New Message screen appears with the original message pasted in the message field.
5. Enter a phone number or the name of a contact. The recipient is selected.
6. Touch the   button. The text message is forwarded.

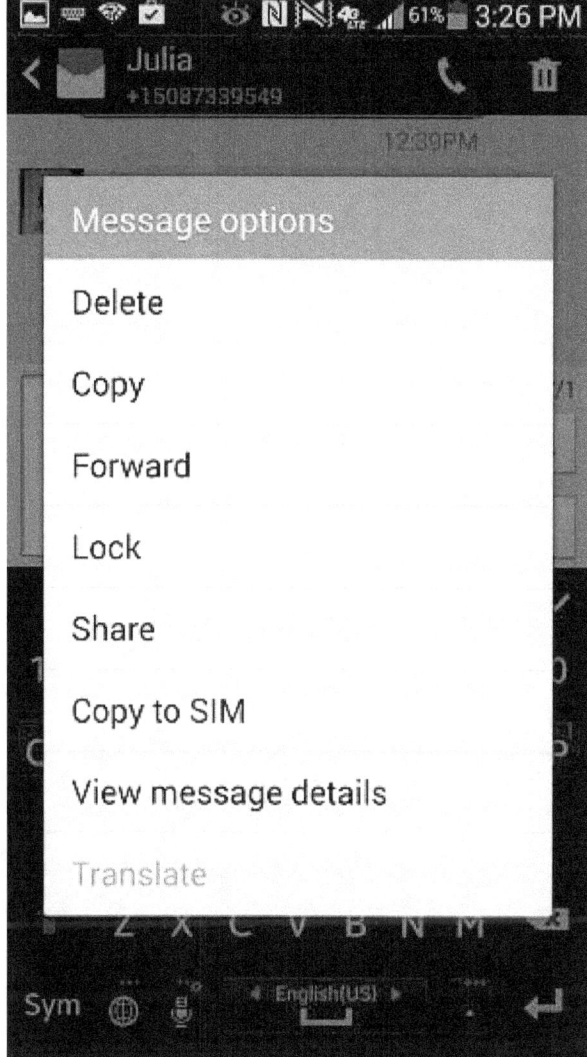

Figure 8: Message Options

8. Calling the Sender from within a Text

After receiving a text message from a contact, you may call that person without exiting the text message. To call someone while viewing a text conversation, put the phone up to your ear. The Galaxy Note 3 automatically dials the contact's number.

9. Viewing Sender Information from within a Text

You can look up a contact's details without exiting the Messaging application. To view the information of the person who sent you a text message, open the text conversation. Refer

to *"Reading Text Messages"* on page 85 to learn how. Touch the 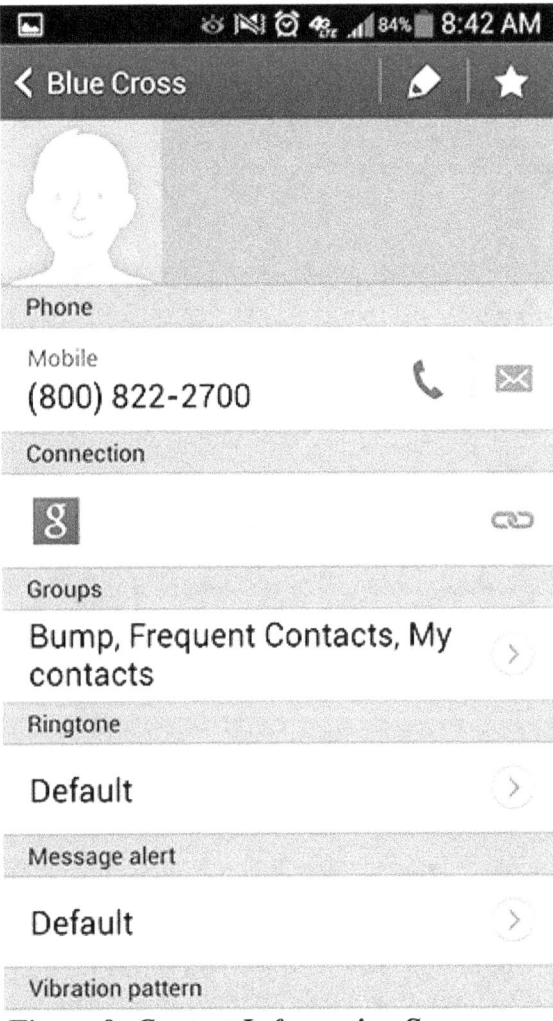 icon or the person's picture next to any one of the messages that he or she has sent. The Contact Information screen appears, as shown in **Figure 9**.

Figure 9: Contact Information Screen

10. Deleting Text Messages

The Galaxy Note 3 can delete separate text messages or an entire conversation, which is a series of text messages between you and one or more contacts.

Warning: Once deleted, text messages cannot be restored.

To delete an entire conversation:

1. Touch the   icon. The Messaging screen appears.
2. Touch and hold a conversation. The Conversation menu appears, as shown in **Figure 10**.
3. Touch **Delete**. A Confirmation dialog appears.
4. Touch **OK**. The conversation is deleted.

To delete a separate text message:

1. Touch the   icon. The Messaging screen appears.
2. Touch a conversation. The conversation opens.
3. Touch and hold a text message. The Message options appear.
4. Touch **Delete**. A confirmation dialog appears.
5. Touch **OK**. The message is deleted.

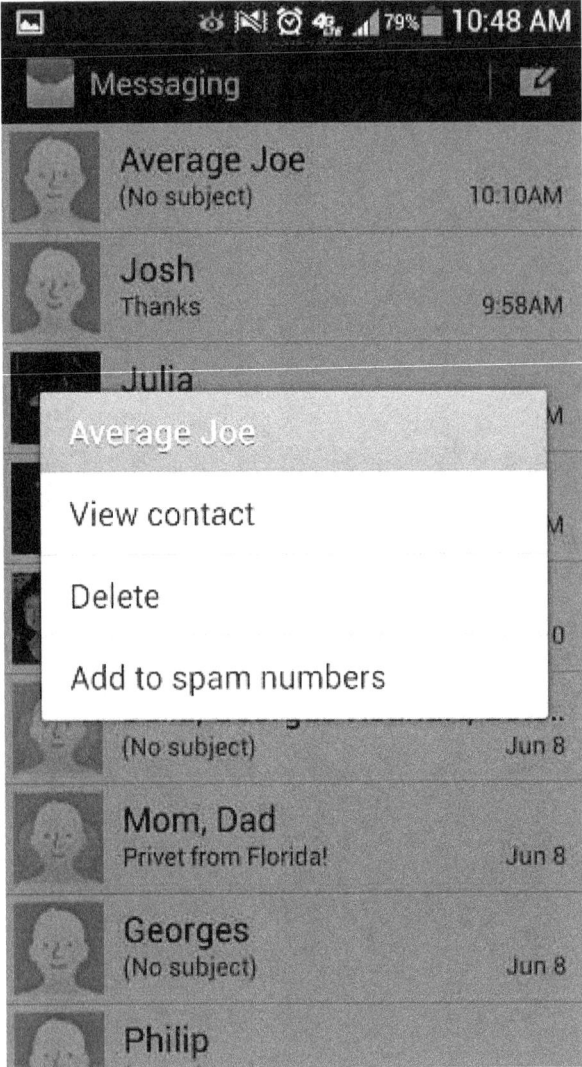

Figure 10: Conversation Menu

11. Adding Texted Phone Numbers to Contacts

A phone number contained in a text message may be immediately added to the phonebook as a new contact. To save a texted phone number as a contact:

1. Touch the   icon. The Messaging screen appears.
2. Touch a conversation. The conversation opens.
3. Touch the phone number in the text message. The Phone Number options appear, as shown in **Figure 11**.

4. Touch **Add to Contacts**. The Create Contact window appears, as shown in **Figure 12**.
5. Touch **Create contact**, in which case the New Contact screen appears, as shown in **Figure 13**. Refer to *"Adding a New Contact"* on page 55 to learn how to add the number to your Phonebook. Alternatively, touch **Update existing**, in which case the Phonebook appears, as shown in **Figure 14**. Touch the name of an existing contact, and then touch **Save** to add the number to the existing contact's information.

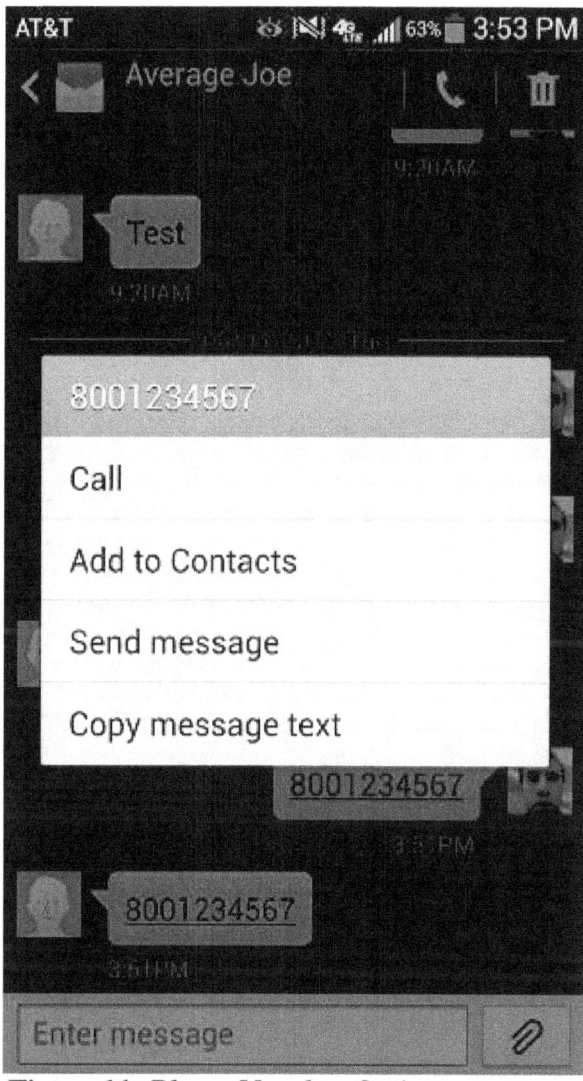

Figure 11: Phone Number Options

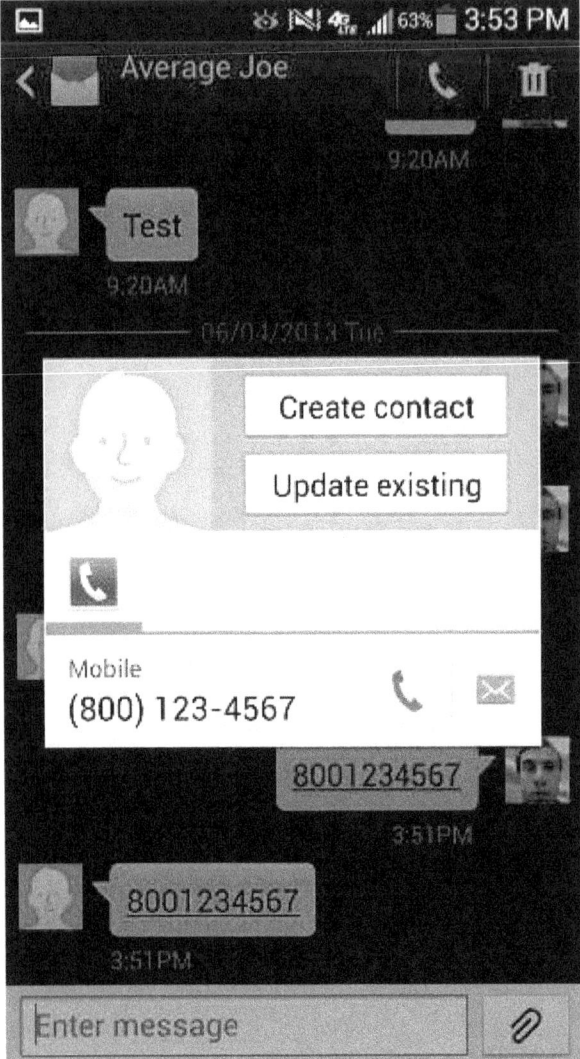

Figure 12: Create Contact Window

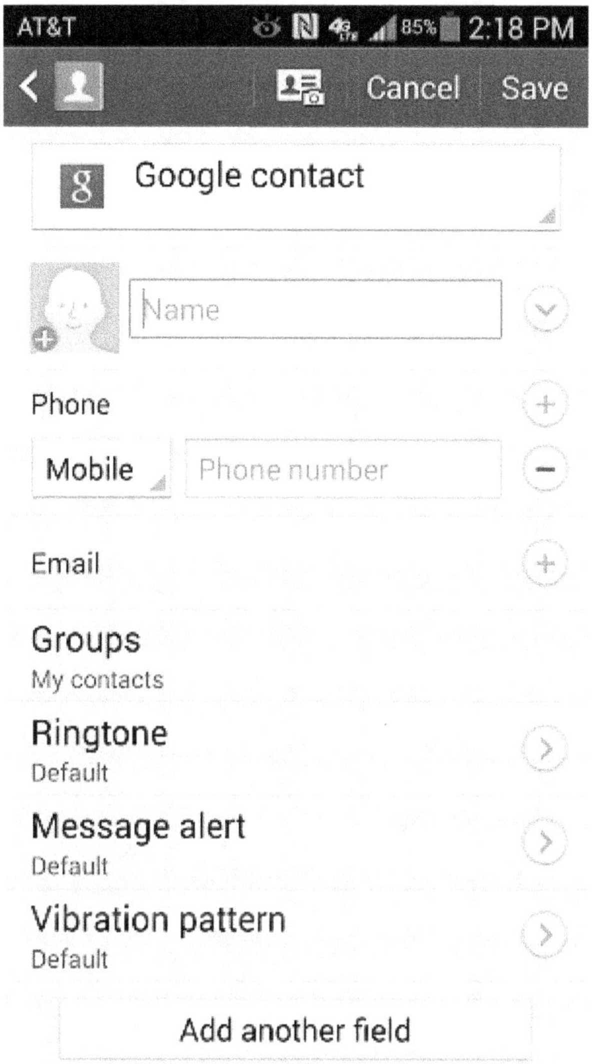

Figure 13: New Contact Screen

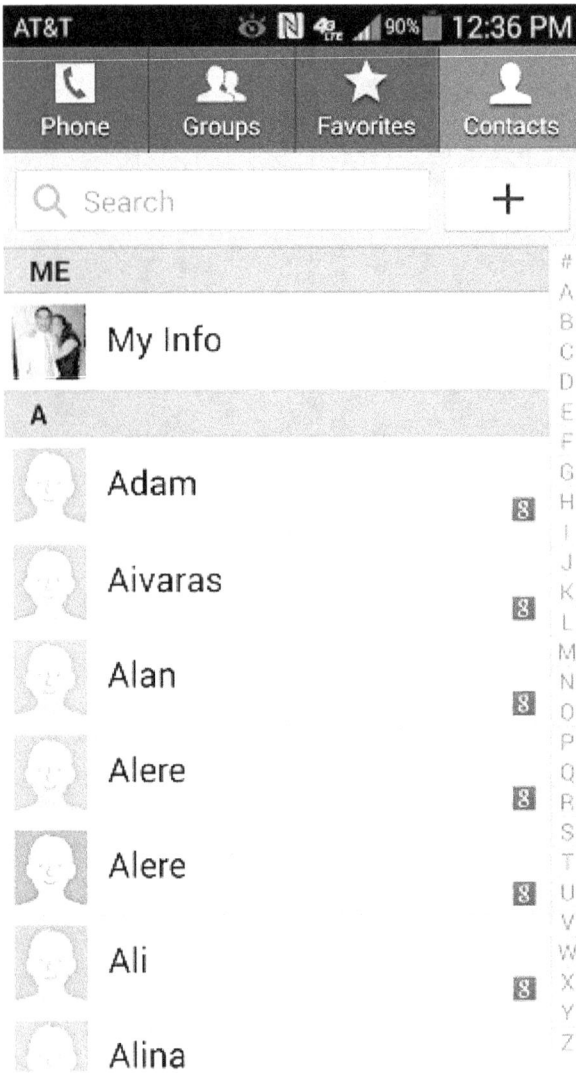

Figure 14: Phonebook

12. Adding an Attachment to a Text Message

A picture, video, or other file can be attached to any text message. To send a text message with an attachment:

1. Refer to *"Composing a New Text Message"* on page 78 and follow steps 1-3.

2. Touch the ✐ icon to the right of the 'Enter message' field. The Attachment menu appears, as shown in **Figure 15**.

3. Touch and hold an attachment and then touch one of the following options to manage it, if desired:

- **View** - Preview the attachment in full-screen mode. Touch the 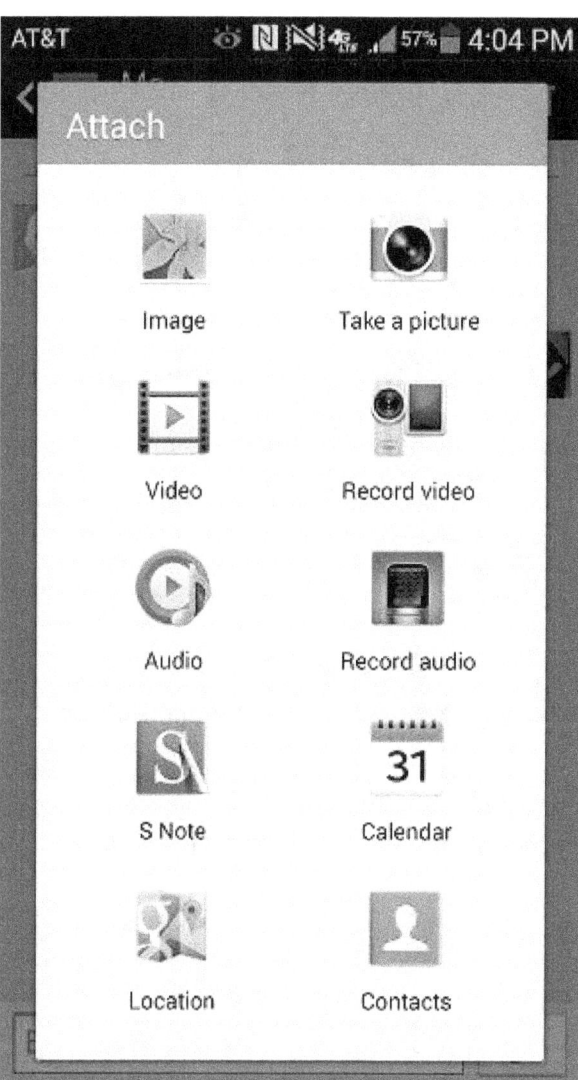 key to return to the text message.
- **Replace** - Replace the attachment with another one.
- **Remove** - Remove the attached file from the text message.

Figure 15: Attachment Menu

13. Attaching a Picture

The Galaxy Note 3 can send media messages containing a picture. To attach a picture to a text message:

1. Refer to *"Adding an Attachment to a Text Message"* on page 94 and follow steps 1-3. The Attachment menu appears.
2. Follow the steps in the appropriate section below:

Taking and Attaching a Picture

1. Touch the icon. The camera turns on.
2. Touch the button. The picture is captured and displayed on the screen for review, as shown in **Figure 16**.
3. Touch **Discard** to retake the photo or touch **Save** to attach it to the text message. The photo is attached and the text message appears, as shown in **Figure 17**.

Attaching a Picture from a Photo Album

1. Touch the icon. The Gallery opens, as shown in **Figure 18**.
2. Touch the album that contains the photo that you wish to attach. The thumbnails of the photos in the album appear.
3. Touch a photo. A mark appears next to the selected photo.
4. Touch the mark in the upper right-hand corner of the screen. The photo is attached and the text message appears.

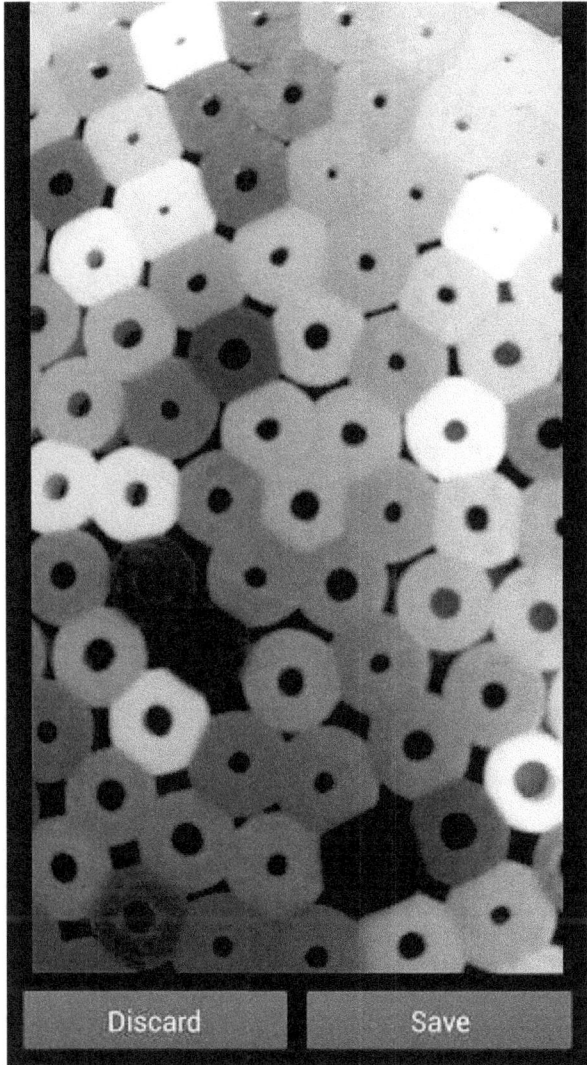

Discard | Save

Figure 16: Picture Review

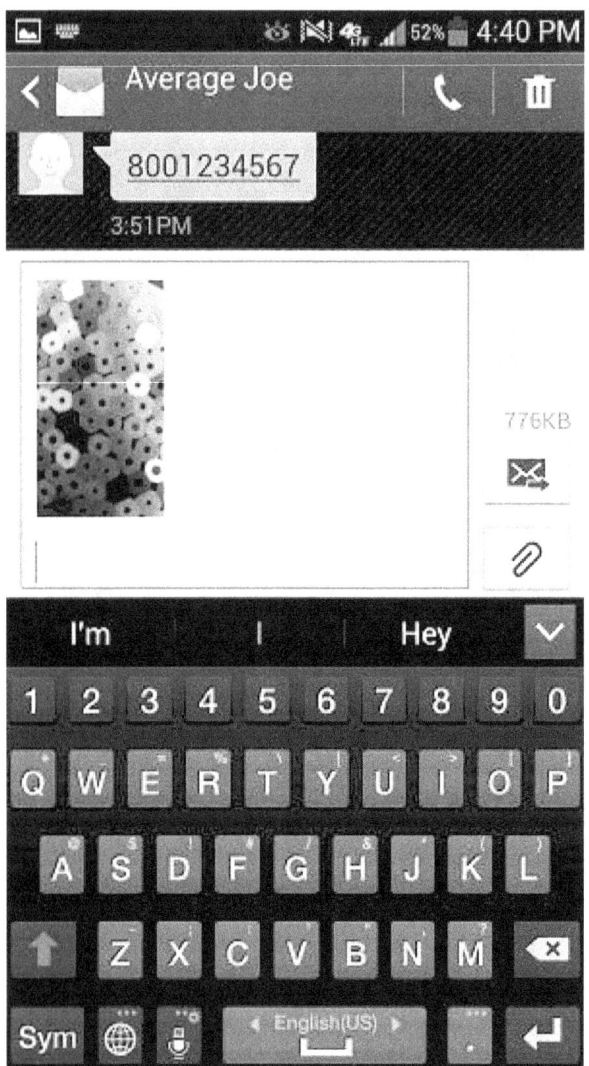

Figure 17: Text Message with Picture Attached

Figure 18: Gallery

14. Attaching a Video

The Galaxy Note 3 can send media messages containing video. To attach a video to a text message:

1. Refer to *"Adding an Attachment to a Text Message"* on page 94 and follow steps 1-3. The Attachment menu appears.
2. Follow the steps in the appropriate section below:

Attaching a Video from the Camcorder

1. Touch the   button. The camcorder turns on.

2. Touch the   button. The video begins to record.

3. Touch the   button. The camcorder stops recording, and the preview screen appears.

4. Touch **Discard** to retake the video or touch the ⏺ icon in the center of the screen to preview it. The video plays.
5. Touch **Save**. The video is attached to the text message, as shown in **Figure 19**.

Attaching a Video from the Videos Gallery (not recommended due to small size limit)

1. Touch the   icon. A list of video albums appears.
2. Touch an album. The thumbnails of the videos in the album appear.
3. Touch a video. The video is attached to the text message.

Note: If the message "Unsupported file" appears at the bottom of the screen, try attaching a shorter video.

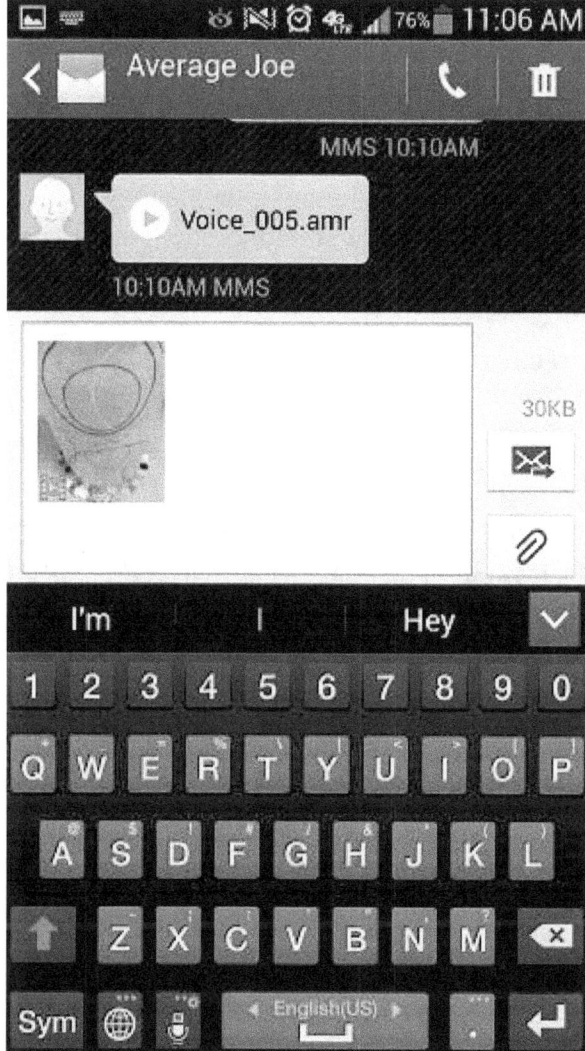

Figure 19: Text Message with Video Attached

15. Attaching a Voice Recording

The Galaxy Note 3 can send media messages containing voice recordings. To attach a voice recording to a text message:

1. Refer to *"Adding an Attachment to a Text Message"* on page 94 and follow steps 1-3. The Attachment menu appears.
2. Touch the ![icon] icon. The voice recorder turns on, as shown in **Figure 20**.
3. Touch the ![button] button. The phone starts recording.
4. Touch the ![button] button to stop recording. The Voice Recorder dialog appears.
5. Touch a recording in the list to preview it. Touch **Done** in the upper right-hand corner of the screen to play the recording. Alternatively, touch **Cancel** to attach the recording without listening to it. The recording is attached to the text message, as shown in

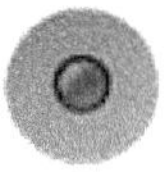

    Figure 21. You can also touch the ![button] button at any time while recording to discard the file.

Figure 20: Voice Recorder

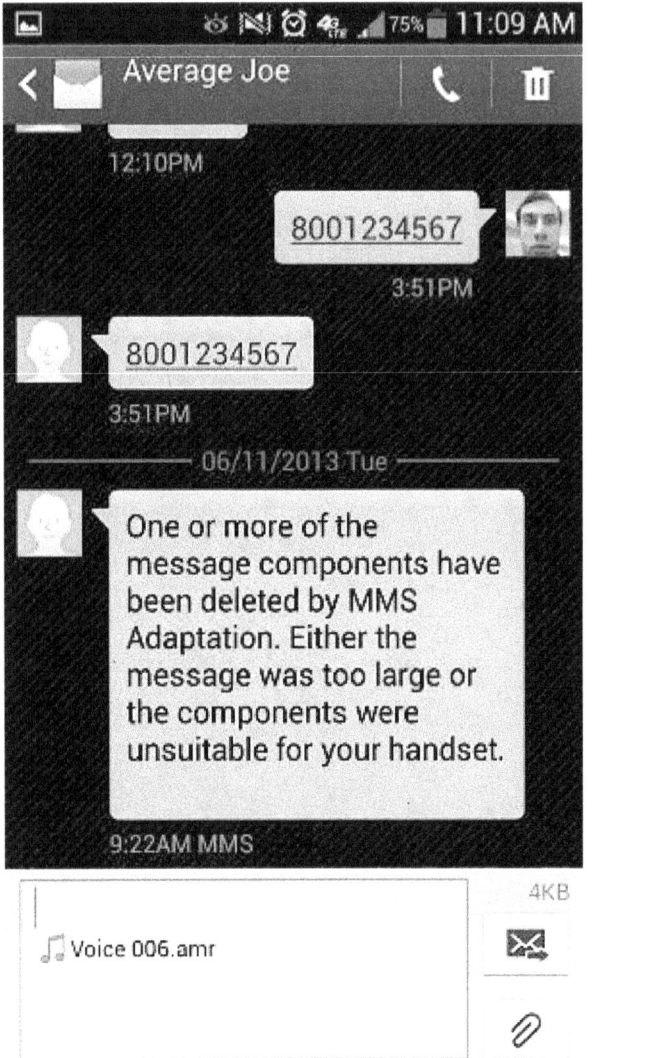

Figure 21: Text Message with Voice Recording Attached

16. Attaching a Note

The Galaxy Note 3 can send a media message containing a note (memo). To attach a note to a text message:

1. Refer to *"Adding an Attachment to a Text Message"* on page 94 and follow steps 1-3. The Attachment menu appears.

2. Touch the ![icon] icon. A list of notes appears, as shown in **Figure 22**. If you have not created any notes in the past, the list will be blank.

3. Touch a note in the list. The note is attached to the text message, as shown in **Figure 23**.

   You can also create a new note to attach by touching the ![plus icon] icon. When you are done composing the note, touch the ![checkmark icon] in the upper right-hand corner of the screen, and then touch **OK** to attach the note.

Figure 22: List of Memos

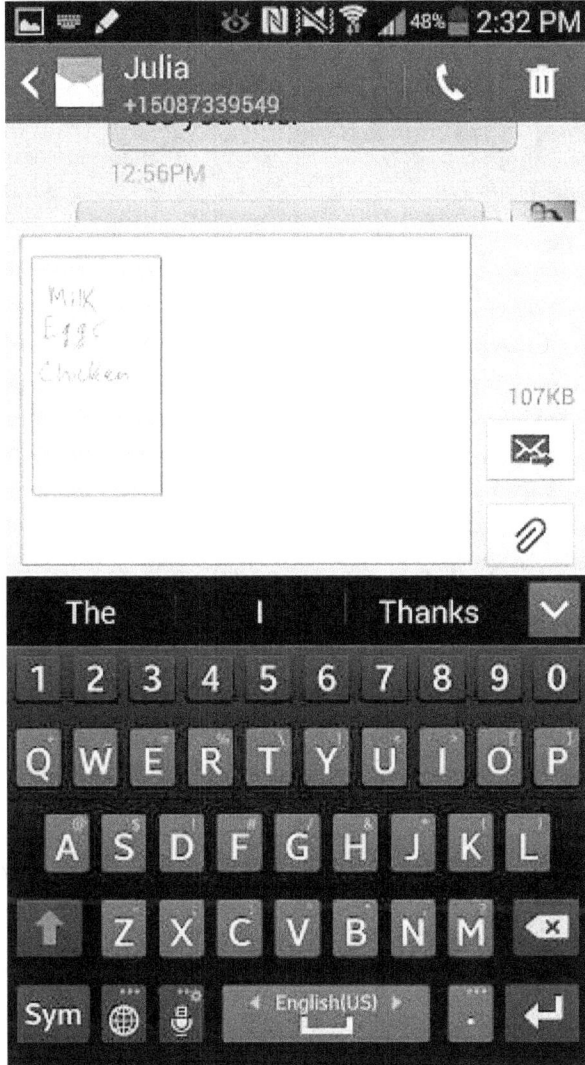

Figure 23: Text Message with Attached Memo

17. Attaching a Calendar Event

The Galaxy Note 3 can send a media message containing the information related to a calendar event, such as the date, time, and location. To attach a calendar event to a text message:

1. Refer to *"Adding an Attachment to a Text Message"* on page 94 and follow steps 1-3. The Attachment menu appears.

2. Touch the **31** icon. A list of events on your calendar appears, as shown in **Figure 24**.

3. Touch each event that you would like to attach. A ✓ appears next to each selected event.

4. Touch **Done** in the upper right-hand corner of the screen. The selected events are attached to the text message, as shown in **Figure 25** (with two events attached).

Note: No more than ten calendar events may be attached to a single text message.

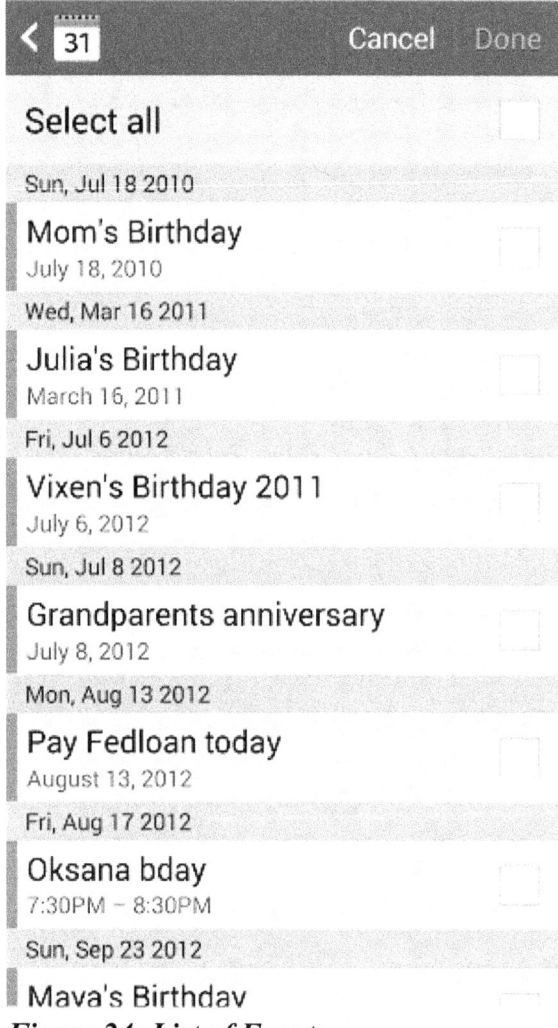

Figure 24: List of Events

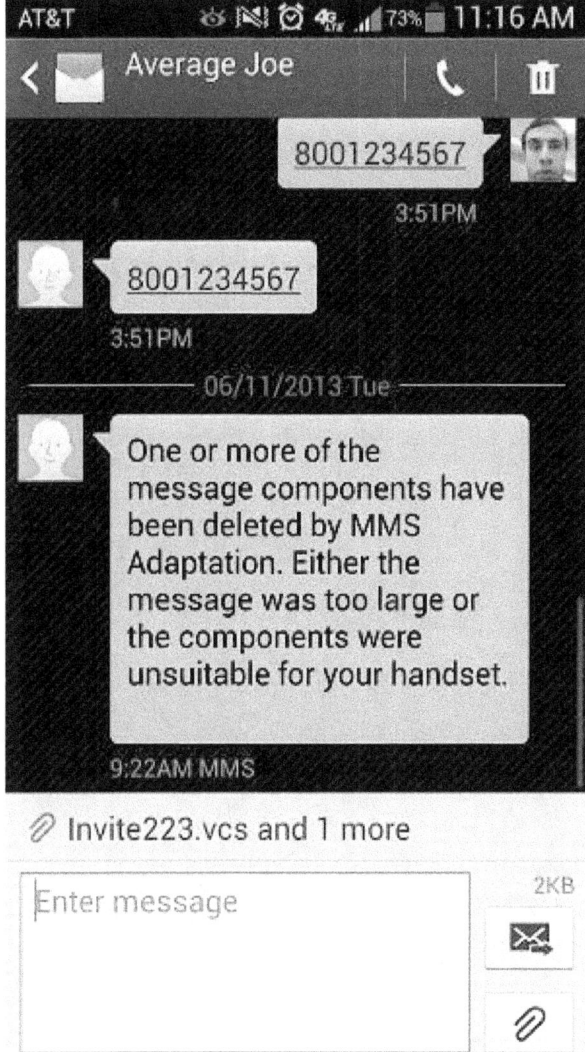

Figure 25: Text Message with Calendar Event Attached

18. Saving Attachments from Text Messages

After receiving an attachment in a text message, it can be saved to your Galaxy Note 3. To save an attachment from a text message:

1. Touch the   icon. The Messaging screen appears.
2. Touch a conversation. The conversation opens.
3. Touch and hold the attachment in the text message. The Message options appear.

4. Touch **Save attachment**. A list of files that are attached to the open conversation appears, as shown in **Figure 26**.
5. Touch an attachment to select it. A ✓ mark appears next to each selected attachment.
6. Touch **Save**. The attachment is saved to the Gallery.

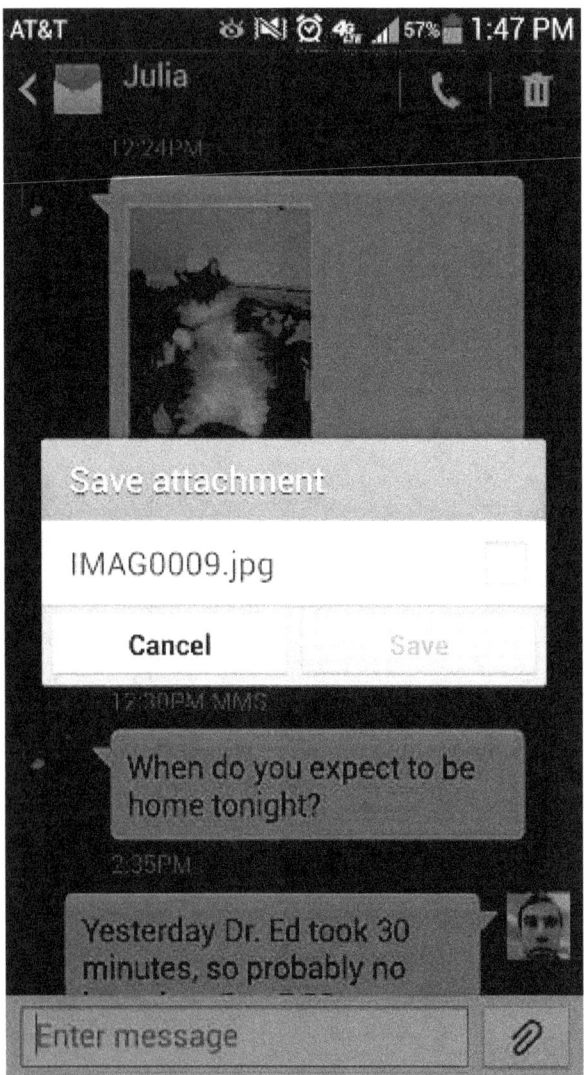

Figure 26: List of Attached Files

19. Sending a Text Message to an Entire Group

Creating contact groups allows you to send text messages to multiple people at a time without having to add each recipient separately. Refer to *"Adding a Contact to a Group"* on page 94 to learn more about groups. To send a text to an entire group:

1. Touch the [icon] icon at the bottom of the Home screen. The Messaging screen appears.
2. Touch the [icon] icon in the upper right-hand corner of the screen. The New Message screen appears.
3. Touch the [icon] button to the right of the 'Enter recipient' field. The Phonebook appears.
4. Touch **Groups** in the upper left-hand corner of the screen. A list of groups appears, as shown in **Figure 27**. If you do not see 'Groups', touch Contacts and slide your finger to the right.
5. Touch the group to which you would like to send a text message. A list of contacts that are contained in the group appears.
6. Touch **Select all**. All of the contacts in the group are selected, provided that there are ten contacts or less.
7. Touch **Done** in the upper right-hand corner of the screen. The selected contacts are added to the recipient field. Refer to *"Composing a New Text Message"* on page 77 to learn how to write and send a text message.

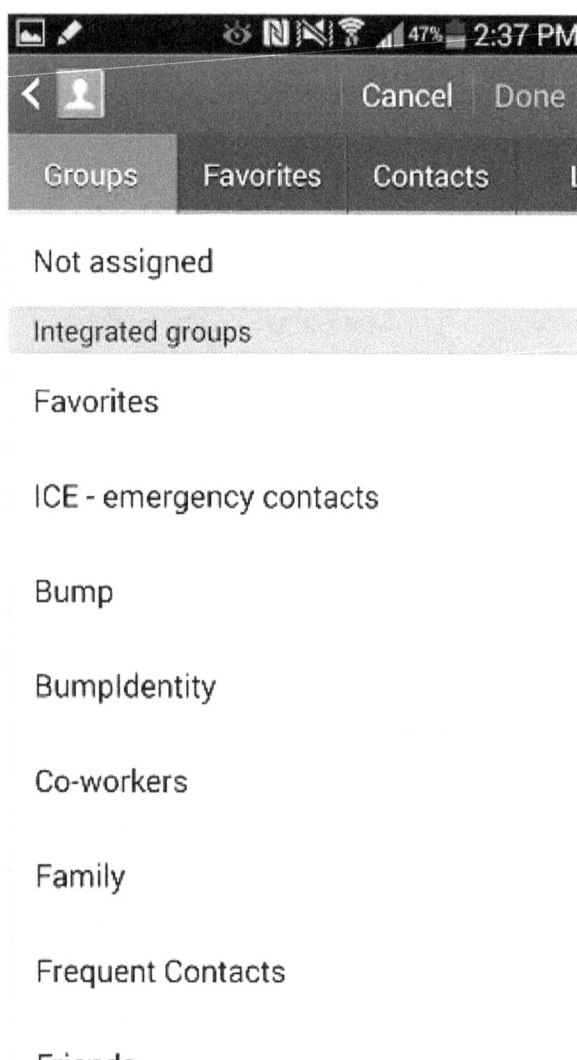

Figure 27: List of Groups

Taking Pictures and Capturing Videos

Table of Contents

1. Taking a Picture

The Galaxy Note 3 has a rear-facing 13 megapixel camera with auto focus and a front-facing 2 megapixel camera. To take a picture, touch the ⬤ icon. The camera turns on, as shown in **Figure 1**. Touch the 🔄 icon to switch cameras. Touch a part of the screen to make the camera focus on that location. Touch the 📷 button. The picture is captured, and stored in the 'Camera' album.

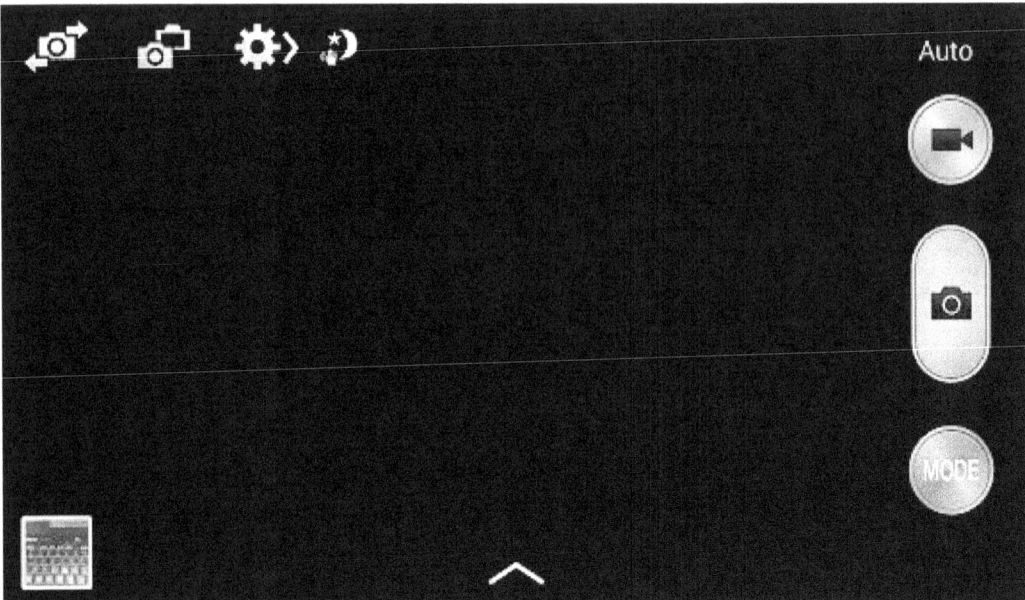

Figure 1: Camera Turned On

2. Using the Digital Zoom

While taking pictures, use the camera's built-in Digital Zoom feature if the subject of the photo is far away. Digital Zoom can also be used while recording a video. To zoom in, touch the screen with two fingers and move them apart. To zoom out, touch the screen with two fingers spread apart and move them together.

Note: Because of its digital nature, the zoom function will not provide the best resolution, and the image may look fuzzy. It is recommended to be as close as possible to the subject of the photo or video.

3. Using Both Cameras at Once

The Galaxy Note 3 has a unique feature that allows you to take two pictures at once using the front and rear cameras at the same time. To use both cameras at once:

1. Touch the icon. The camera turns on.
2. Touch the icon in the upper left-hand corner of the screen. A stamp appears on the screen, as shown in **Figure 2**.

3. Touch the stamp and move it to the desired location on the screen. You can also resize it by touching one of the corners and moving your finger.

4. Touch the ◤◥ icon at the bottom of the screen to replace the stamp with another shape. A list of available front camera shapes appears, as shown in **Figure 3**. Touch a shape to select it.

5. Touch the 📷 button. The picture is captured and stored in the 'Camera' album.

Figure 2: Front Camera Stamp

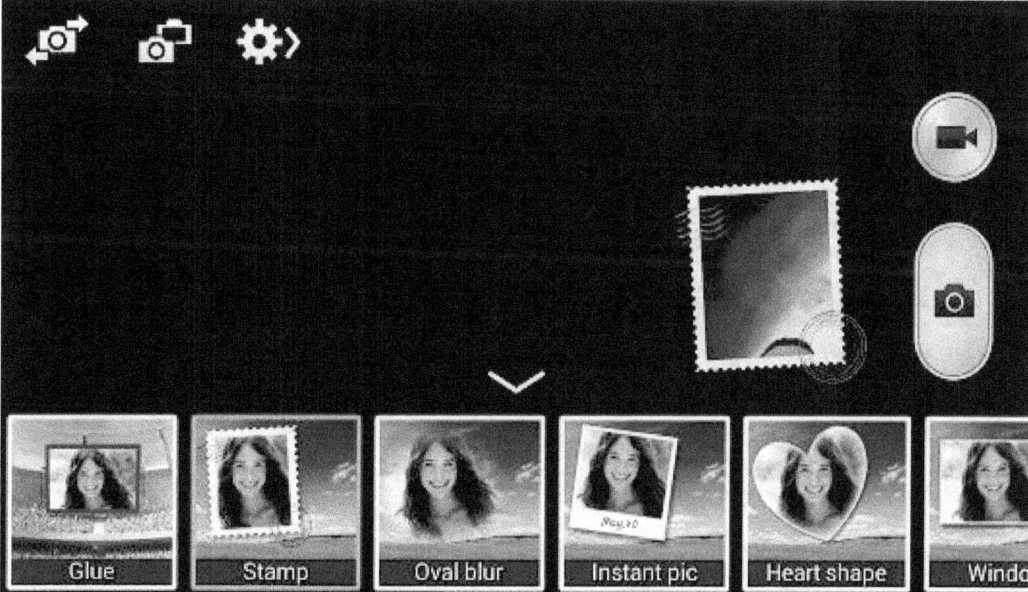

Figure 3: Front Camera Shapes

4. Using the Flash

The Galaxy Note 3 has a built-in flash, which can be used along with the rear-facing camera. When shooting a video with the flash turned on, it will remain on. To use the flash:

1. Touch the ![icon] icon. The camera turns on.

2. Touch the ![icon] icon. The Camera Quick settings appear, as shown in **Figure 4**.

3. Touch the ![icon] icon. The flash is turned on and will be used every time a picture is taken.

4. Touch the ![icon] icon. The flash is set to automatic and the surrounding light determines whether it is used.

5. Touch the ![icon] icon. The flash is turned off and will never be used.

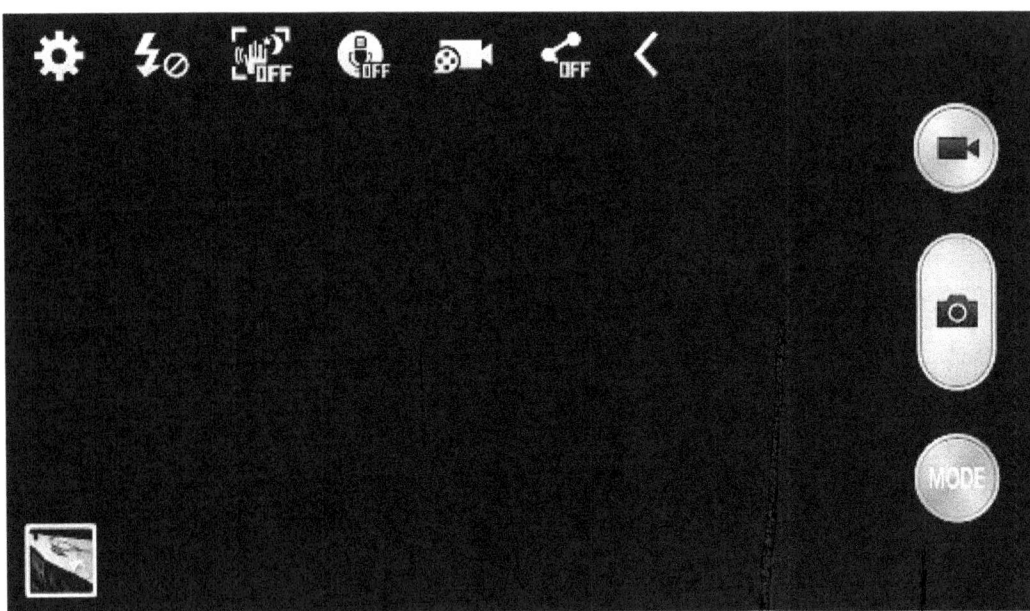

Figure 4: Camera Quick Settings

5. Applying an Effect before Taking a Picture

In order to avoid having to apply an effect after taking a picture, you may apply certain simple effects before taking one. To apply an effect before taking a picture, touch the ▰ icon at the bottom of the screen. A list of camera effects appears, as shown in **Figure 5**. Touch an effect and then take a picture by touching the ⬭ button to instantly apply it.

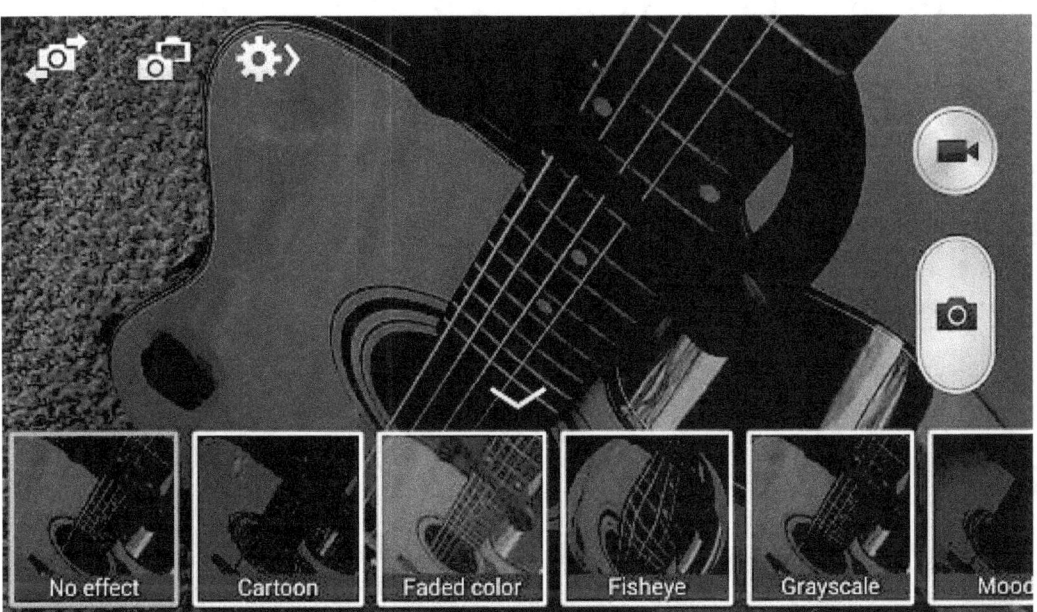

Figure 5: Camera Effects

6. Setting the Camera Mode

You may wish to set a different camera mode depending on the environment, such as when taking a picture at night or at a sporting event. To set the camera mode, touch the 🔘 button in the lower right-hand corner of the screen. The Camera Mode list appears, as shown in **Figure 6**. Touch one of the following modes. The selected mode is turned on. A description of each mode appears when you view it.

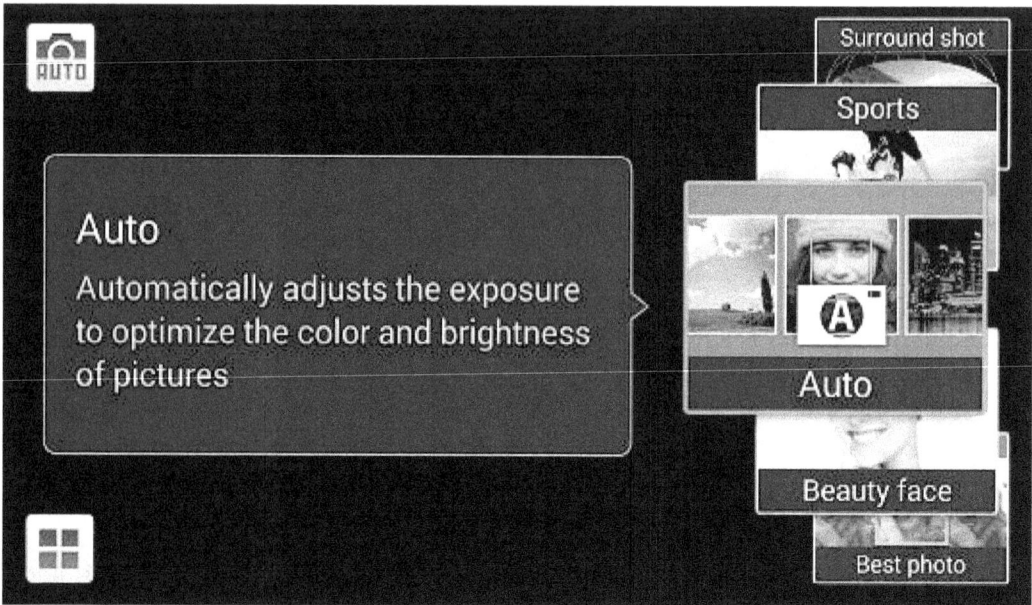

Figure 6: Camera Mode List

7. Creating an Animated Photo

The camera allows you to create pictures that have animated elements, such as people or animals performing stunts. To create an animated photo:

1. Select the **Animated Photo** mode. Refer to *"Setting the Camera Mode"* on page 176 to learn how.
2. Touch the [camera] button. The camera analyzes the scene searching for moving objects. Hold the phone steady while analyzing. The Animation Editing screen appears, as shown in **Figure 7**.
3. Touch the screen and select the part of the screen that you would like to animate by scrubbing it with your finger.
4. Touch **Freeze** at the top of the screen and then select the part of the screen that you would like to keep from animating.
5. Touch **Save** in the upper right-hand corner of the screen. The animated photo is saved in the 'Camera' album.

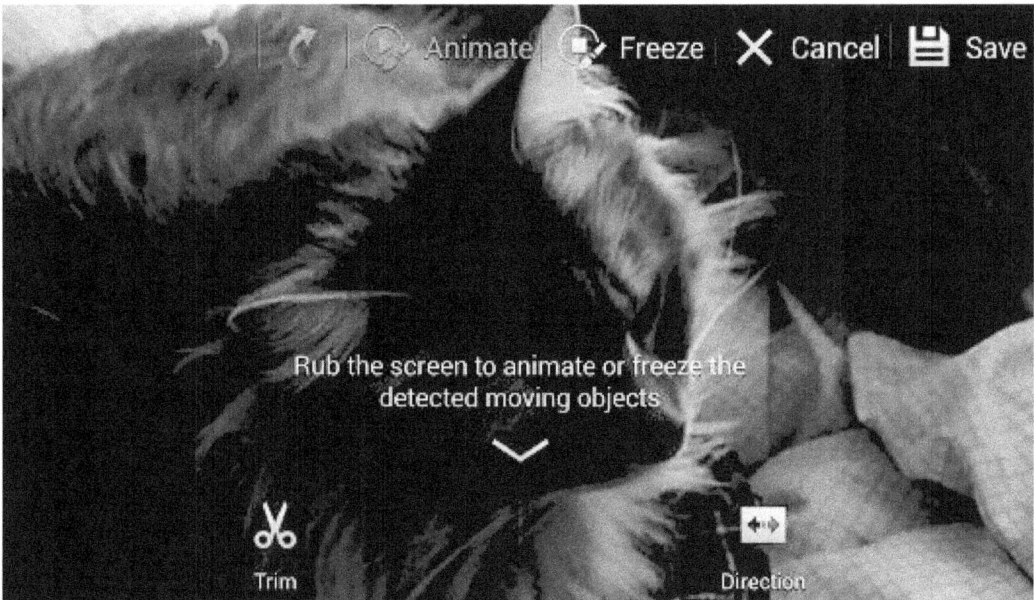

Figure 7: Animation Editing Screen

8. Creating a Panoramic Photo

The camera allows you to take pictures of panoramic scenes that are too wide to fit in a normal picture, such as a landscape. To create a panoramic photo:

1. Select the **Panorama** mode. Refer to *"Setting the Camera Mode"* on page 167 to learn how.
2. Move the camera to the left-most part of the scene that you wish to capture. Touch the ⬚ button. The camera captures the first frame, as shown in **Figure 8**.
3. Slowly move the camera to the right-most part of the scene. When the camera has finished capturing as much as it can store, the photo is automatically stored in the 'Camera' album.

Figure 8: First Frame of a Panoramic Photo

9. Capturing a Video

The Galaxy Note 3 has a built-in camcorder that allows you to capture videos. To capture a video:

1. Touch the ⬤ icon. The camera turns on.

2. Touch the 🎥 button. The camcorder begins to record video, as shown in **Figure 9**.

3. Touch the ⏸ button at any time to pause the camcorder.

4. Touch the ⏹ button. The camcorder stops recording, and the video is stored in the 'Camera' album.

Figure 9: Camcorder Recording a Video

10. Taking a Picture while Capturing a Video

While capturing a video, you may take a quick snapshot of the screen. To take a picture while

capturing a video, touch the [camera icon] button. A photo is taken, and stored in the 'Camera' album.

11. Setting the Camcorder Mode

You may wish to set a different camcorder mode depending on your preferences, such as when sending a video in a text message. To set the camcorder mode:

1. Touch the [icon] icon. The camera turns on.
2. Touch the [icon] icon. The Camera Quick settings appear.
3. Touch the [icon] icon at the top of the screen. The Recording Mode menu appears, as shown in **Figure 10**.
4. Touch one of the following options to select the corresponding mode:

   - **Normal** - Default recording mode with no effects.

121

- **Limit for MMS** - Limits the size of the video so that it can be attached to a text message.
- **Slow motion** - Makes the moving objects in the video move at a slower rate. Touch the ⬛ icon to adjust the slow motion setting.
- **Fast Motion** - Makes the moving objects in the video move at a faster rate. Touch the ⬛ icon to adjust the fast motion setting.
- **Smooth Motion** - Reduces jerky movements of the objects in the video.

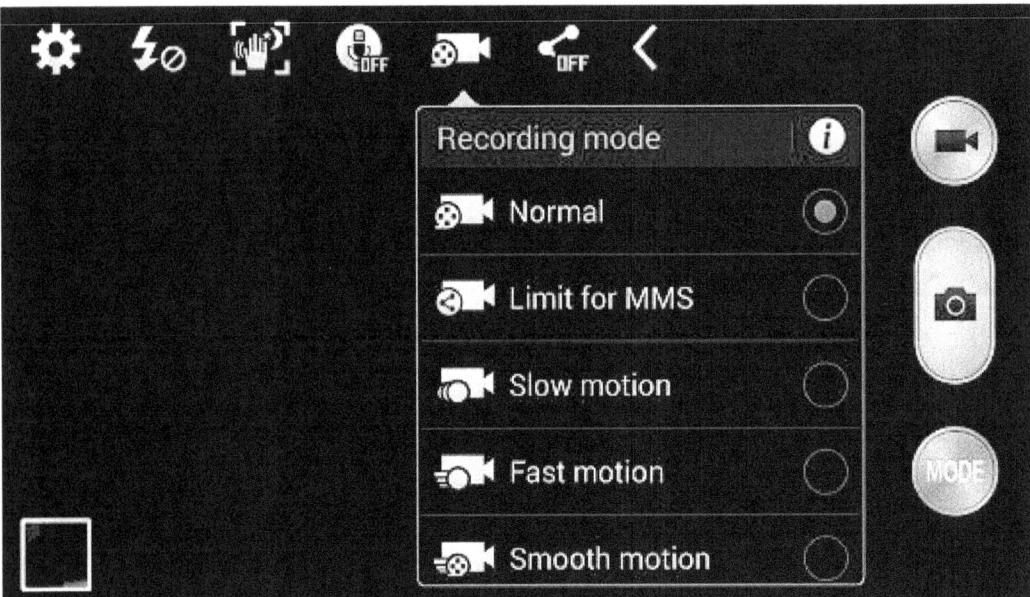

Figure 10: Recording Mode Menu

12. Editing Camera and Camcorder Settings

The camera and camcorder settings on the phone can be adjusted to essentially edit a photo or video before it is taken. Settings include changing the brightness, adding an effect, or changing the image quality.

Adjusting Camera Settings

To adjust the camera settings when the camera is turned on:

1. Touch the ⬛ icon. The Camera Quick settings appear.

2. Touch the ⬛ icon. The Camera settings appear, as shown in **Figure 11**.
3. Touch one of the following to adjust the corresponding setting:

- **Photo size** - Set the resolution of the photo. A higher resolution will produce a higher quality photo, but will take up more memory.
- **Burst Shot** - Quickly takes several photos of a moving target.
- **Tap to take pics** - Allows you to touch an area on the screen to focus on it, and immediately capture a photo. You do not need to touch the button to capture photos when this feature is turned on.
- **Face Detection** - Allows the camera to automatically detect and focus on people's faces.
- **Metering** - Determines how the camera measures light. Center-weighted metering measures background light in the center of the scene. Spot metering measures light around the subject of the photo. Matrix metering averages the light in the entire scene.
- **ISO** - Controls the camera's sensitivity to light. Use lower values for subjects that are not moving or those that are already brightly lit. Use higher values for subjects that are moving quickly or those that are poorly lit.
- **Smart stabilization** - Prevents blurriness that occurs when your hand shakes while taking a picture.

Touch the icon in the upper right-hand corner of the Camera settings to adjust these additional settings:

- **Location tag** - Assigns a location to each photo that you take, provided that you have GPS services turned on.
- **Review** - Display a photo in the Gallery after it is taken. If 'Review' is turned on, you will need to navigate back to the camera every time that you take a picture.
- **Volume key** - Assigns one of the following functions to the volume button: zooming in or out, taking a picture, or capturing a video.
- **Timer** - Delays the shot by the specified number of seconds.
- **White balance** - Select the correct white balance to match the environment and create a true-to-life color range. The White Balance setting is similar to the Heat Range setting on professional cameras.
- **Exposure value** - Adjusts the amount of light that enters the camera's sensor. Use a higher exposure for low-light environments and vice versa.
- **Guidelines** - Activates gridlines to help you align the subjects in your shot.
- **Voice control** - Allows you to take pictures using voice commands, such 'Cheese' and 'Shoot'.
- **Contextual filename** - Gives each picture a file name based on its contents. Activate this feature to use the Tag Buddy feature in the Gallery.
- **Storage** - Determines where each captured photo is saved. Choose 'Memory card' to store photos on a microSD card that you have inserted. Choose 'Device' to store photos on the device's internal storage.
- **Shutter sound** - Causes the phone to make a camera shutter sound every time a picture is taken.

- **Reset** - Resets all camera and camcorder settings to factory defaults.

Adjusting Camcorder Settings

Touch the [icon] icon at the top of the Camera settings to adjust these camcorder settings:

- **Video size** - Set the resolution of the video. A higher resolution will produce a higher quality video, but will take up more memory.
- **Video stabilization** - Prevents the motion blur that occurs when your hand shakes while capturing a video.
- **Audio zoom** - Zooming in on a specific area causes the microphone to focus on the area in order to capture sound more clearly.

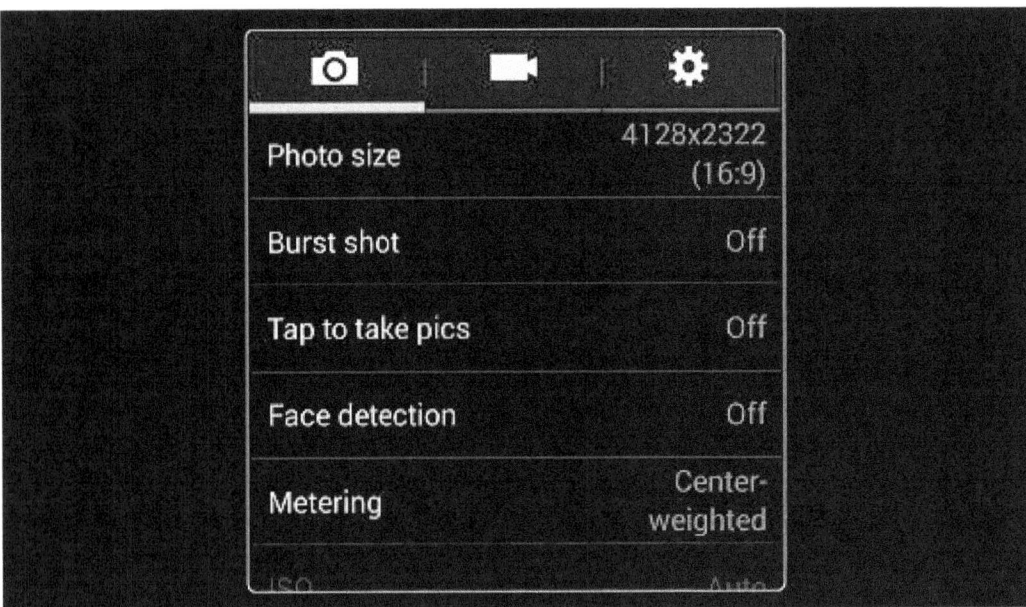

Figure 11: Camera Settings

Managing Photo and Video Albums

Table of Contents

1. Browsing Photos and Videos

You can browse pictures without activating the camera. To view saved images:

1. Touch the ▨ icon. The Gallery opens, as shown in **Figure 1**.
2. Touch an album. The album opens and the thumbnails of the photos in it appear, as shown in **Figure 2**.
3. Touch a photo or video. The photo appears in full-screen mode or the video begins to play.
4. Touch the screen and move your finger to the left or right. Other photos and videos in the same album appear.
5. Touch the ◀ button. The thumbnails of the pictures in the current album appear.

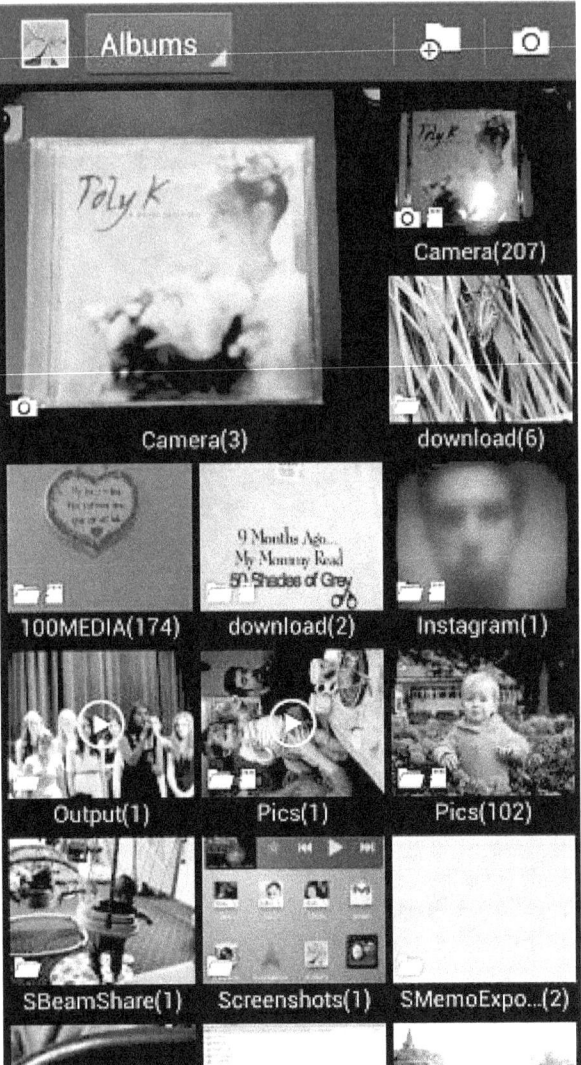

Figure 1: Gallery

Figure 2: Photo Thumbnails

2. Starting a Slideshow

The Galaxy Note 3 can play slideshows using the pictures stored in the Gallery. To start a slideshow:

1. Touch the ![icon] icon. The Gallery opens.
2. Touch an album. The album opens.
3. Touch the ![key] key. The Album menu appears, as shown in **Figure 3**.
4. Touch **Slideshow**. The Slideshow Settings window appears, as shown in **Figure 4**.
5. Touch one of the following effects in the list to use it as a transition between photos during the slideshow:

   - **Flow** - No effect. Moves to the next photo by sliding the previous one horizontally to the left.
   - **Fade** - Slowly fades into the next photo while leaving the previous one on the screen.
   - **Zoom** - Slowly zooms into the current photo and then switches abruptly to the next one.
   - **Drop** - Several photos drop down from the top of the screen at once.
   - **Zoom in on faces** - Slowly zooms in on the photo, focusing on the faces.
   - **Cube** - Three-dimensional cube effect.
   - **Perspective shuffle** - Shows a small version of each photo while showing several upcoming photos in the background.
   - **Random** - Applies a random effect from this list every time the slideshow transitions to a new photo.

6. Touch **Music** at the top of the Slideshow Settings window. Touch one of the options in the list to play music during the slideshow.
7. Touch **More** at the top of the Slideshow Settings window to select the number of seconds each photo stays on the screen, under 'Speed', and the order in which the photos are shown, under 'Playing order'.
8. Touch **Start**. The slideshow begins.
9. Touch the screen anywhere. The slideshow ends, and the photo album appears.

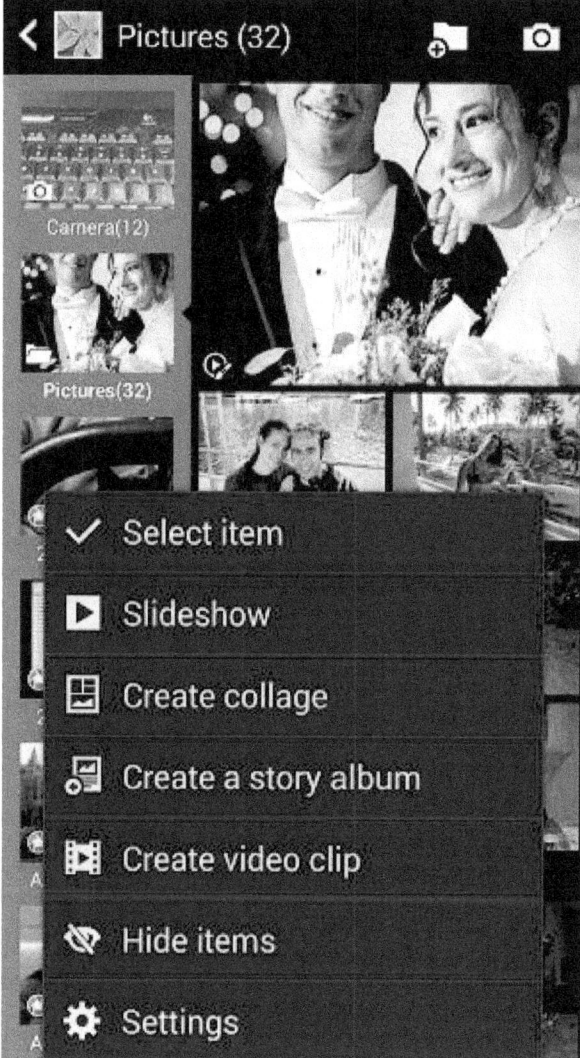

Figure 3: Album Menu

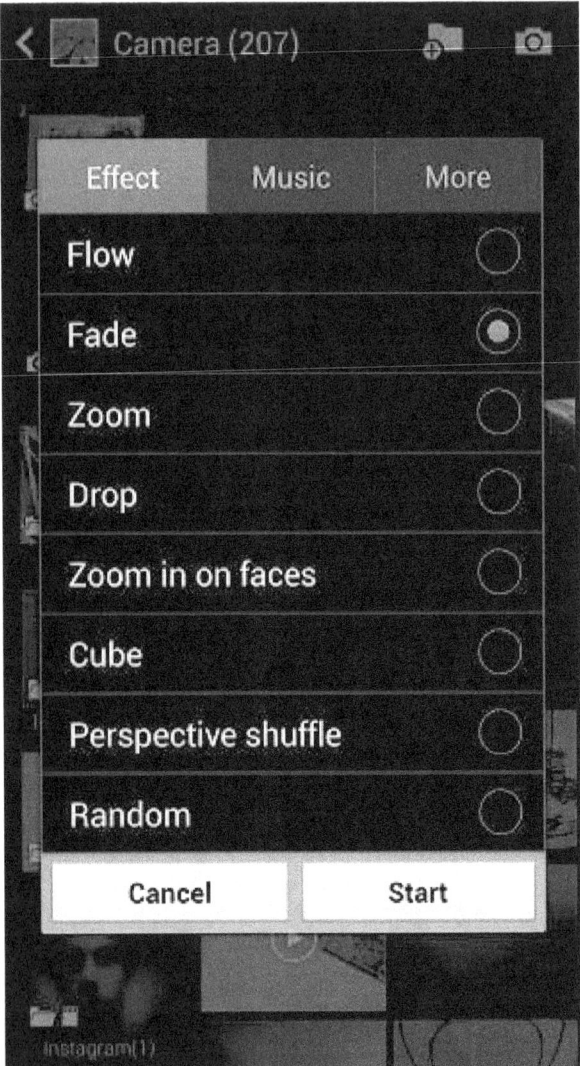

Figure 4: Slideshow Settings Window

3. Editing a Photo

After taking a picture, you can use the Galaxy Note 3 to crop it, rotate it, or enhance it with effects. To edit pictures in the Gallery:

1. Touch the ![icon] icon. The Gallery opens.
2. Touch an album. The album opens.
3. Touch a photo. The photo appears in full-screen mode.
4. Touch the ![key] key. The Photo menu appears, as shown in **Figure 5**.
5. Touch **Edit**. The Photo Editing screen appears, as shown in **Figure 6**.
6. Follow the steps in one of the following sections to edit the photo:

Rotating a Photo

You may wish to rotate a photo to orient it vertically or horizontally. To rotate a photo:

1. Touch the ![icon] icon at the bottom of the screen. Photo rotation is enabled.
2. Touch the photo and move your finger in a clockwise or counter-clockwise motion to rotate the photo accordingly. The photo is rotated.
3. You can also touch one of the following icons to rotate the photo accordingly:

![icon] - Rotates the photo 90 degrees counter-clockwise.

![icon] - Rotates the photo 90 degrees clockwise.

![icon] - Flips the photo 180 degrees horizontally. This means that any objects pointing to the right will now point to the left, and vice versa.

![icon] - Flips the photo 180 degrees vertically. This means that any objects pointing down will now point up, and vice versa.

4. Touch **Save** in the upper right-hand corner of the screen when you are finished. The photo is saved as a copy of the original in the same album. The original photo is left in its original location. Alternatively, touch **Cancel** at the top of the screen to discard the rotated photo and leave the original as it is.

Cropping a Photo

Crop a photo to use only a portion of it. To crop a photo:

1. Touch the ![icon] icon at the bottom of the screen. A blue cropping rectangle appears on the photo. The portion of the photo that will be included in the crop is in color, while the rest is in black and white. If the photo is already in black and white, the previous sentence does not apply.
2. Use the following tips when cropping a photo:

   - Touch the ![icon] icons and drag them in any direction to change the size of the cropped area.
   - Touch inside the cropped area and move it to select the part of the photo that you wish to keep.
   - Touch the ![icon] icon and move your finger clockwise or counter-clockwise to rotate the cropping rectangle accordingly.
   - Touch one of the aspect ratio icons at the bottom of the screen, such as 1:1 or 16:9, to select a cropping rectangle with preset dimensions.
   - Touch the ![icon] icon in the lower left-hand corner of the screen to preview the cropped picture before saving it.

3. Touch **Save** in the upper right-hand corner of the screen when you are finished. The photo is saved as a copy of the original in the same album. The original photo is left in its original location. Alternatively, touch **Cancel** at the top of the screen to discard the cropped photo and leave the original as it is.

Adjusting the Color Balance

You can manually adjust the color balance to achieve the desired appearance in a photo. To adjust the color balance:

1. Touch the ![icon] icon at the bottom of the screen. The Color Balance menu appears at the bottom of the screen.
2. Touch one of the following options below to adjust the corresponding color setting:

   - **Auto adjust** - Automatically adjusts the color balance to achieve the best picture.
   - **Brightness** - Adjust the brightness of the photo.
   - **Contrast** - Increases or decreases the difference between the darkest and lightest areas of the photo.

- **Saturation** - Increases or decreases the difference between the colors in the photo. A minimum saturation will produce a black and white photo.
- **Adjust RGB** - Adjust the amount of red, green, and blue color in the photo.
- **Temperature** - Increases or decreases the amount of blue and white colors, or red and yellow colors. A low temperature will produce a scene that imitates overcast conditions or winter, while a high temperature will produce a scene that looks like summer, or a sunny day.
- **Exposure** - Adjusts the amount of light that is allowed to fall on each part of the photo.
- **Hue** - Adjusts the tint of the colors in the photo. This tool can completely alter the color of your photo.

3. Touch **Save** in the upper right-hand corner of the screen when you are finished. The photo is saved as a copy of the original in the same album. The original photo is left in its original location. Alternatively, touch **Cancel** at the top of the screen to discard the adjusted photo and leave the original as it is.

Adding Effects

To add effects to a photo, touch the ⬛ icon at the bottom of the screen, and then touch the desired effect. The effect is applied. Some effects require adjustment. Touch **Save** in the upper right-hand corner of the screen. The photo is saved as a copy of the original in the same album. The original photo is left in its original location. Alternatively, touch **Cancel** at the top of the screen to discard the adjusted photo and leave the original as it is.

Touching Up Faces

You may wish to perform some touch up on the faces in a photo, especially for formal occasions. To touch up a face:

1. Touch the ⬛ icon at the bottom of the screen. The Portrait options appear at the bottom of the screen.
2. Touch one of the options below and then use the + and - to apply and adjust the corresponding effect:

   - **Red-eye fix** - Removes red eyes from a photo. Touch an eye to remove the red-eye effect.
   - **Airbrush face** - Removes imperfections, including pimples and even minor facial hair, from the entire face.
   - **Face brightness** - Increases or decreases the amount of light shed on a face.
   - **Out-of-focus** - Increases or decreases the focus on the background of the photo.
   - **Spot healing** - Removes imperfections in selected locations on the face.

Adding a Clip-Art Sticker

Just for fun, you may wish to add a sticker to a photo. Touch the ⭐ icon at the bottom of the screen, and then choose a sticker to do so. Touch the sticker and then drag it to the desired location on the photo. Touch **Save** in the upper right-hand corner of the screen. The photo is saved as a copy of the original in the same album. The original photo is left in its original location. Alternatively, touch **Cancel** at the top of the screen to discard the clip art and leave the original as it is.

Adding a Drawing

Just for fun, you may wish to add a drawing to a photo. Touch the ✎ icon at the bottom of the screen, and then choose a pen to do so. Use the eraser to erase anything you have drawn. The eraser will not erase the photo. Touch **Save** in the upper right-hand corner of the screen. The photo is saved as a copy of the original in the same album. The original photo is left in its original location. Alternatively, touch **Cancel** at the top of the screen to discard the drawing on the photo and leave the original as it is.

Adding a Frame

Just for fun, you may wish to add a frame to a photo. Touch the ◻ icon at the bottom of the screen, and then choose a frame to do so. Touch **Save** in the upper right-hand corner of the screen. The photo is saved as a copy of the original in the same album. The original photo is left in its original location. Alternatively, touch **Cancel** at the top of the screen to discard the framed photo and leave the original as it is.

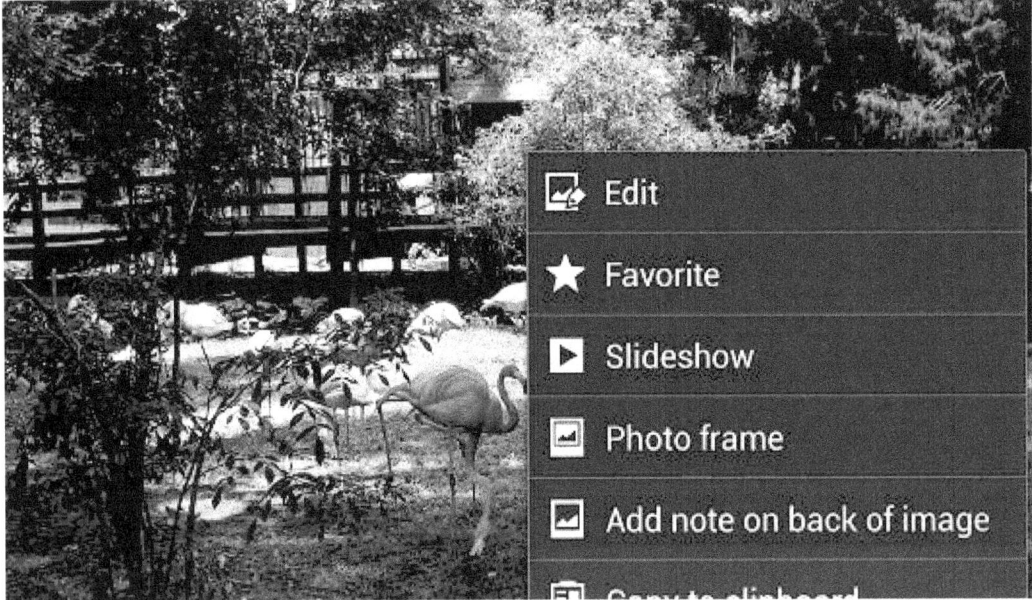

Figure 5: Photo Menu

Figure 6: Photo Editing Screen

4. Adding a Note on the Back of a Photo

For your reference, you may wish to add a note to a photo. To add a note:

1. Open a photo. Refer to *"Browsing Photos and Videos"* on page 125 to learn how.
2. Touch the ▦ key. The Photo menu appears.
3. Touch **Add note** on the back of the image. The Pen tools appear at the top of the screen, as shown in **Figure 7**.
4. Write a note on the picture using your finger like a pen (or use the S Pen).
5. Touch the ✔ icon in the upper right-hand corner of the screen. The note is saved. While

   viewing a photo, touch the ✎ icon in the upper right-hand corner to view the note.

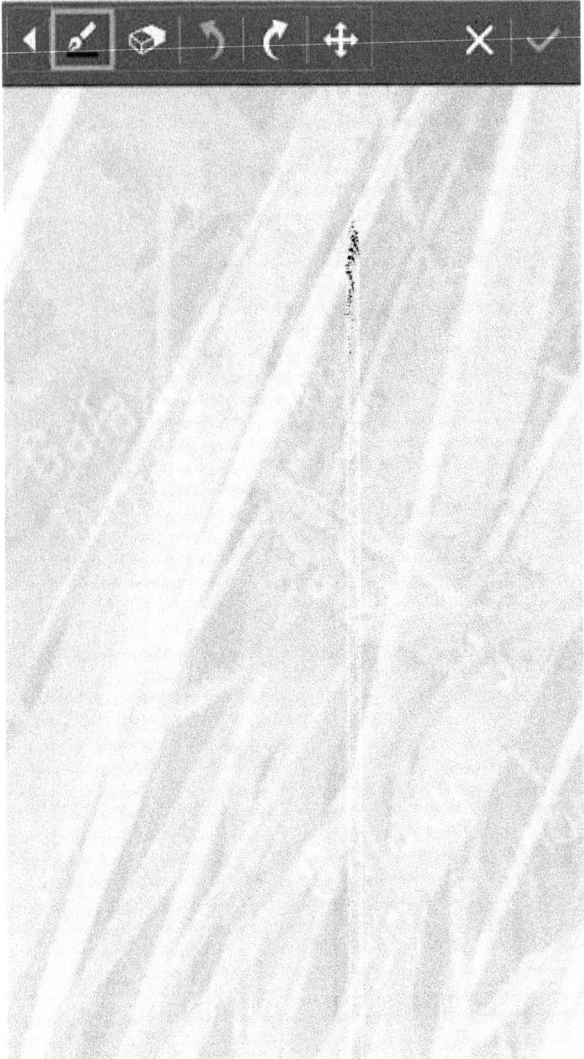

Figure 7: Pen Tools

5. Tagging a Person in a Photo

You may tag specific people in photos in order to find them more quickly or to share photos with them. To tag a person in a photo:

1. Open a photo. Refer to *"Browsing Photos and Videos"* on page 125 to learn how.
2. Touch the ▤ key. The Photo menu appears.
3. Scroll down and touch **Settings**. The Gallery Settings screen appears, as shown in **Figure 8**.

4. Touch **Face Tag**. A ✓ mark appears next to 'Face Tag', and Face Tagging is turned on. Touch the ⬅ key to return to the photo.
5. Touch a face in the photo. A yellow rectangle appears around the face.
6. Touch anywhere inside the yellow rectangle. 'Add name' and 'Me' appears.
7. Touch **Me** if you wish to tag yourself. Otherwise, touch **Add name**. The Phonebook appears.
8. Touch the name of a contact. The face is tagged as the contact that you selected. If the contact does not exist in the Phonebook, touch the ➕ button to add him or her.

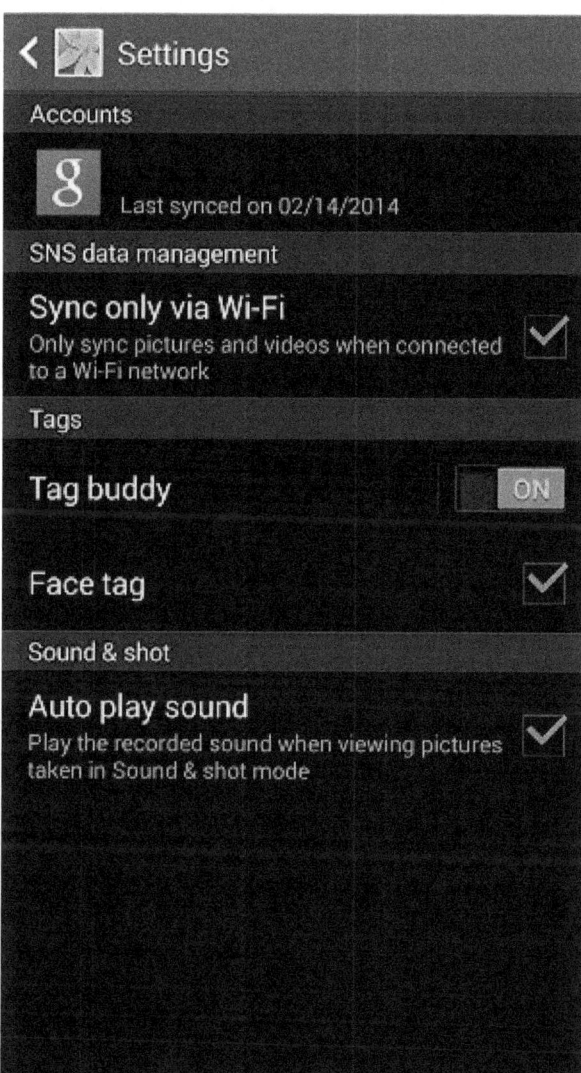

Figure 8: Gallery Settings Screen

6. Sharing a Photo with the People Tagged in It

Tagging people in a photo can be useful because you can quickly share photos with them. Refer to *"Tagging a Person in a Photo"* on page 136 to learn how. To share a photo with a tagged person:

1. Open a photo. Refer to *"Browsing Photos and Videos"* on page 125 to learn how.
2. Touch the ▤ key. The Photo menu appears.
3. Scroll down and touch **Buddy photo share**. A list of tagged people appears, as shown in **Figure 9**.
4. Touch the name of each tagged person with whom you would like to share the photo. The Sharing options appear.
5. Touch the @ icon to share the photo via email or touch the   icon to share via text message. The Sharing method is selected.
6. Touch **OK**. The photo is shared with the selected contacts.

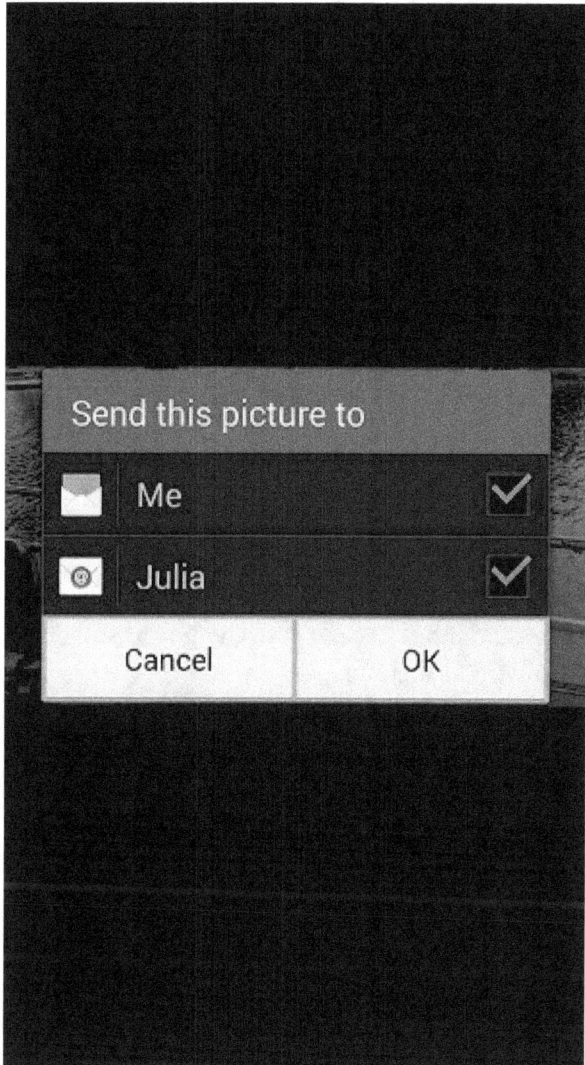

Figure 9: List of Tagged People

7. Trimming a Video

You may trim a video in order to keep only the segment that you want. To trim a video:

1. Open the video that you would like to trim. Refer to *"Browsing Photos and Videos"* on page 125 to learn how.

2. Touch the ✄ icon at the top of the screen, as outlined in **Figure 10**. The Video Trimming screen appears, as shown in **Figure 11**. If you do not see the ✄ icon, touch the screen anywhere.

3. Touch the icon and drag it to the right to select the beginning of the video and cut out the rest of the content at the beginning. Touch the icon and drag it to the left to select the end of the video and cut out the rest of the content at the end.

4. Touch **Done** in the upper right-hand corner of the screen. The New File name dialog appears.

5. Enter a name for the new video and touch **Done** in the lower right-hand corner of the screen. The new video is saved in the same album. The original video remains untouched.

Figure 10: Video Trimming Icon Outlined

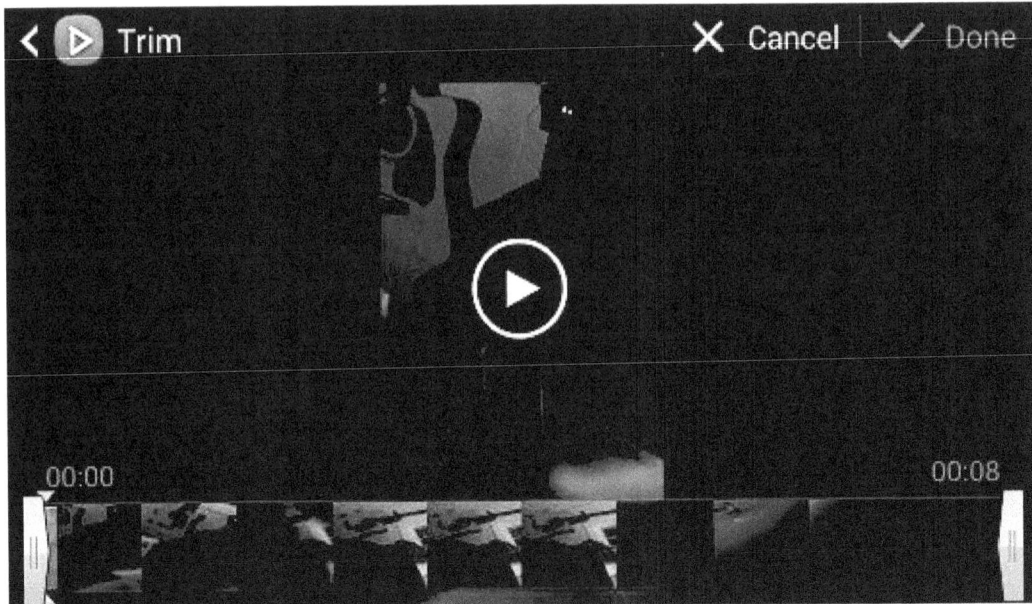

Figure 11: Video Trimming Screen

8. Deleting Photos and Videos

Warning: Once a photo or video is deleted, there is no way to restore it, so make sure you do not want the selected files.

To free up some space in the phone's memory, try deleting photos or videos from the Gallery. To delete a photo or video:

1. Open a photo album. Refer to *"Browsing Photos and Videos"* on page 125 to learn how.
2. Touch and hold a photo or video. The photo is selected and a ✓ mark appears next to it, as outlined in **Figure 12**.
3. Touch as many photos and videos as desired. The items are selected.
4. Touch the 🗑 icon in the upper right-hand corner of the screen. A confirmation dialog appears.
5. Touch **OK**. The selected items are deleted.

Figure 12: Selected Photo

Using the Chrome Browser

Table of Contents

1. Navigating to a Web Page

You can surf the Web using your Galaxy Note 3. It is highly recommended that you use the Google Chrome browser for the best Web experience. To navigate to a Web page using a web address, or URL:

1. Touch the icon, or touch the icon and then touch the icon. The Chrome browser opens, as shown in **Figure 1**.
2. Touch the address bar at the top of the screen, as outlined in **Figure 1**. The address is highlighted in blue and the virtual keyboard appears.
3. Enter the Web address and touch the button. The phone navigates to the corresponding website.

Note: Refer to "Tips and Tricks" *on page 318 to learn more about using the address bar.*

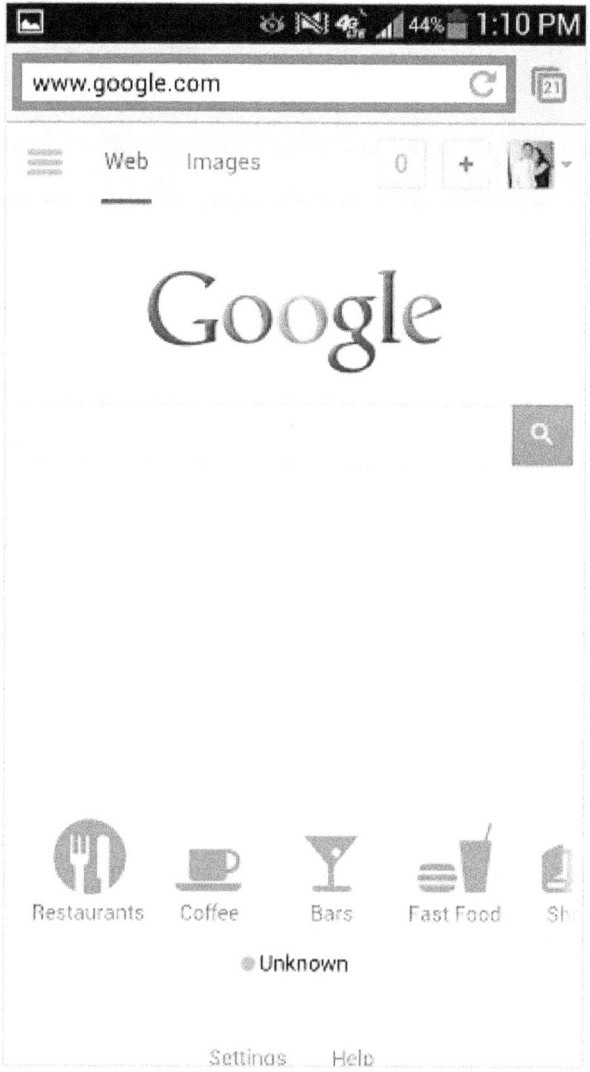

Figure 1: Chrome Browser Open

2. Adding and Viewing Bookmarks

The Galaxy Note 3 can store favorite web pages as bookmarks to allow you to access them faster in the future. To add a bookmark:

1. Navigate to a web page. Refer to *"Navigating to a Web Page"* on page 144 to learn how.
2. Touch the ▭ key. The Chrome menu appears, as shown in **Figure 2**.

3. Touch the ⭐ icon. The Add Bookmark screen appears, as shown in **Figure 3**.

4. Enter a name for the bookmark and touch **Save**. The web page is saved to your bookmarks. You can also save the bookmark to a specific folder by touching **Mobile bookmarks** and selecting a different folder.

To view saved bookmarks:

1. Touch the 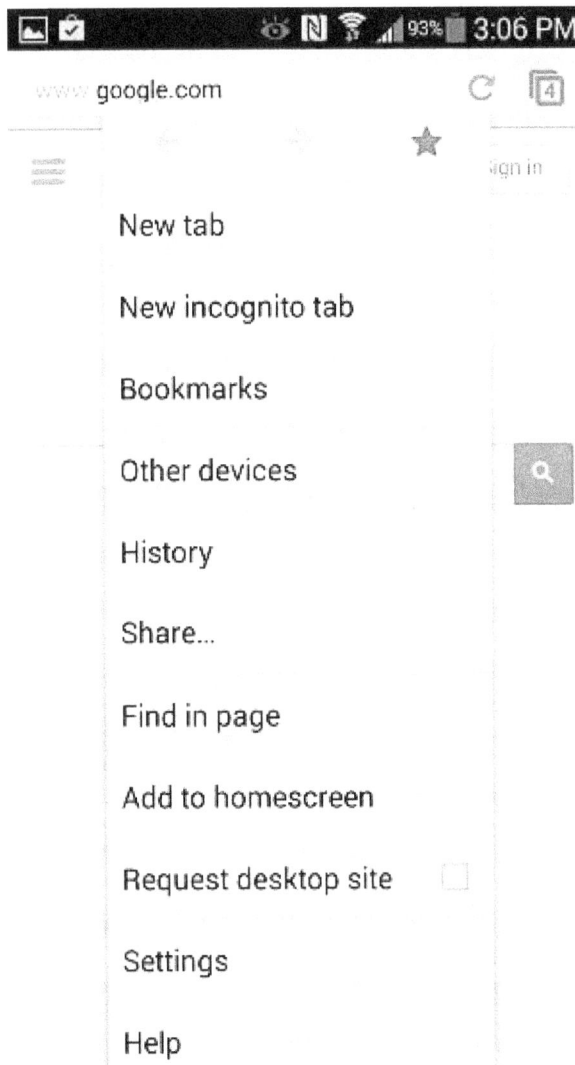 key. The Chrome menu appears.

2. Touch **Bookmarks**. A list of bookmarks appears, as shown in **Figure 4**.
3. Touch a bookmark. Chrome navigates to the web page.

Figure 2: Chrome Menu

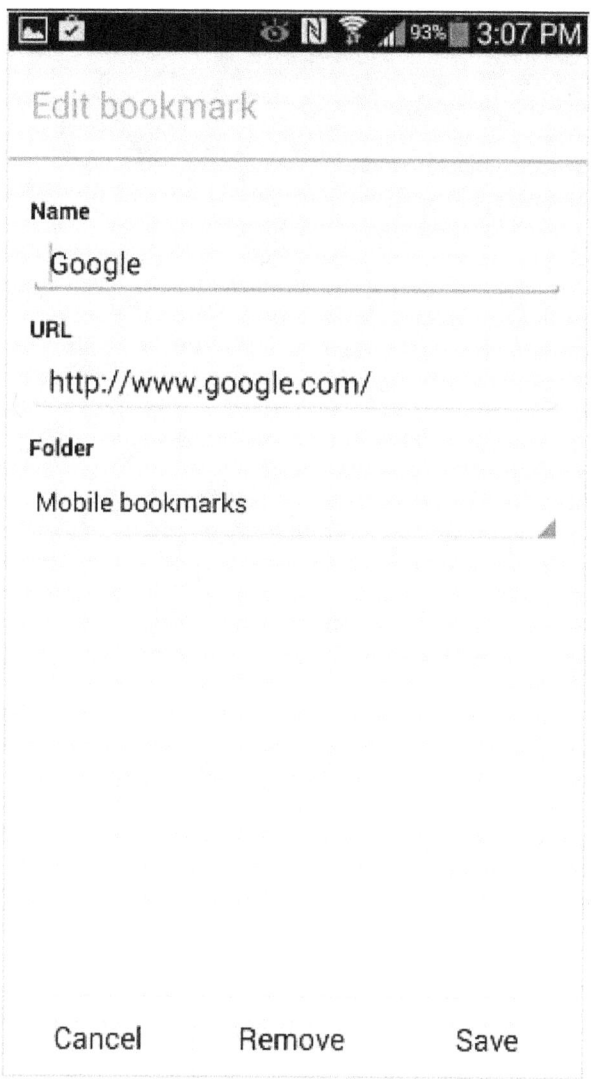

Figure 3: Add Bookmark Screen

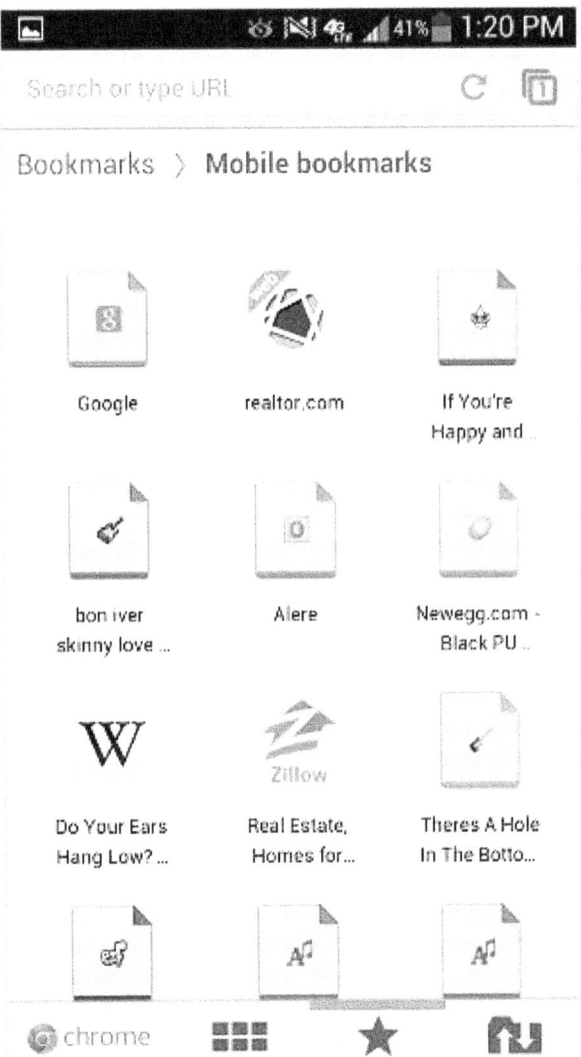

Figure 4: List of Bookmarks

3. Managing Browser Tabs

The Chrome browser supports an unlimited number of tabs. Use the following tips when working with open browser windows:

1. Touch the  icon. The open tabs appear, as shown in **Figure 5**.
2. Touch **New Tab**. A new tab is created.
3. Touch and hold a tab while viewing all open tabs, and slide your finger to the left or right. The selected tab is closed.
4. Touch a tab while viewing all open tabs. The tab opens.

Figure 5: Open Tabs

4. Working with Links

In addition to touching a link to navigate to its destination, there are other link options. Touch and hold a link to see all link options, as shown in **Figure 6**. The following options are available:

- **Open in new tab** - Opens the link in a new tab, so as not lose the current web page. Refer to *"Managing Browser Tabs"* on page 149 to learn how to view all open tabs.
- **Open in incognito tab** - Opens the link in a new incognito tab, so as not lose the current web page. An incognito tab is not recorded in your browsing history for increased privacy. Refer to *"Managing Browser Tabs"* on page 149 to learn how to view all open tabs.
- **Copy link address** - Copies the web address to the clipboard. Touch and hold an empty space in any application and touch **Paste** to paste the link. Refer to *"Navigating to a Web Page"* on page 144 to learn how to visit a website using the URL.
- **Copy link text** - Selects the text in the link to be copied and pasted in another location. Refer to *"Copying, Cutting, and Pasting Text"* on page 80 to learn more. You can also touch and hold plain text to achieve the same effect.
- **Save Link** - Downloads the web page to the phone. To view a list of downloads, touch the ▦ icon at the bottom of the Home screen and then touch the ⬇ icon. The Downloads screen appears, as shown in **Figure 7**. Touch a web page in the list. The Chrome browser opens and navigates to the Web page.

Figure 6: Link Options

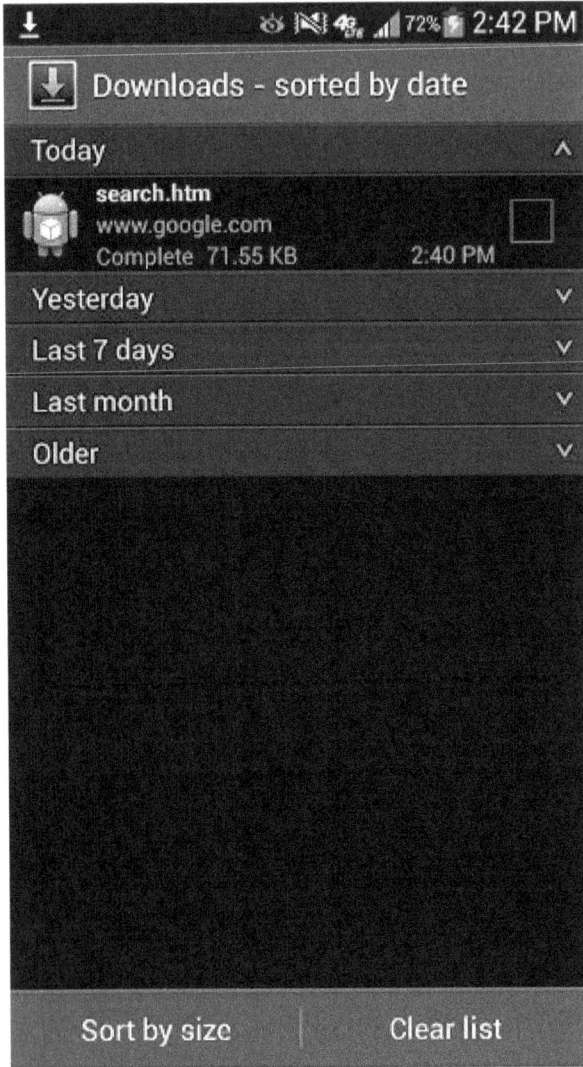

Figure 7: Downloads Screen

5. Searching a Web Page for a Word or Phrase

While surfing the web, you may search any page for a word or phrase. To perform a search on a web page:

1. Navigate to a web page. Refer to *"Navigating to a Web Page"* on page 144 to learn how.
2. Touch the ▤ key. The Browser menu appears.
3. Touch **Find in page**. 'Find in page' appears at the top of the screen.

4. Enter the search term or phrase. The matching results are highlighted in orange and yellow on the web page as you type, as shown in **Figure 8**. Alternatively, 'No matches' appears at the top of the screen if no matches are found.

5. Touch the ⌃ or ⌄ arrow to select the previous or next matching result, respectively. The currently selected result is highlighted in orange.

6. Touch the 🔍 key. The virtual keyboard is hidden so that you can review the search results.

Figure 8: Search Results on a Web Page

6. Viewing the Browsing History

The Galaxy Note 3 stores all recently visited web pages in its Browsing History. Since Chrome will match a Web address as you type, you will rarely need to manually view the history. To view the Browsing History while using the Chrome browser:

1. Touch the address bar at the top of the screen. The web address is highlighted in blue.
2. Enter **chrome:history**. The Browsing History appears, as shown in **Figure 9**.
3. Touch a web page in the list. Chrome navigates to the selected web page.

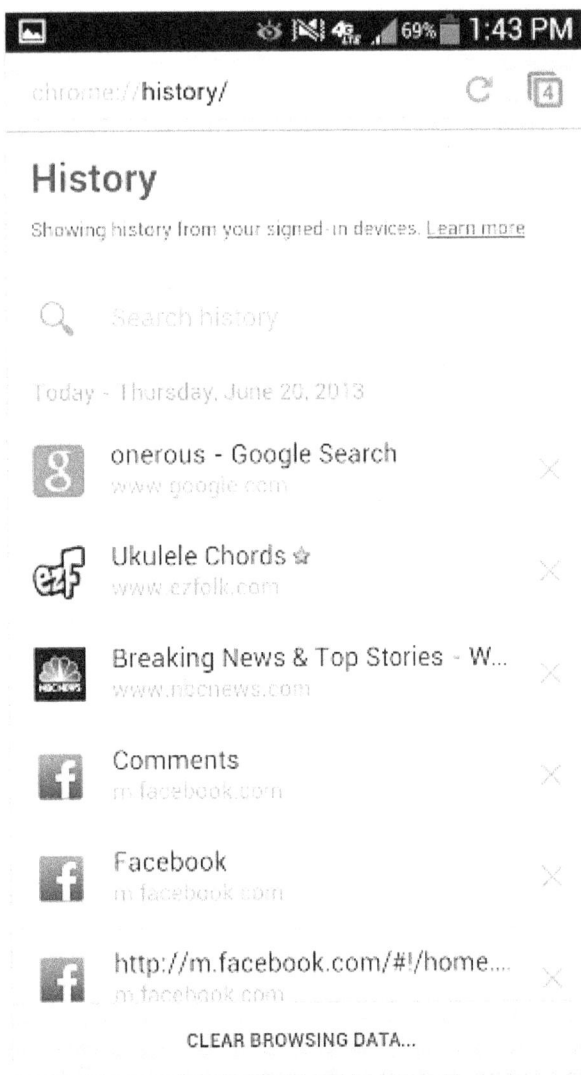

Figure 9: Browsing History

7. Sharing a Web Page

If you find a particularly interesting web page, you can share it with a friend. To share a web page:

1. Navigate to the web page. Refer to *"Navigating to a Web Page"* on page 144 to learn how.
2. Touch the ▦ key. The Browser menu appears.
3. Touch **Share**. The Web Page Sharing menu appears, as shown in **Figure 10**.
4. Touch an option in the list to share the web page. When sharing it via Email or Text Message, you will need to enter the recipient's address or phone number, respectively. When sharing it via social applications, such as Flipboard or Google+, you will need to log in before you can share.

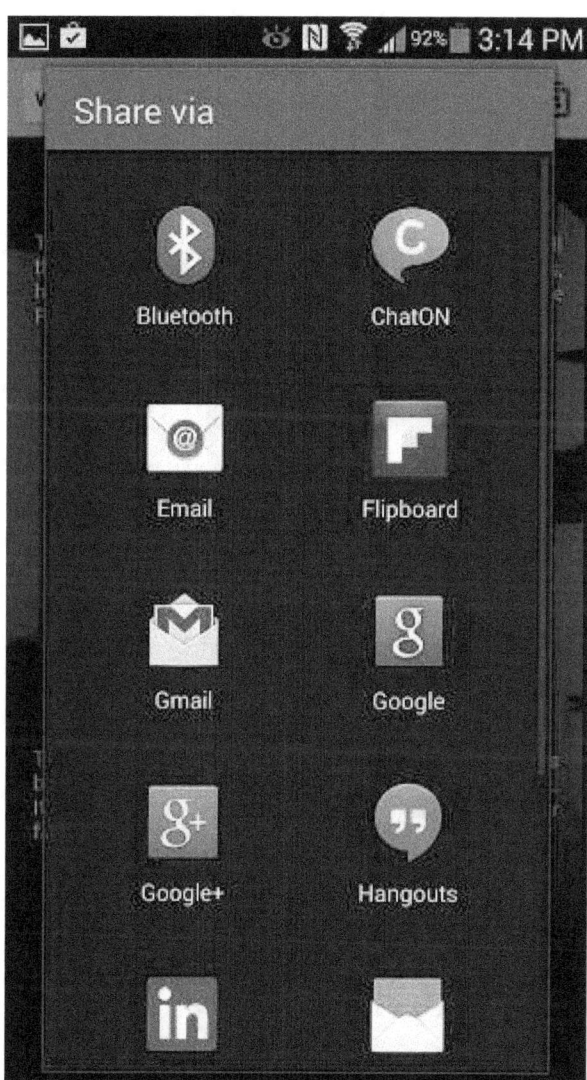

Figure 10: Web Page Sharing Menu

8. Setting the Search Engine

By default, the Chrome browser uses Google as the search engine, but you can also use Bing or Yahoo. To perform a search, enter the search terms in the address bar at the top of the screen and touch the [Go] button. To set the search engine that is used when you perform a search:

1. Touch the [☰] key. The Browser menu appears.
2. Touch **Settings**. The Chrome Settings screen appears, as shown in **Figure 11**.
3. Touch **Search engine**. A list of available search engines appears.
4. Touch the search engine that you prefer. The selected search engine will be used every time you perform a search from the address bar.

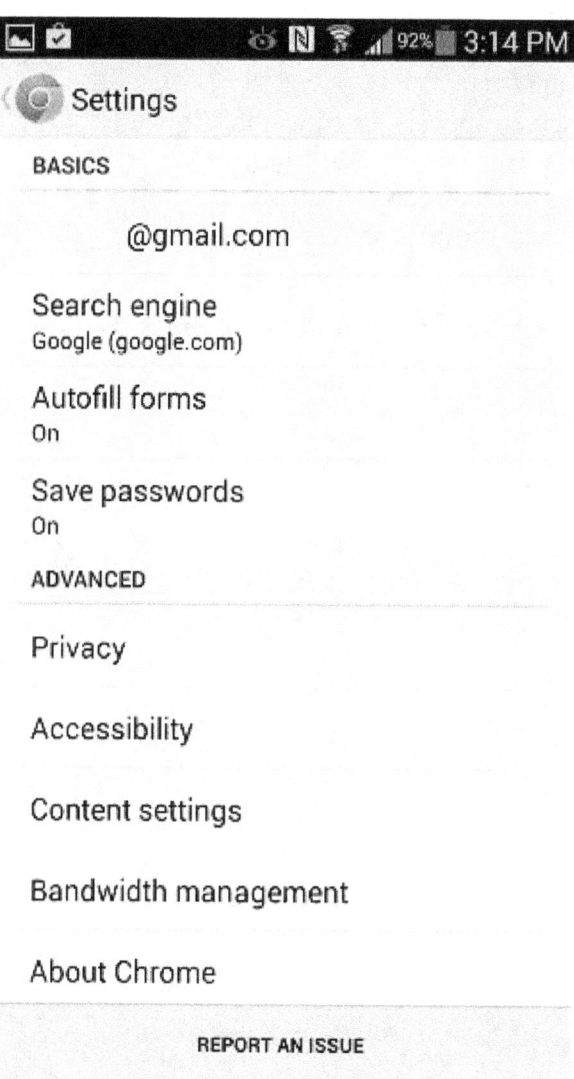

Figure 11: Chrome Settings Screen

9. Turning Autofill On or Off

Chrome can automatically fill in certain personal information to save you time. By default, Autofill is turned on. To turn Autofill on or off:

Warning: Using Autofill to enter personal information may be dangerous, as hackers may gain access to your credentials and use them to steal your identity. Always use strong passwords with a combination of numbers, letters, and symbols.

1. Touch the ▤ key. The Browser menu appears.
2. Touch **Settings**. The Chrome Settings screen appears.
3. Touch **Autofill forms**. The Autofill Profiles screen appears, as shown in **Figure 12**.
4. Touch **Add profile**. The Add Profile screen appears, as shown in **Figure 13**.
5. Enter your personal information. Scroll down and touch **Save** when you are finished. The new profile is saved. You can also add credit card information by repeating this process, and touching **Add credit card** in step 4.

6. Touch the ⬜ **ON** switch in the upper right-hand corner of the screen if you wish to stop using Autofill. Autofill is turned off.

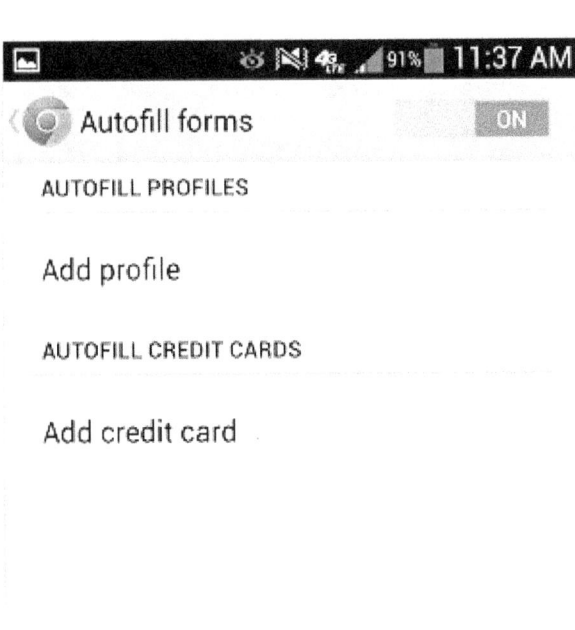

Figure 12: Autofill Profiles Screen

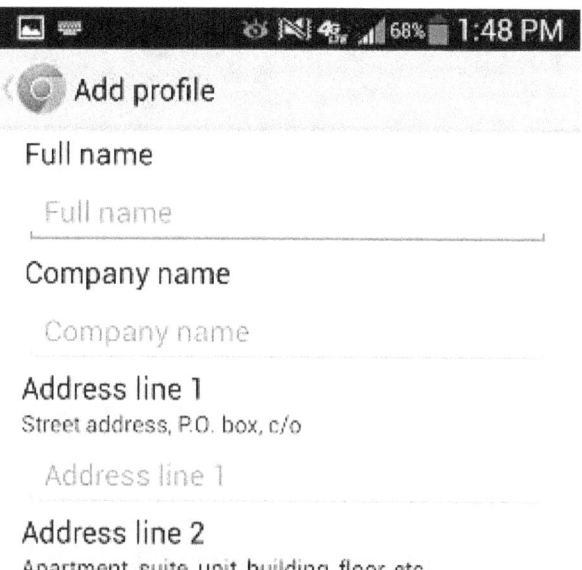
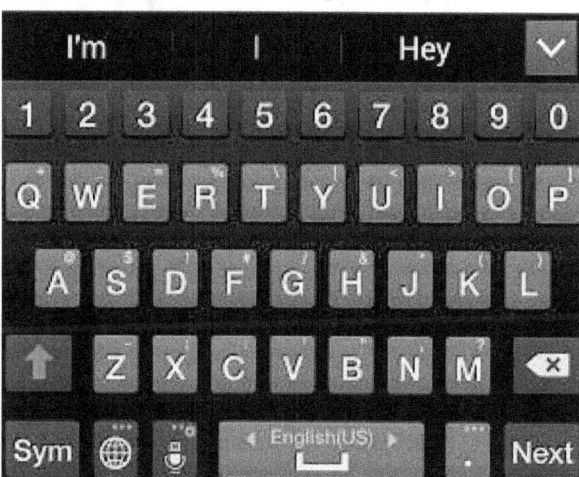

Figure 13: Add Profile Screen

10. Saving Passwords

Chrome can save passwords for you in order to save time when logging in to protected services. When this feature is turned on, the Password Saving dialog will appear every time that you enter a password, as shown in **Figure 14**. By default, this feature is turned on. To turn password saving on or off:

Warning: Using saved passwords may be dangerous, as hackers may gain access to your credentials and use them to steal your identity. Always use strong passwords with a combination of numbers, letters, and symbols.

1. Touch the ▦ key. The Browser menu appears.
2. Touch **Settings**. The Chrome Settings screen appears.
3. Touch **Save passwords**. The Saved Passwords screen appears, as shown in **Figure 15**.
4. Touch the **ON** switch in the upper right-hand corner of the screen. Saving Passwords is turned off and Chrome will no longer offer to save any passwords.
5. Touch the **OFF** switch in the upper right-hand corner of the screen. Saving Passwords is turned on. You may also delete a saved password for a particular website by touching the URL in the list, and then touching **Delete**.

Figure 14: Password Saving Dialog

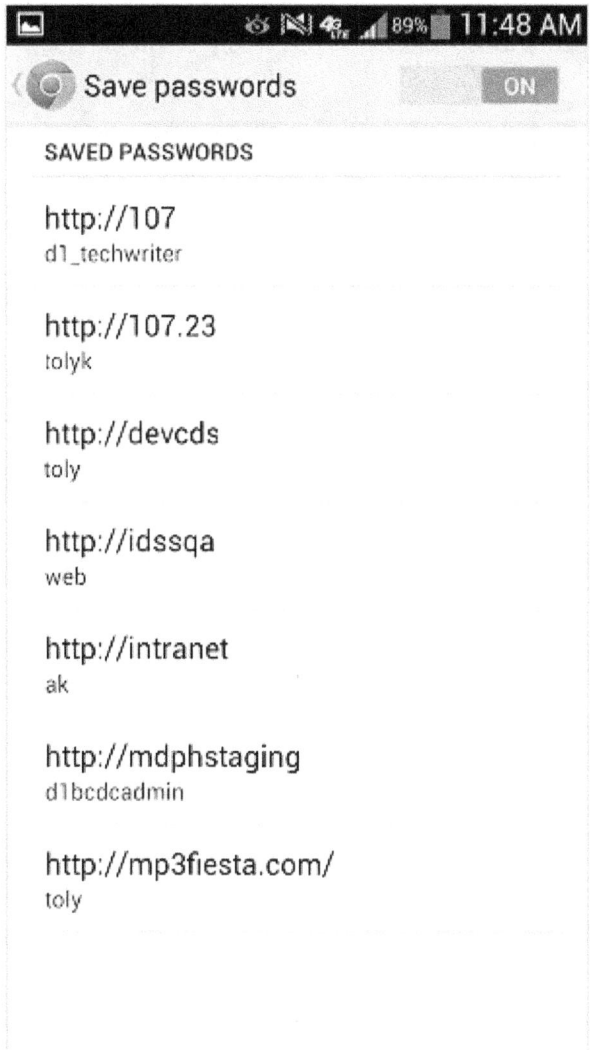

Figure 15: Saved Passwords Screen

11. Turning Pop-Up Blocking On or Off

Some web pages may cause annoying pop-ups to appear. Chrome can automatically prevent these pop-ups from appearing. However, some sites may need to open additional legitimate pages in new tabs. For this reason, you may wish to turn the pop-up blocker off. By default, the pop-up blocker is turned on. To turn pop-up blocking on or off:

1. Touch the ⊟ key. The Browser menu appears.
2. Touch **Settings**. The Chrome Settings screen appears.
3. Touch **Content settings**. The Content Settings screen appears, as shown in **Figure 16**.

4. Touch **Block pop-ups**. The ☑ mark disappears, and Chrome will no longer block any pop-ups.

5. Touch **Block pop-ups** again. The ☑ mark appears, and Chrome will block all pop-ups.

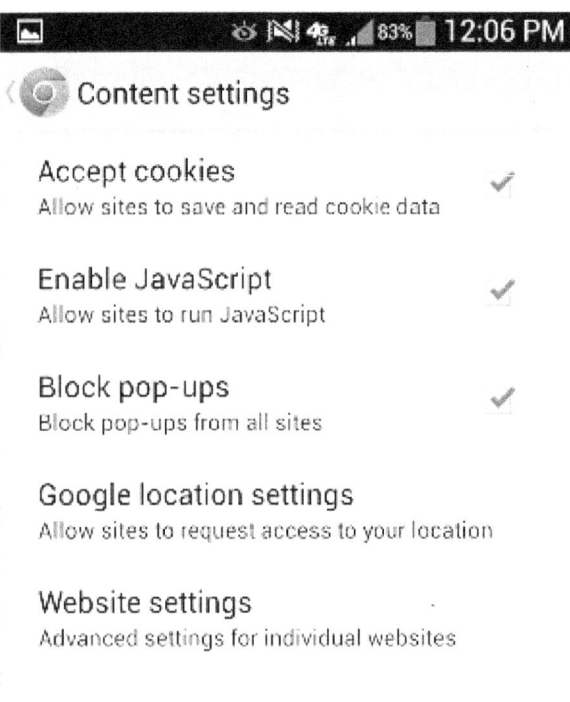

Figure 16: Content Settings Screen

12. Changing the Text Size

If you have trouble seeing small text in Chrome, you may wish to increase the text size. On the other hand, if you wish to see more text on a single screen you may wish to decrease its size. To change the text size:

1. Touch the ▣ key. The Browser menu appears.
2. Touch **Settings**. The Chrome Settings screen appears.
3. Touch **Accessibility**. The Chrome Accessibility Settings screen appears, as shown in **Figure 17**.

4. Touch the ⬤ slider below 'Text scaling', and drag it to the left to decrease the text size or to the right to increase it. The text size is adjusted accordingly and a preview of the actual size of the text in the Chrome browser is shown above 'Text scaling'.

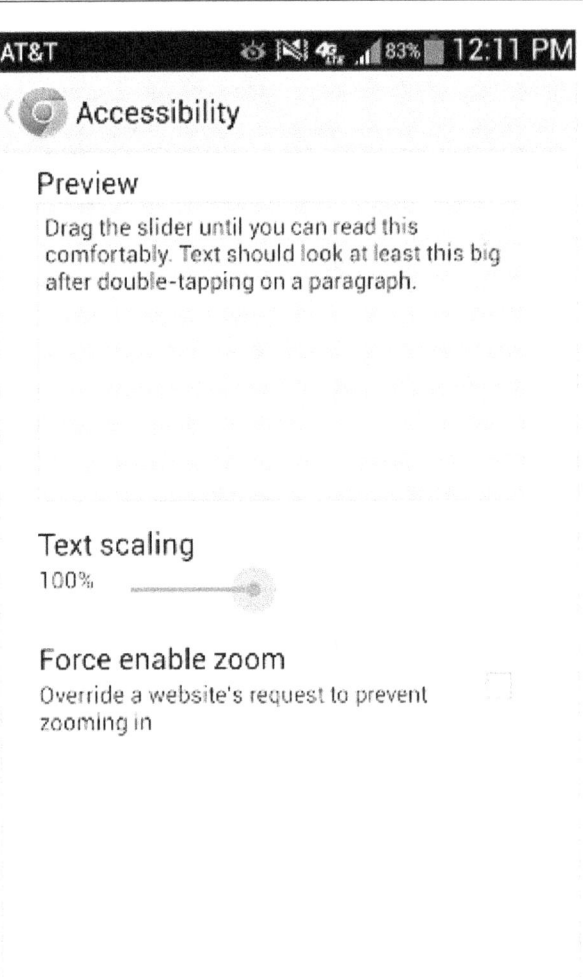

Figure 17: Chrome Accessibility Settings Screen

13. Clearing Personal Data

In order to protect your privacy, Chrome can clear your personal data, such as the list of recently visited websites, known as the History. The phone can also clear other data, such as saved passwords and Autofill forms. To clear personal data while using the Chrome browser:

1. Touch the ▤ key. The Browser menu appears.
2. Touch **Settings**. The Chrome Settings screen appears.
3. Touch **Privacy**. The Privacy Settings screen appears, as shown in **Figure 18**.
4. Touch **CLEAR BROWSING DATA** at the bottom of the screen. The Clear Browsing Data window appears, as shown in **Figure 19**.
5. Touch one or more of the following options to select the data that you wish to erase:

   - **Clear browsing history** - Deletes all history files, which include the addresses of recently visited websites.
   - **Clear the cache** - Deletes all web page data, such as image files and other files that comprise a web page.
   - **Clear cookies, site data** - Deletes all text data, such as site preferences, authentication, and shopping cart contents.
   - **Clear saved passwords** - Deletes all stored passwords for various websites, such as online email clients, marketplaces, and banking clients.
   - **Clear autofill data** - Deletes all form data, such as screen names, addresses, and phone numbers.

6. Touch **Clear**. The selected data is permanently erased.

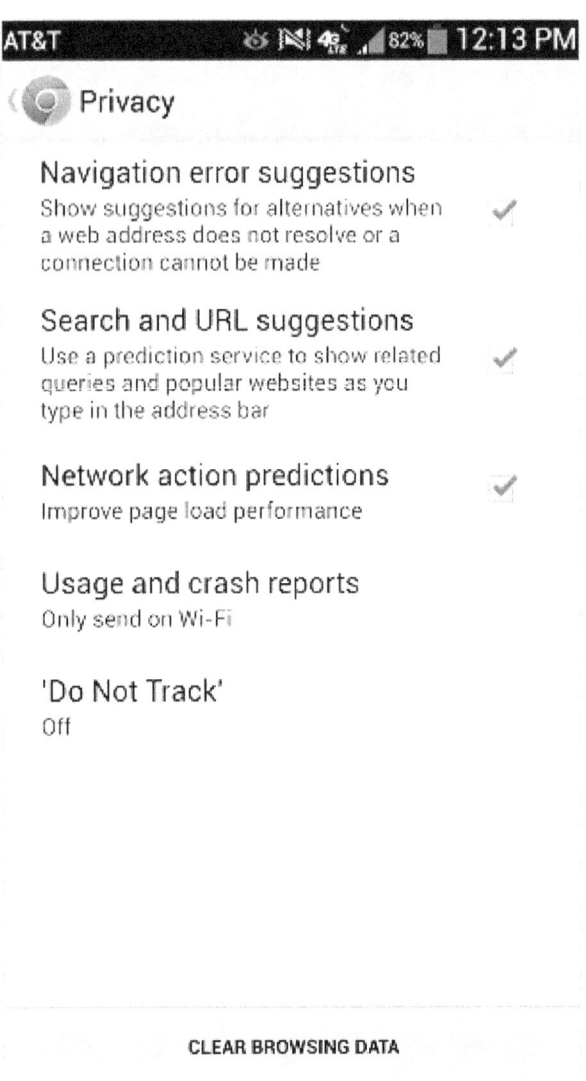

Figure 18: Privacy & Security Settings Screen

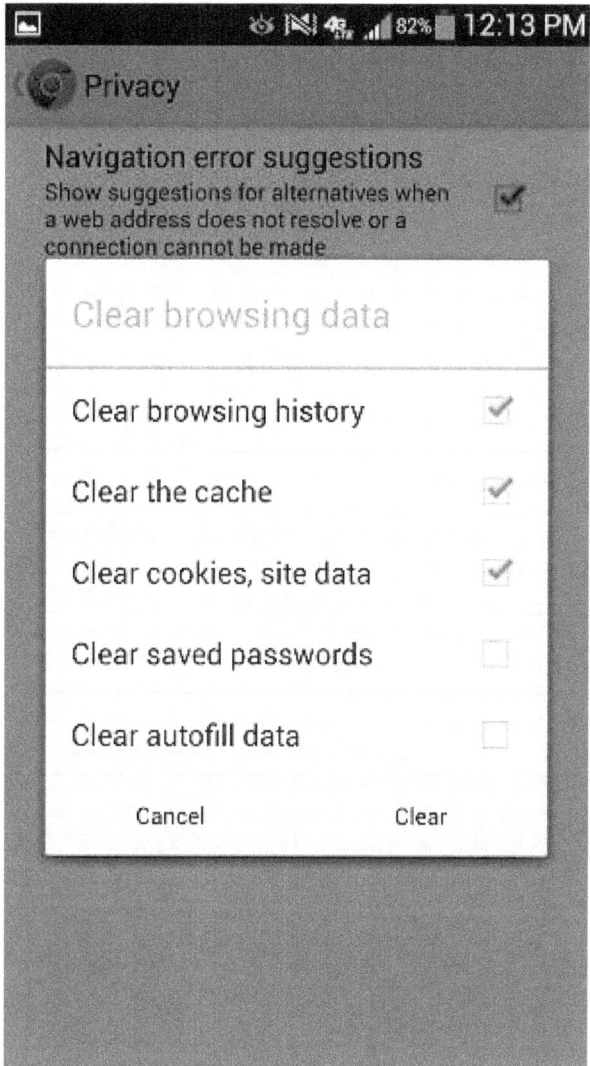

Figure 19: Browsing Data Window

Using the Gmail Application

Table of Contents

1. Adding a Google Account to the Phone

Before using the Gmail application, add at least one Google account to the Galaxy Note 3. It is highly recommended to use the Gmail service with the phone, since a Gmail account is required to use the application store (Play Store) anyway. To add a Google account to the phone:

1. Touch the ▤ key. The Home menu appears, as shown in **Figure 1**.
2. Touch **Settings**. The Settings screen appears, as shown in **Figure 2**.
3. Touch **General** at the top of the screen. The General Settings screen appears, as shown in **Figure 3**.
4. Touch the 🔑 icon at the top of the list. The Accounts screen appears, as shown in **Figure 4**.
5. Touch **Add account**. The Add Account screen appears, as shown in **Figure 5**.
6. Touch **Google**. The Add Google Account screen appears, as shown in **Figure 6**.
7. Touch **New** at the bottom of the screen if you do not yet have a Google account. Enter all of the required information on the following screens to create your account. Otherwise, touch **Existing** and enter your Google credentials to log in to your existing account.

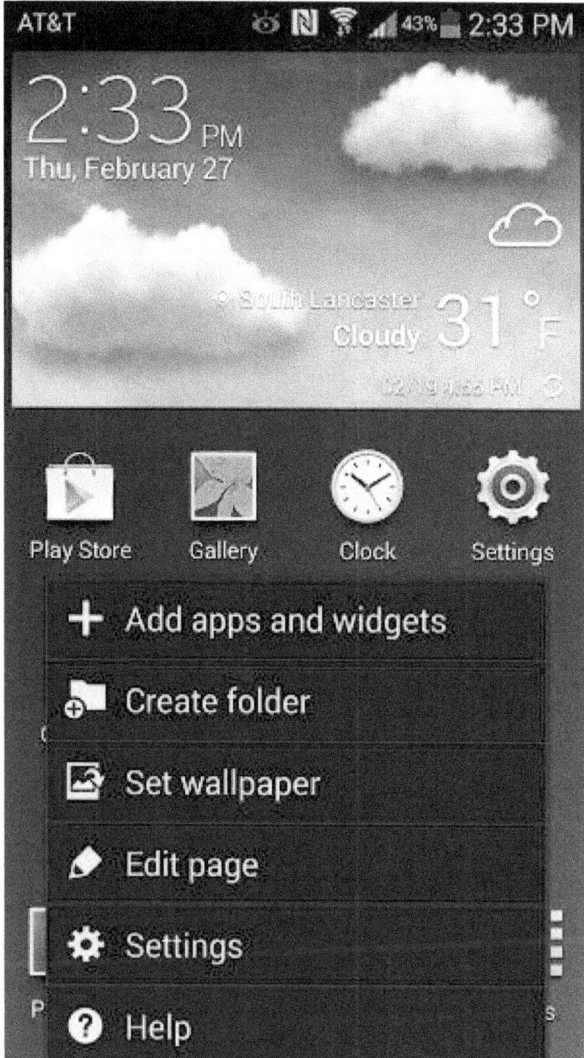

Figure 1: Home Menu

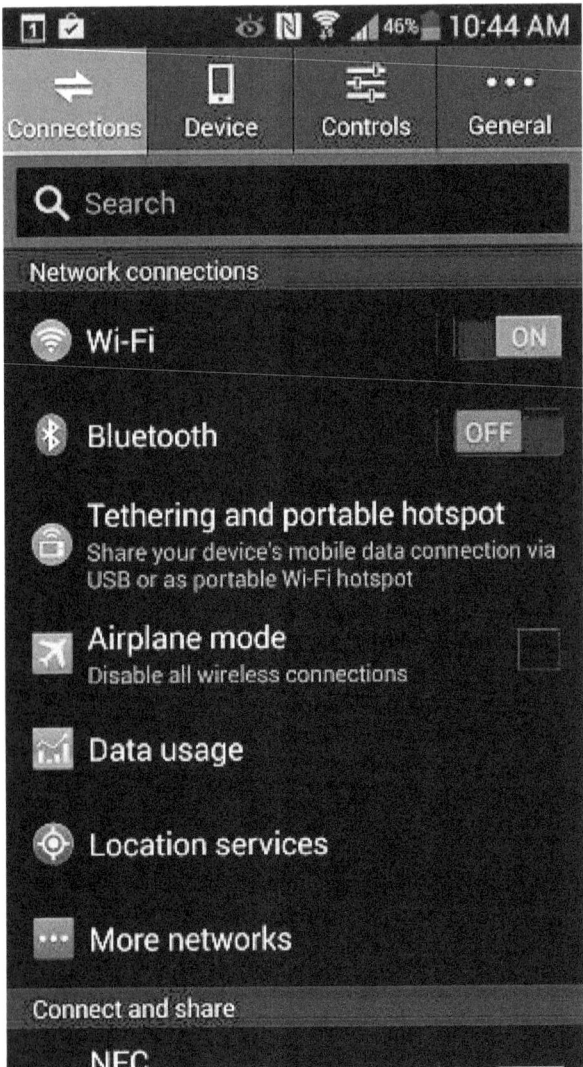

Figure 2: Settings Screen

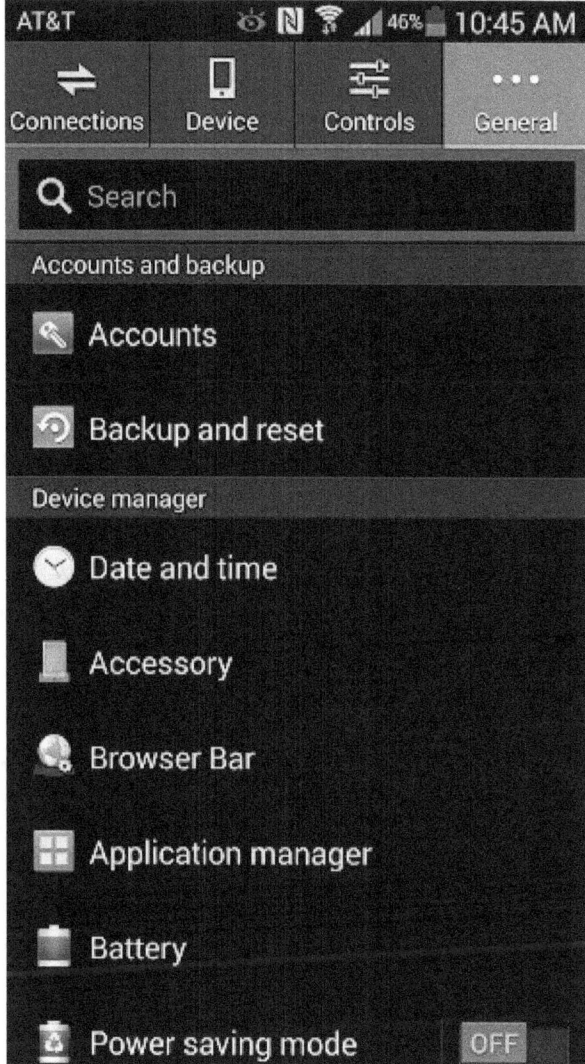

Figure 3: General Settings Screen

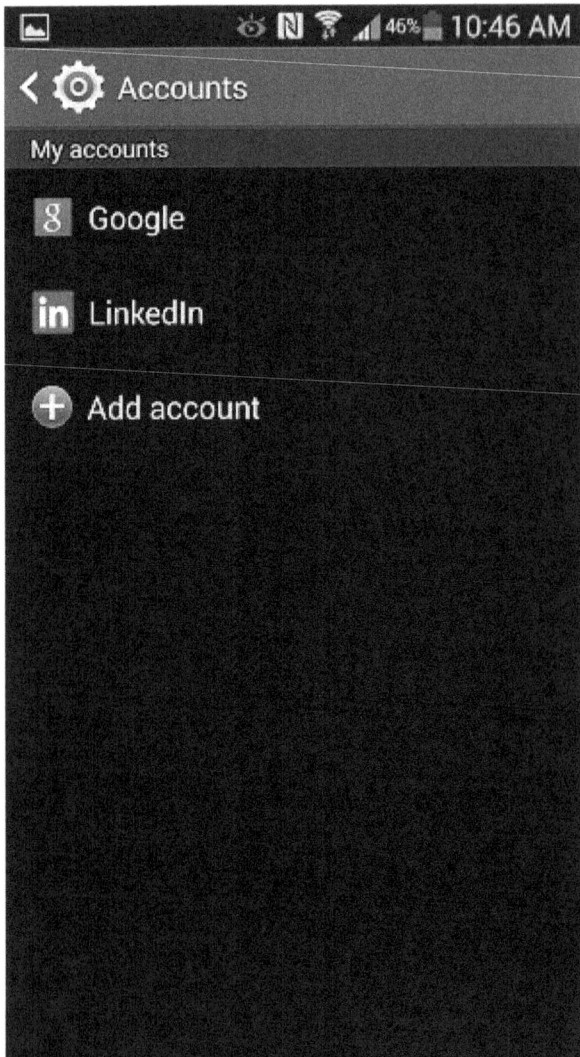

Figure 4: My Accounts Screen

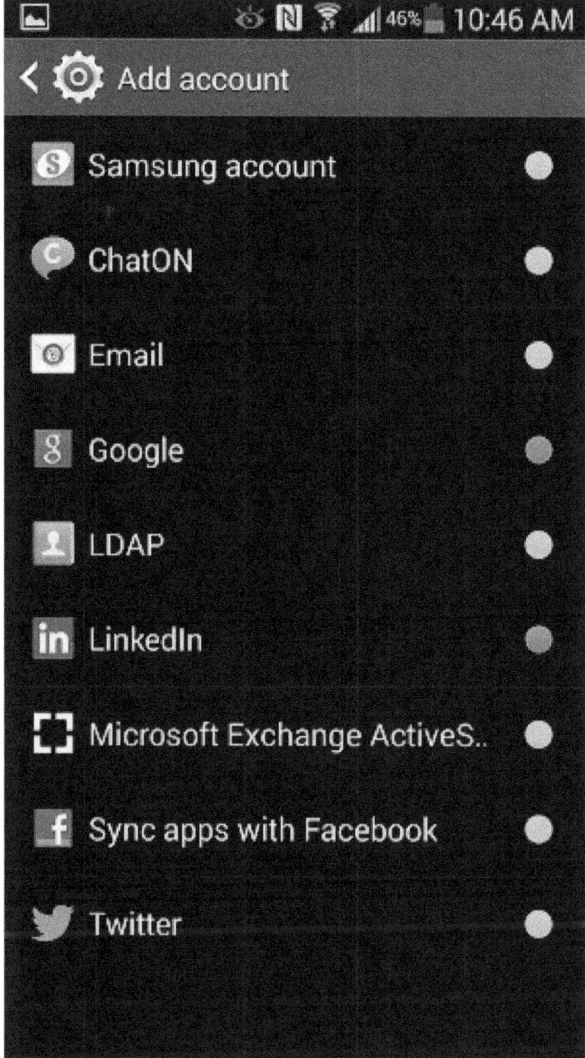

Figure 5: Add Account Screen

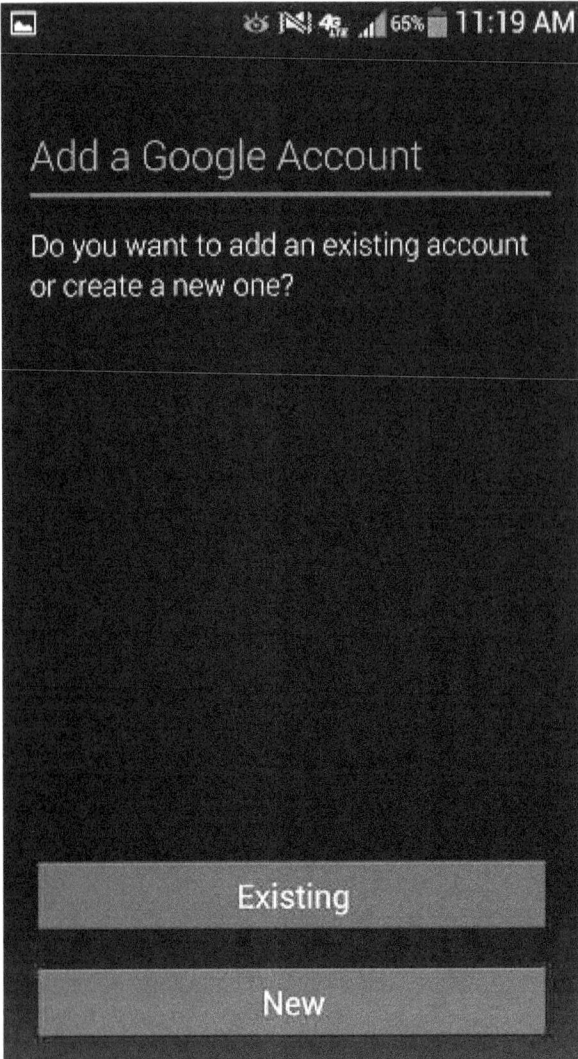

Figure 6: Add Google Account Screen

2. Reading Email

You can read your email on the Galaxy Note 3 using the Gmail application. To read email:

1. Touch the ![M] icon on the Home screen or touch the ![grid] icon and then touch the ![M] icon. The Gmail application opens and the Inbox appears, as shown in **Figure 7**.
2. Touch an email in the list. The email opens.
3. Touch the screen and move your finger to the left or right to view the previous or next email, respectively. The email appears.

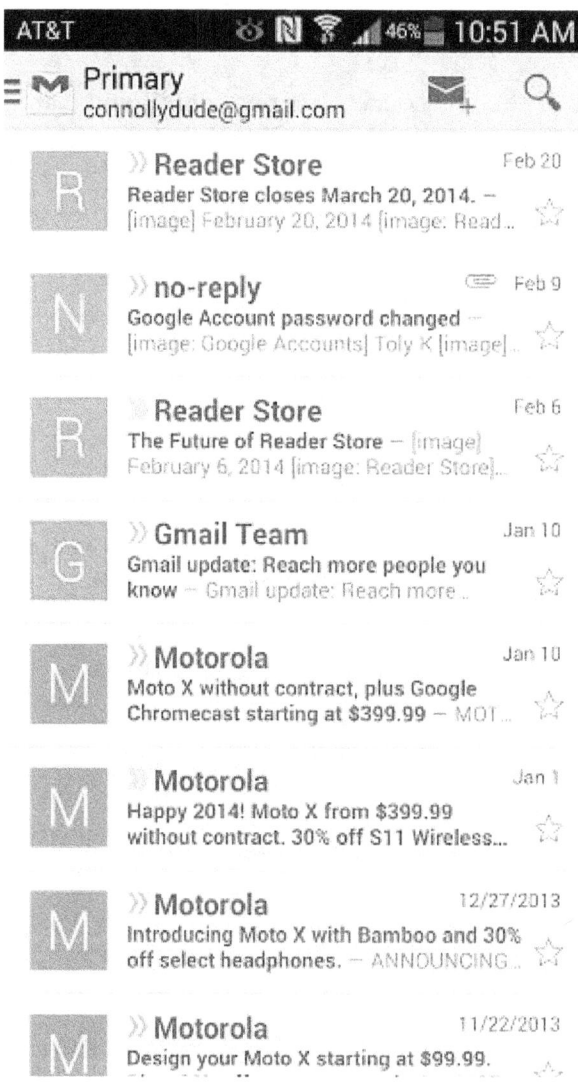

Figure 7: Gmail Inbox

3. Sending an Email

Compose email directly from the Galaxy Note 3 using the Gmail application. To write an email while using the Gmail application:

1. Open the Inbox. Refer to *"Reading Email"* on page 174 to learn how.
2. Touch the ![icon] icon. The Compose screen appears, as shown in **Figure 8**.
3. Start typing the name of a contact for whom you have a saved email address. A list of suggestions appears.

4. Touch the contact's name. The contact's email address is inserted. Alternatively, you may enter an email from scratch in the 'To' field.
5. Touch **Subject** and enter an optional topic for the email. Touch **Compose email** and enter a message. The subject and message are entered.
6. Touch the ➤ button in the upper right-hand corner of the screen. The email is sent.

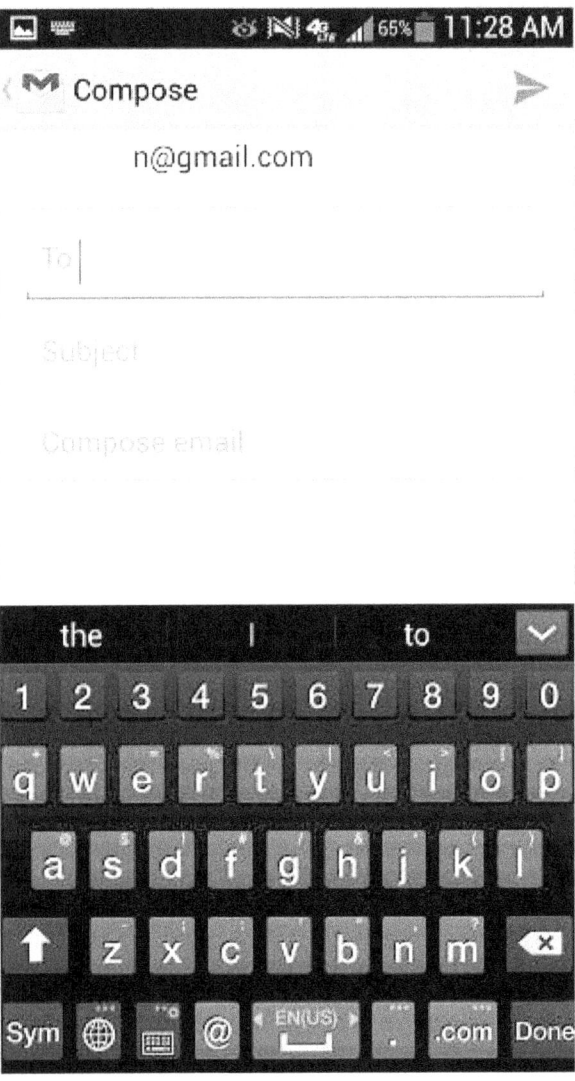

Figure 8: Compose Screen

4. Replying to and Forwarding Emails

After receiving an email, you can reply to the sender or forward the email to a new recipient. To reply to, or forward, an email while using the Gmail application:

1. Open the Inbox. Refer to *"Reading Email"* on page 174 to learn how.
2. Touch an email. The email opens.
3. Touch the ↰ icon next to the sender's email address, as outlined in **Figure 9**. A new email is generated with the sender's email address already entered in the 'To' field.

4. Enter a message and touch the ➤ button. The reply is sent.

5. Alternatively, touch the icon to the right of the ⋮ icon in step 3, and then touch **Reply all** or **Forward**. Choosing 'Reply all' will send a reply to all recipients of the original email. Choosing 'Forward' will send a copy of the message to a different recipient, requiring you to enter an email address in the 'To' field. Follow step 4 to reply to all recipients or to forward the email.

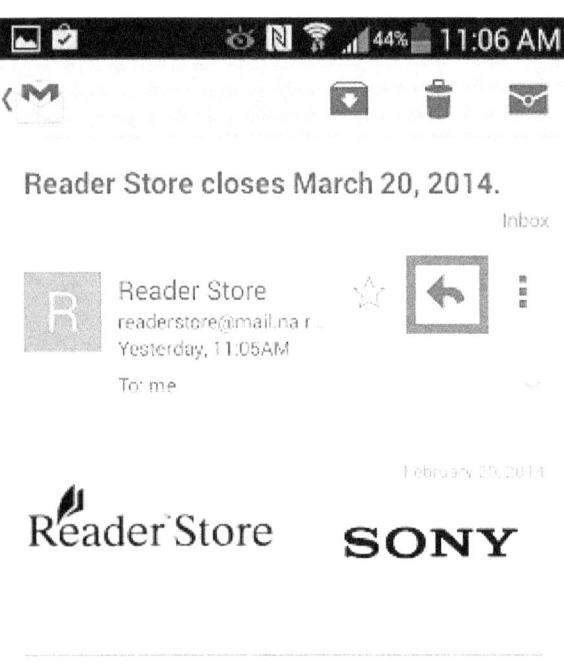

Figure 9: Reply Icon Outlined

5. Deleting Emails and Restoring Deleted Emails to the Inbox

Deleting an email sends it to the Trash folder. To completely delete an email, the Trash folder must be emptied. To delete emails while using the Gmail application:

Warning: Emails in the Trash folder are permanently deleted after 30 days. Make sure that you retrieve the message before 30 days if you still need it.

1. Open the Inbox. Refer to *"Reading Email"* on page 174 to learn how.
2. Touch the letter or picture to the left of the emails that you wish to delete. The letter will always be the first letter of the name or service involved in the email conversation. For instance, if it is an email conversation with George, touch the ⬜ icon. Touch the letter to the left of each email that you wish to delete. The selected email conversations are highlighted in blue, as shown in **Figure 10**.

3. Touch the 🗑 icon at the top of the screen, as outlined in **Figure 11**. The selected emails are deleted.

Note: To clean up the Inbox without deleting emails, try archiving them. Archiving an email removes it from the Inbox and places it in the 'All Mail' folder. To archive an email, touch the email in the Inbox and slide your finger to the left or right. 'Archived' appears in place of the email in the Inbox. Touch **undo** *to return the email to the Inbox.*

To restore deleted emails to the Inbox:

1. Open the Inbox. Refer to *"Reading Email"* on page 174 to learn how.
2. Touch **Primary** in the upper left-hand corner of the screen. A list of email folders appears, as shown in **Figure 12**.
3. Scroll down and touch **Trash**. The Trash folder appears.
4. Touch the letter or picture to the left of the email that you wish to restore to the Inbox. The selected emails are highlighted.
5. Touch the 📁 icon in the upper right-hand corner of the screen. The Move To options appear, as shown in **Figure 13**.
6. Touch **Primary**. The selected emails are moved to the Primary Inbox.

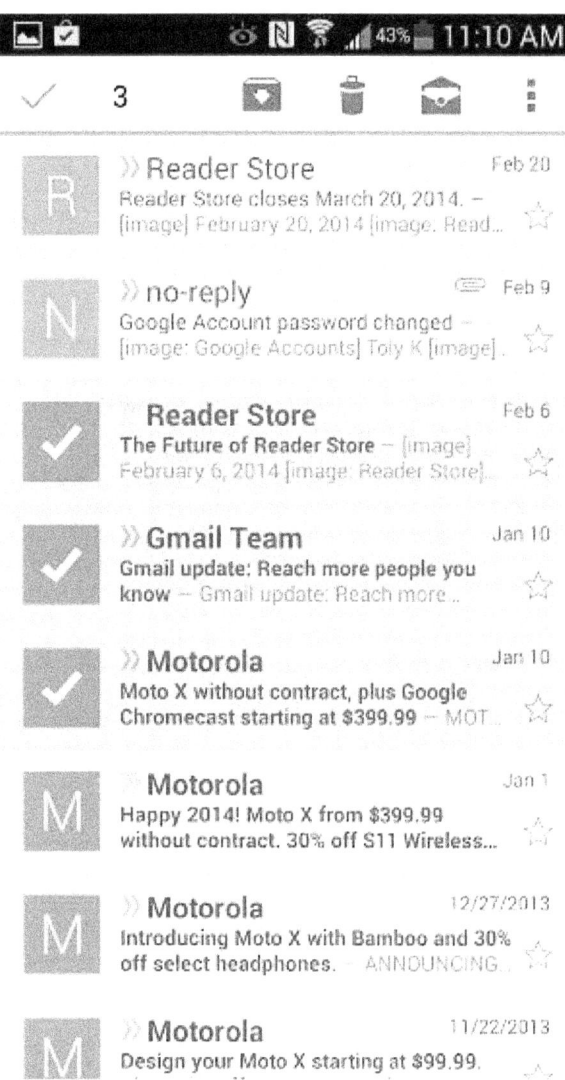

Figure 10: Selected Emails

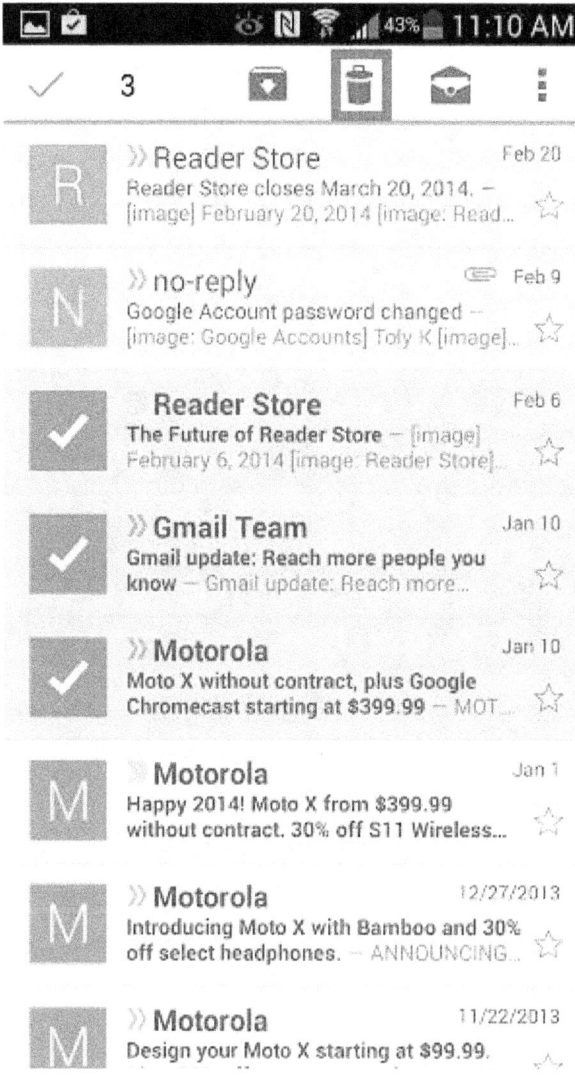

Figure 11: Trash Icon Outlined

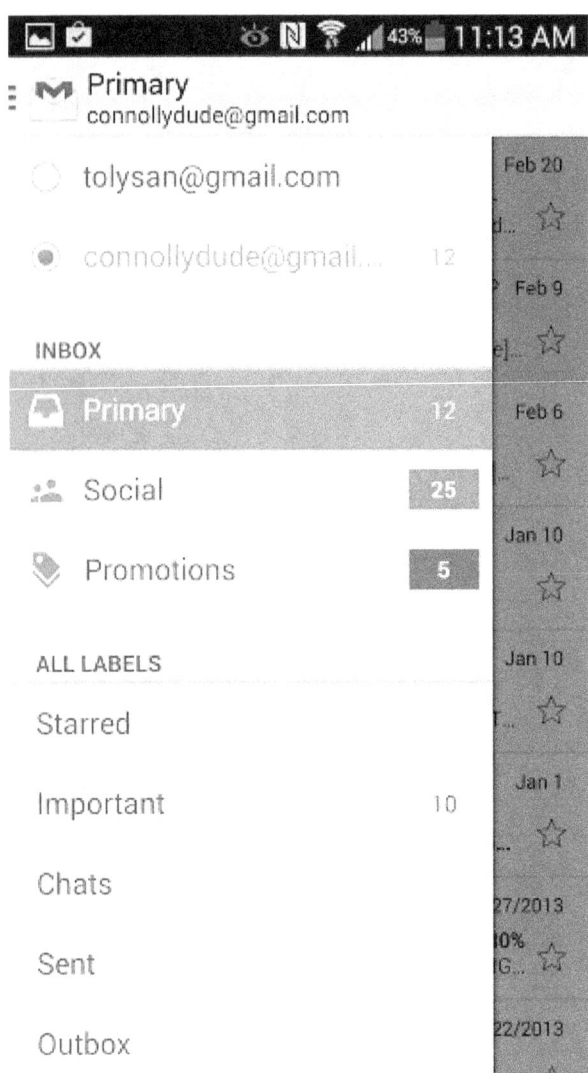

Figure 12: List of Email Folders

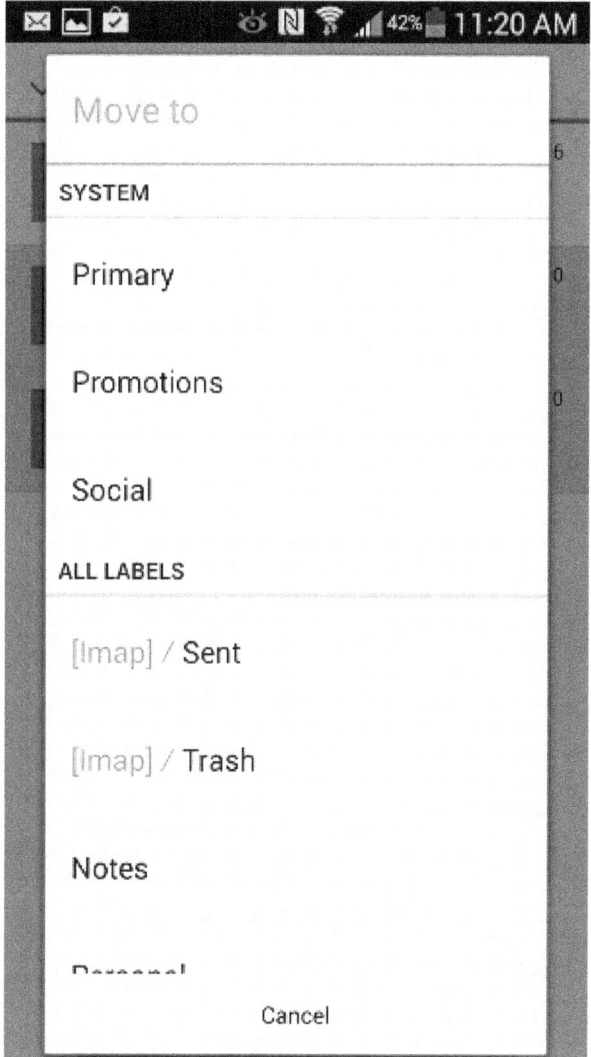

Figure 13: Move To Options

6. Adding Labels to Emails

Emails can be classified according to the nature of the message, such as 'work' or 'personal'. To add labels to emails while using the Gmail application:

1. Open the Inbox. Refer to *"Reading Email"* on page 174 to learn how.

2. Touch the letter or picture to the left of the emails to which you wish to add a label. The letter will always be the first letter of the name or service involved in the email conversation. For instance, if it is an email conversation with George, touch the ⬜ icon. The selected email conversations are highlighted in blue.

3. Touch the ⋮ icon in the upper right-hand corner of the screen. The Inbox options appear, as shown in **Figure 14**.

4. Touch **Change labels**. A list of Gmail labels appears, as shown in **Figure 15**.

5. Touch as many labels as you wish. Touch **OK**. The labels are applied to the selected emails.

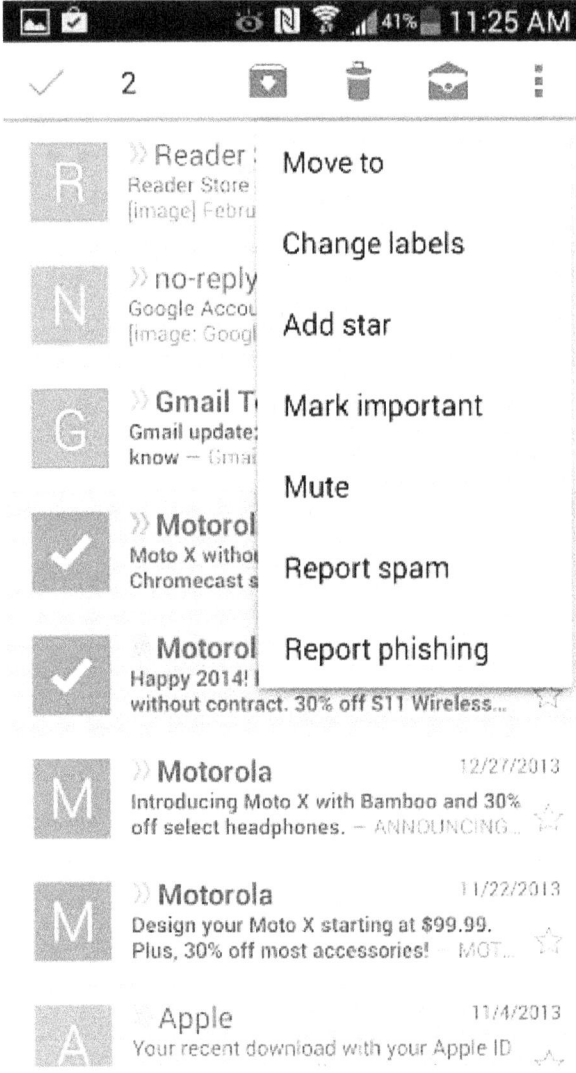

Figure 14: Inbox Options

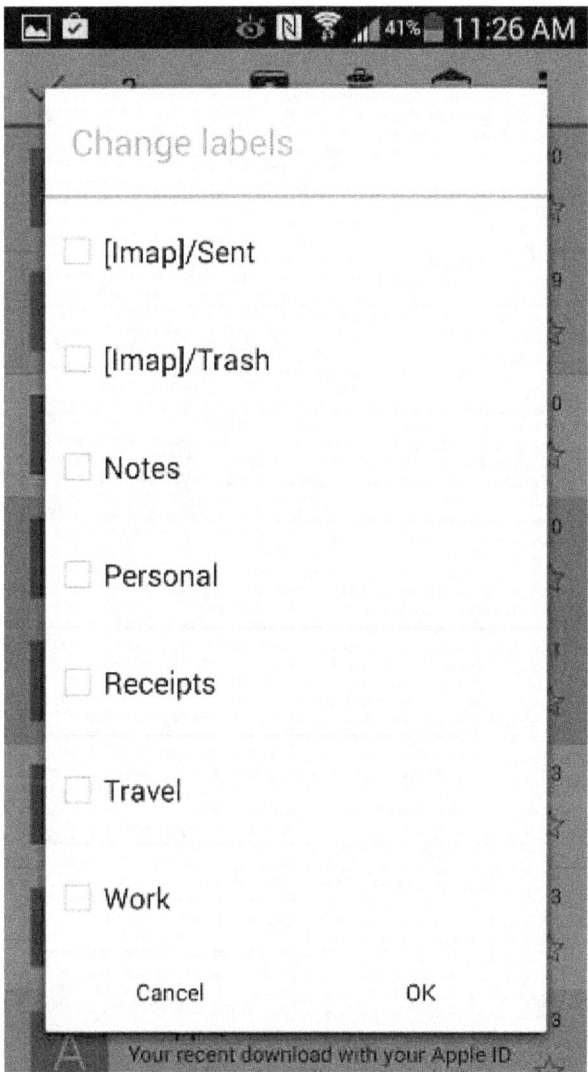

Figure 15: List of Gmail Labels

7. Searching the Inbox

To find an email in the Inbox, use the search function, which searches email addresses, message content, and subject lines. To search the Inbox while using the Gmail application:

1. Open the Inbox. Refer to *"Reading Email"* on page 174 to learn how.
2. Touch the 🔍 icon in the upper right-hand corner of the screen. The virtual keyboard appears.
3. Enter a search word or phrase and touch the 🔍 button. The Galaxy Note 3 searches the Inbox and a list of matching results appears.

8. Ignoring New Messages in a Conversation

If you are included in an email conversation between multiple people that no longer pertains to you, you can set Gmail to prevent all emails in that conversation from reaching your Inbox. This action is called 'Muting' a conversation. To mute a conversation:

Note: Any new emails in the conversation that are addressed only to you will still appear in your inbox.

1. Open the Inbox. Refer to *"Reading Email"* on page 174 to learn how.
2. Touch the letter or picture to the left of the emails that you wish to mute. The letter will always be the first letter of the name or service involved in the email conversation. For

   instance, if it is an email conversation with George, touch the 🅖 icon. The selected emails are highlighted in blue.
3. Touch the ⁝ icon in the upper right-hand corner of the screen. The Inbox options appear.
4. Touch **Mute**. The conversation is muted and only emails addressed solely to you will appear.

9. Blocking All Emails from a Specific Sender

If you receive unwanted emails from the same email address, such as a solicitor of unwanted products or services, you may block the sender altogether by marking the email as 'Spam'. To block emails from a specific sender:

1. Open the Inbox. Refer to *"Reading Email"* on page 174 to learn how.
2. Touch the letter or picture to the left of the emails that you wish to report as spam. The letter will always be the first letter of the name or service involved in the email

   conversation. For instance, if it is an email conversation with George, touch the 🅖 icon. The selected email conversations are selected and highlighted in blue.

3. Touch the ▤ icon in the upper right-hand corner of the screen. The Inbox options appear.
4. Touch **Report spam**. The selected emails and all future emails from the selected senders are moved to the Spam folder.

10. Adjusting the General Gmail Preferences

You may customize the Gmail application by adjusting its settings. To adjust the general Gmail preferences while using the Gmail application:

1. Touch the ▤ key while using the Gmail application. The Gmail menu appears, as shown in **Figure 16**.
2. Touch **Settings**. The Gmail Settings screen appears, as shown in **Figure 17**.
3. Touch **General settings**. The General Gmail Settings screen appears, as shown in **Figure 18**.
4. Touch one of the following options to adjust the corresponding setting:

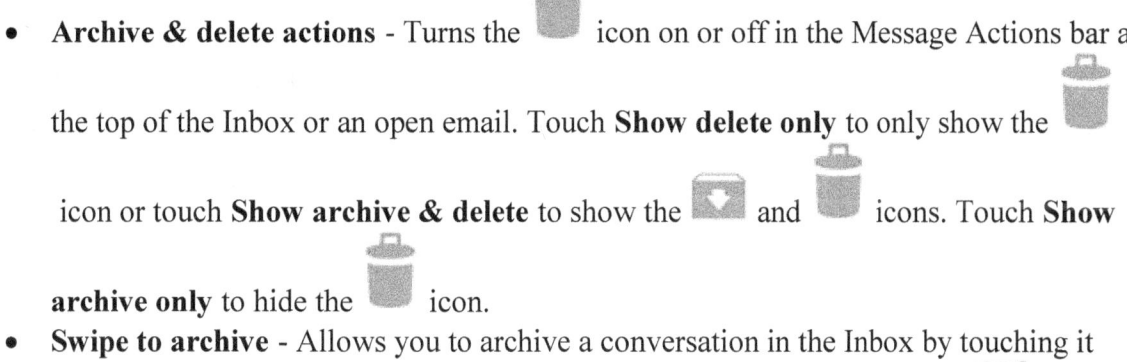

- **Archive & delete actions** - Turns the 🗑 icon on or off in the Message Actions bar at the top of the Inbox or an open email. Touch **Show delete only** to only show the 🗑 icon or touch **Show archive & delete** to show the 🗄 and 🗑 icons. Touch **Show archive only** to hide the 🗑 icon.
- **Swipe to archive** - Allows you to archive a conversation in the Inbox by touching it and swiping your finger to the left or right. This feature is enabled when a ✔ icon appears next to 'Swipe to archive'.
- **Sender image** - Displays the picture that you have assigned to the sender to the left of their name in the Inbox and in open emails. This feature is enabled when a ✔ icon appears next to 'Sender image'.
- **Reply all** - Turns the ↩ icon, used by default to reply only to the original sender, into a 'Reply all' icon, which is used to reply to all recipients of the email by default. This feature is enabled when a ✔ icon appears next to 'Reply all'. Refer to *"Replying to and Forwarding Emails"* on page 177 to learn more. When this feature is turned on, touch the ▤ icon and then touch **Reply** to reply only to the original sender.

- **Auto-fit messages** - Resizes emails that cannot fit to the width of the screen. You will still need to scroll down to read a long email. This feature is enabled when a ☑ icon appears next to 'Auto-fit messages'.
- **Auto-advance** - Selects the screen that is displayed after deleting or archiving an open email. Touch **Auto-advance** and then touch **Newer**, **Older**, or **Conversation list** to select the next screen that will be displayed.
- **Message Actions** - Pins the message actions to a bar at the top of the screen when scrolling through an email. Touch **Message Actions** and then touch **Always show**, **Only show in portrait**, or **Don't show** to select when the message actions should remain pinned at the top of the screen.
- **Confirm before deleting** - Displays a confirmation dialog before deleting an email. This feature is enabled when a ☑ icon appears next to 'Confirm before deleting'. Refer to *"Deleting Emails and Restoring Deleted Emails to the Inbox"* on page 180 to learn how to delete an email.
- **Confirm before archiving** - Displays a confirmation dialog before archiving an email. This feature is enabled when a ☑ icon appears next to 'Confirm before archiving'.
- **Confirm before sending** - Displays a confirmation dialog before sending an email. This feature is enabled when a ☑ icon appears next to 'Confirm before sending'. Refer to *"Sending an Email"* on page 175 to learn more about sending email.

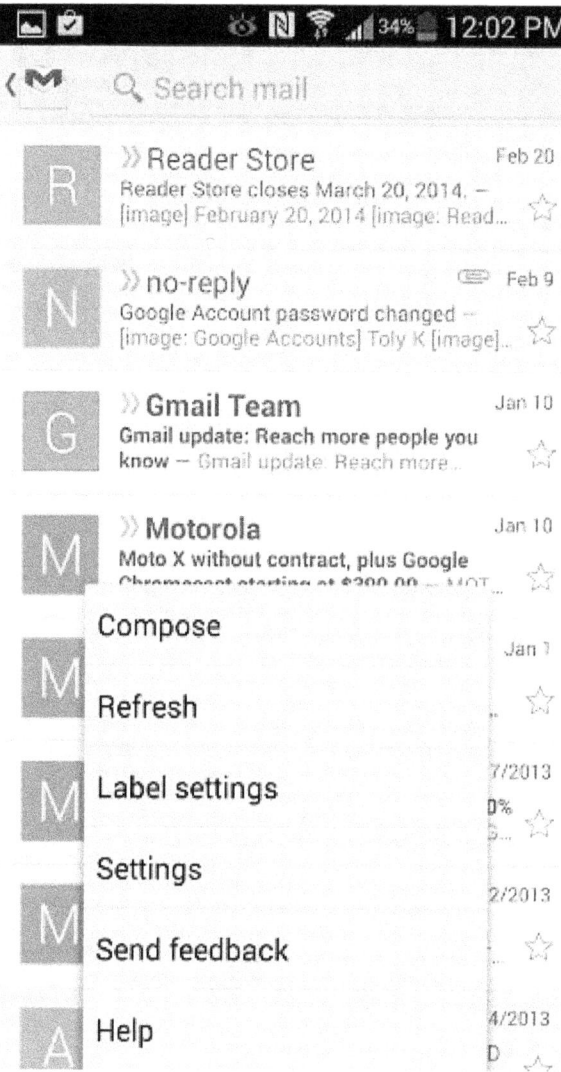

Figure 16: Gmail Menu

General settings

connollydude@gmail.com

About Gmail

Figure 17: Gmail Settings Screen

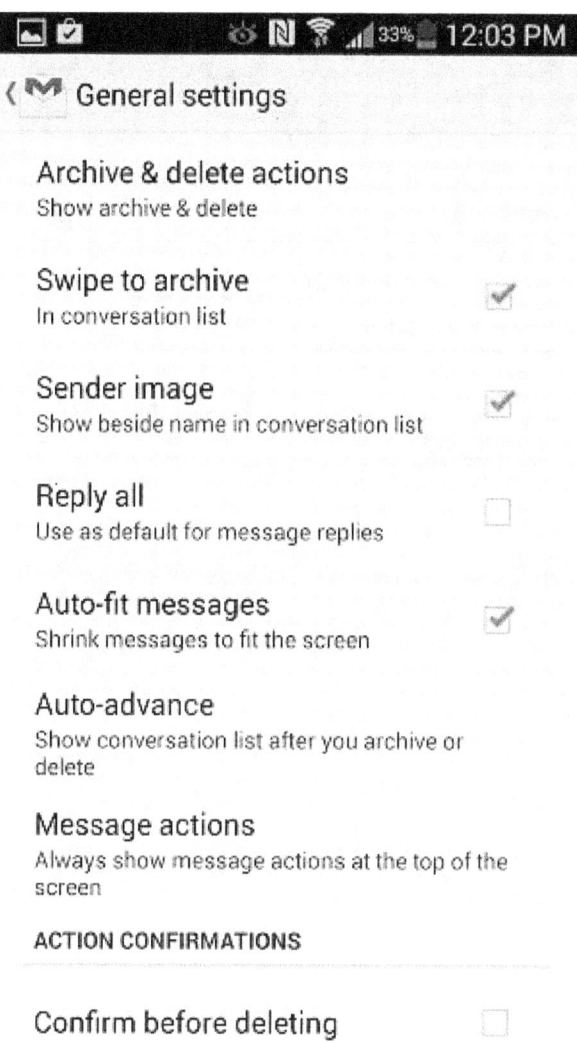

Figure 18: General Gmail Settings Screen

11. Adjusting Gmail Account Preferences

You may adjust the settings particular to your Gmail account. To adjust Gmail account preferences:

1. Touch the ▤ key while using the Gmail application. The Gmail menu appears.
2. Touch **Settings**. The Gmail Settings screen appears.
3. Touch your email address. The Account Preferences screen appears, as shown in **Figure 19**.
4. Touch one of the following options to adjust the corresponding setting:

- **Notifications** - Displays the M icon in the status bar when a new email arrives. This feature is enabled when a ✓ icon appears next to 'Notifications'.
- **Inbox sound & vibrate** - Allows you to customize the notification method for newly received emails. Touch **Sound** or touch **Vibrate** on the following screen to select the sound your phone will make when a new email arrives, and whether the phone will vibrate.
- **Signature** - Allows you to customize the signature that is attached to the end of every email you send using your Galaxy Note 3. Enter a signature and touch **OK** to set it.
- **Vacation Responder** - Allows you to set an automatic email responder that will send the message that you type in the 'Message' field as a reply to every incoming email.

  Enter the start and end dates, and touch the OFF switch to turn on the Vacation Responder.

Note: The Data Usage settings on the Account Preferences screen are for advanced users only. It is not necessary to adjust these settings.

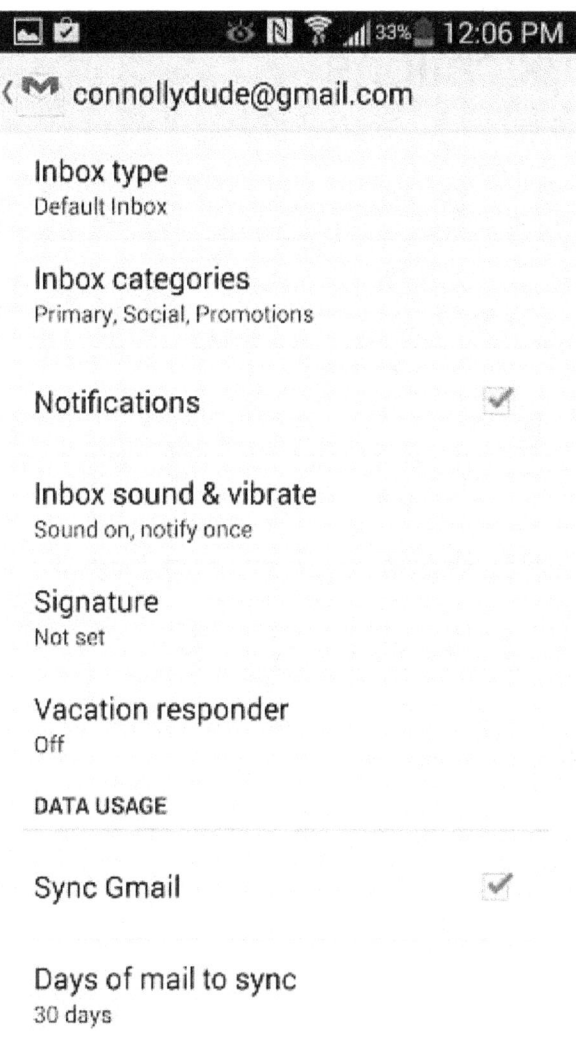

Figure 19: Account Preferences Screen

Managing Applications

Table of Contents

1. Setting up a Google Account

In order to buy applications, you will need to assign a Google account to the Galaxy Note 3. Refer to *"Adding a Google Account to the Phone"* on page 168 to learn how.

2. Searching for an Application

You can search for applications in the Play Store. There are two ways to search for applications:

Manual Search

To manually search for an application:

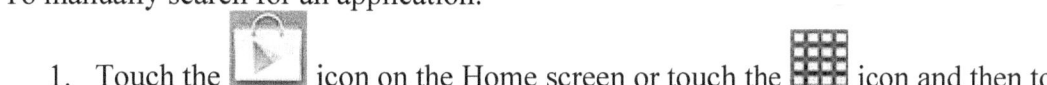

1. Touch the [icon] icon on the Home screen or touch the [icon] icon and then touch the [icon] icon. The Play Store opens, as shown in **Figure 1**.
2. Touch the [icon] icon in the upper right-hand corner of the screen. The virtual keyboard appears.
3. Enter the name of an application or developer and touch the [icon] button in the bottom right-hand corner of the keyboard. The matching results appear grouped by media type, as shown in **Figure 2**.
4. Touch **APPS**. A list of matching application results appears, as shown in **Figure 3**.
5. Touch the name of an application. A description of the application appears.

Browse by Category

To browse applications by category:

1. Touch the [icon] icon on the Home screen or touch the [icon] icon and then touch the [icon] icon. The Play Store opens.
2. Touch **Apps**, **Games**, or any other category. A list of featured applications appears, as shown in **Figure 4** (Apps Category).
3. Touch the screen and move your finger to the left or right to browse the most popular paid or free applications. Keep swiping your finger to the right to select the Categories tab, where you can browse the application categories.
4. Touch the name of an application. A description of the application appears.

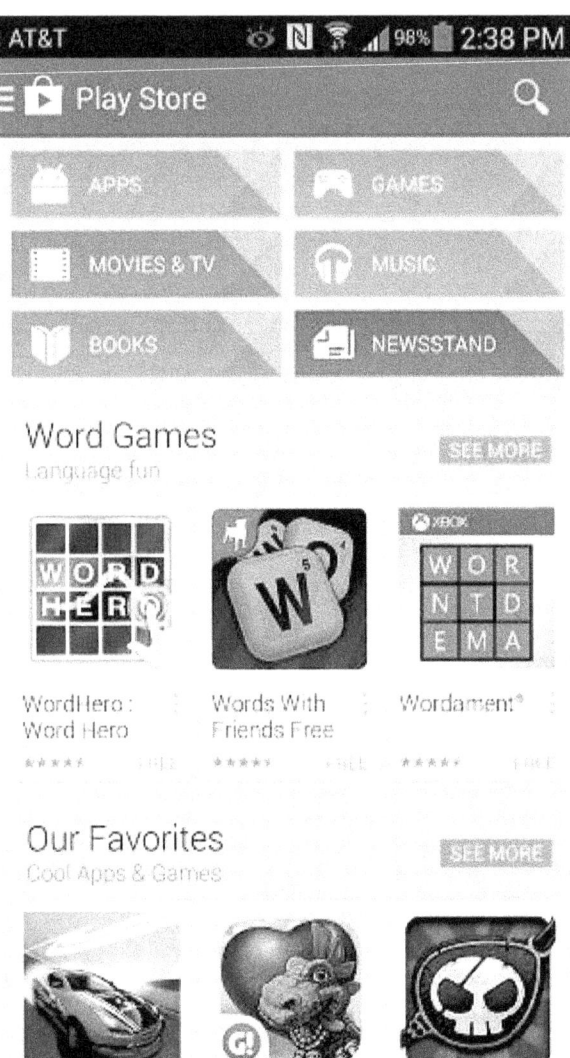

Figure 1: Play Store

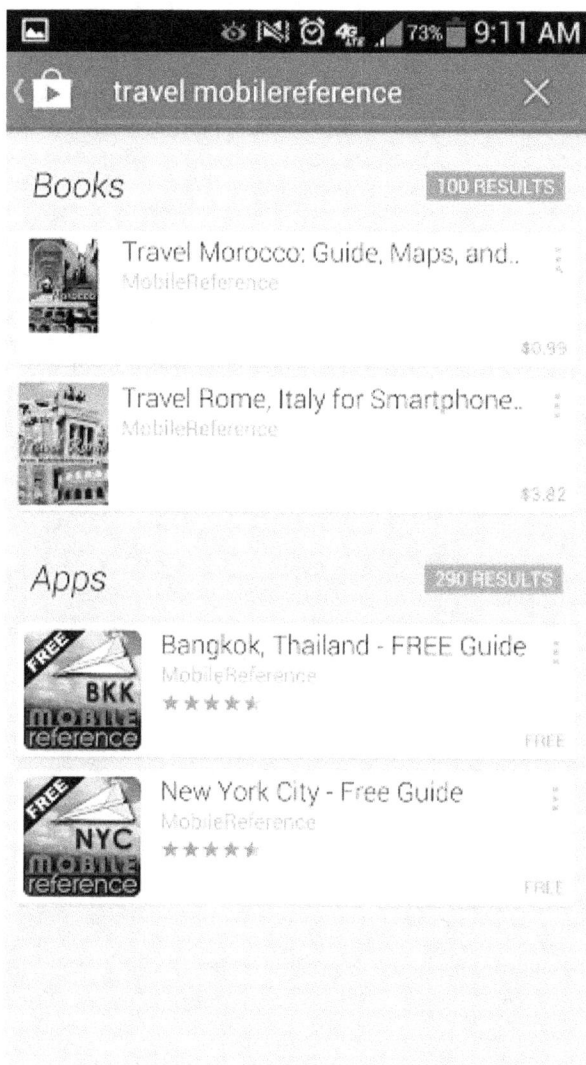

Figure 2: Matching Results Grouped by Media Type

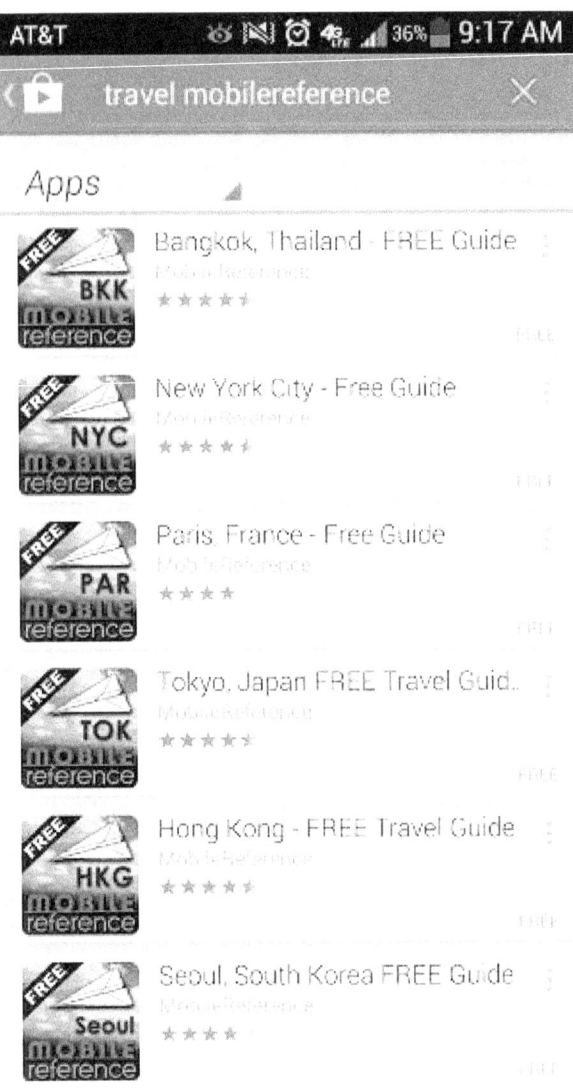

Figure 3: Matching Application Results

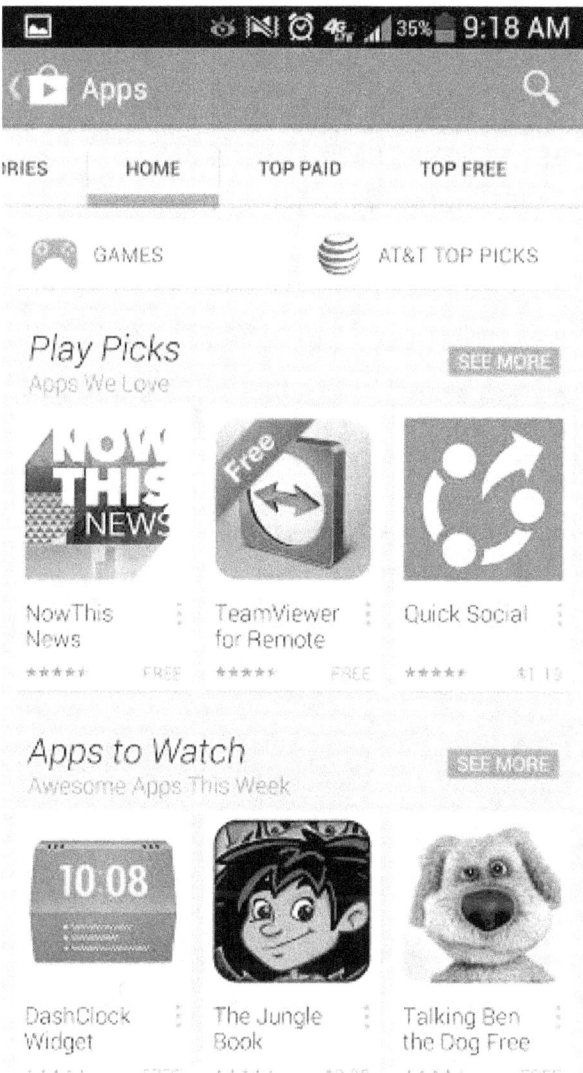

Figure 4: List of Featured Applications (Apps Category)

3. Buying an Application

Applications can be purchased directly from the Galaxy Note 3 using the Play Store. To purchase an application from the Play Store:

1. Find an application. Refer to *"Searching for an Application"* on page 195 to learn more.
2. Touch the name of an application. The Application Description screen appears, as shown in **Figure 5**.
3. Follow the instructions below to download the application:

Installing Free Applications

Touch the [INSTALL] button. The Permissions screen appears, as shown in **Figure 6**. Touch the [ACCEPT] button. The application begins to download and the progress is shown. Touch **OPEN** to run the application when it is finished downloading and installing.

Installing Paid Applications

Touch the price of the application. The Permissions screen appears. Touch the [ACCEPT] button. The application begins to download and the progress is shown. You may also need to enter your Google password before the application can be purchased. Touch **OPEN** to run the application when it is finished downloading and installing.

Note: When purchasing an application for the first time, Google Checkout asks for your credit card information. The information is saved and used for all subsequent purchases.

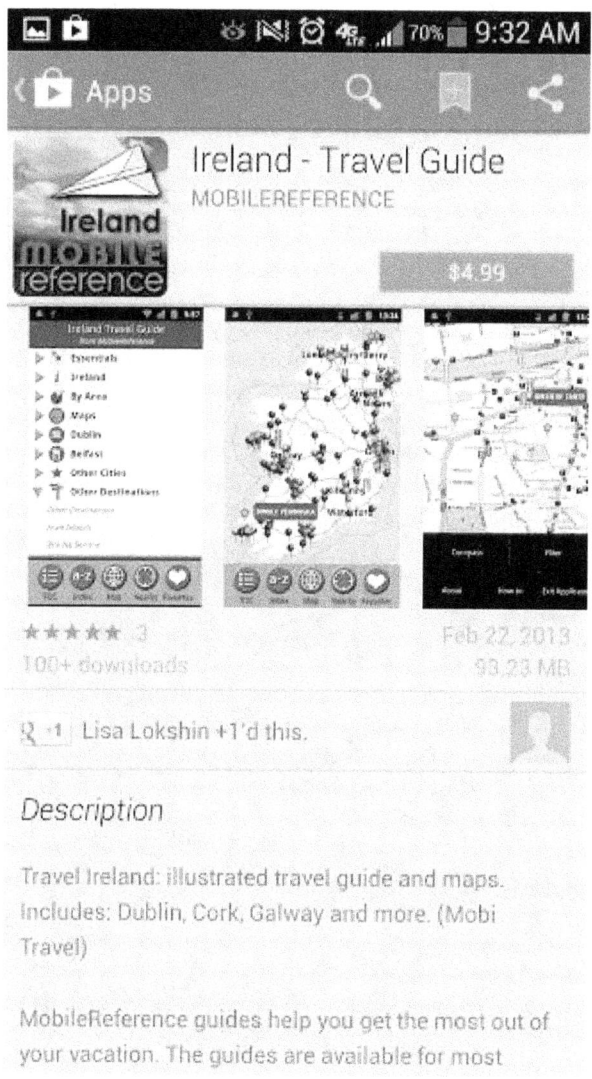

Figure 5: Application Description

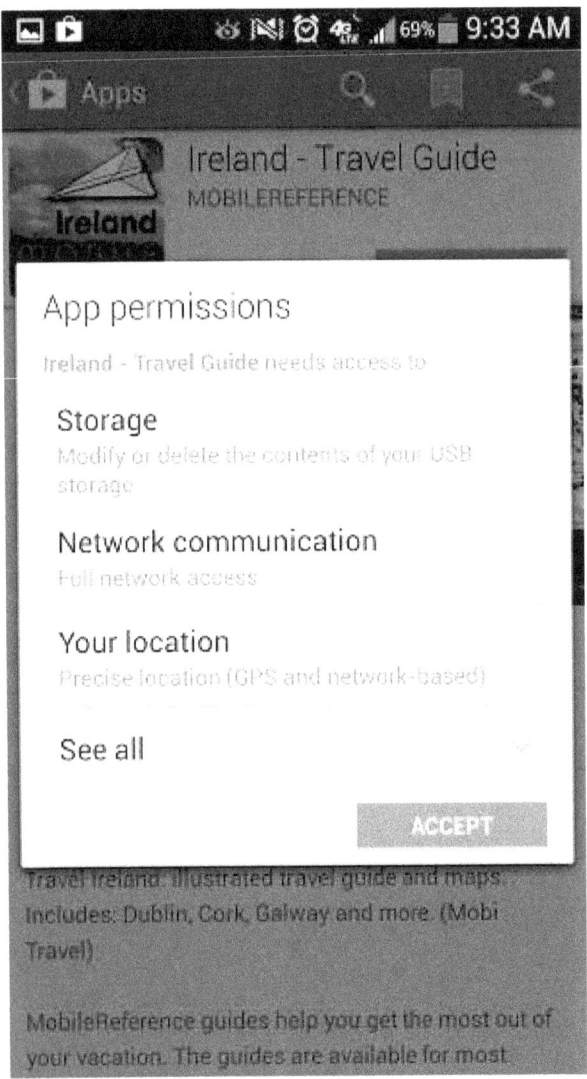

Figure 6: Permissions Screen

4. Uninstalling an Application

Within the first 15 minutes of purchasing an application, it can be uninstalled for a full refund. After 15 minutes have passed, the following instructions only apply to uninstalling an application without receiving a refund. To request a refund and uninstall an application while using the Play Store:

1. Touch the left edge of the screen and slide your finger to the right. The Play Store menu appears, as shown in **Figure 7**.
2. Touch **My Apps**. The My Apps screen appears, as shown in **Figure 8**.

3. Touch the application that you wish to remove. The application description appears.
4. Touch **REFUND** if less than 15 minutes have passed. Otherwise, touch **UNINSTALL**. The application is uninstalled and a refund is given if less than 15 minutes have passed since you purchased it.

*Note: If uninstalling without a refund, a confirmation dialog appears after touching Uninstall. Touch **OK**. The application is uninstalled. You can always re-download an application that was purchased and uninstalled for free. Refer to* "Installing a Previously Purchased Application" *on page 212 to learn how to re-download an application.*

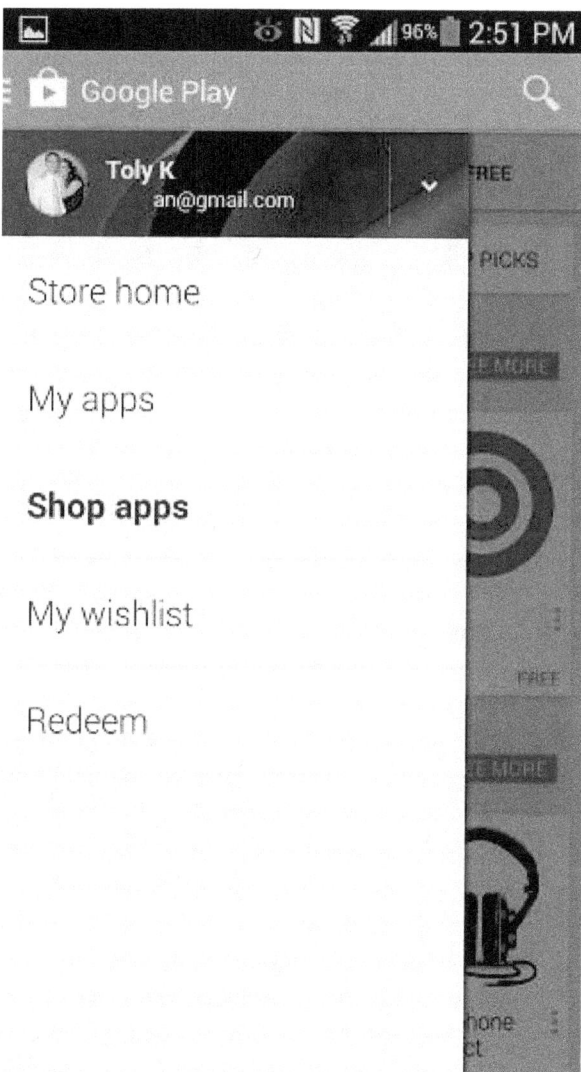

Figure 7: Play Store Menu

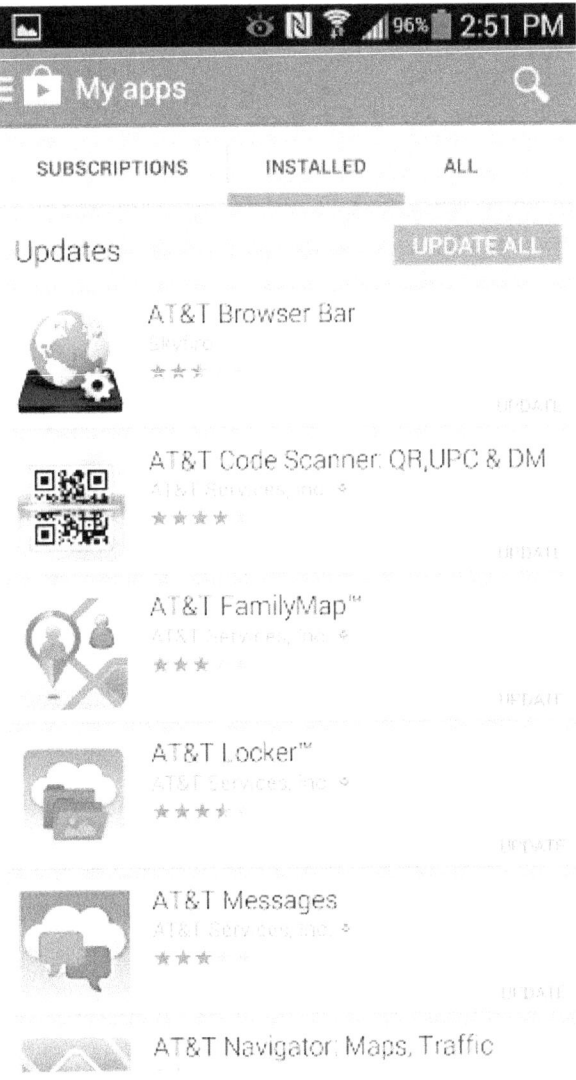

Figure 8: My Apps Screen

5. Adding an Application to Your Wishlist

You may find an application that you like but do not wish to purchase it right away. If you wish to save an application as a favorite, you may add it to your Wishlist. To add an application to your Wishlist:

1. Find an application. Refer to *"Searching for an Application"* on page 195 to learn more.
2. Touch the name of an application. The Application Description screen appears.

3. Touch the ⊞ icon at the top of the screen. The application is added to your Wishlist.

4. Touch the left edge of the screen and slide your finger to the right, and then touch **My wishlist** while using the Play Store. The Wishlist appears, as shown in **Figure 9**.

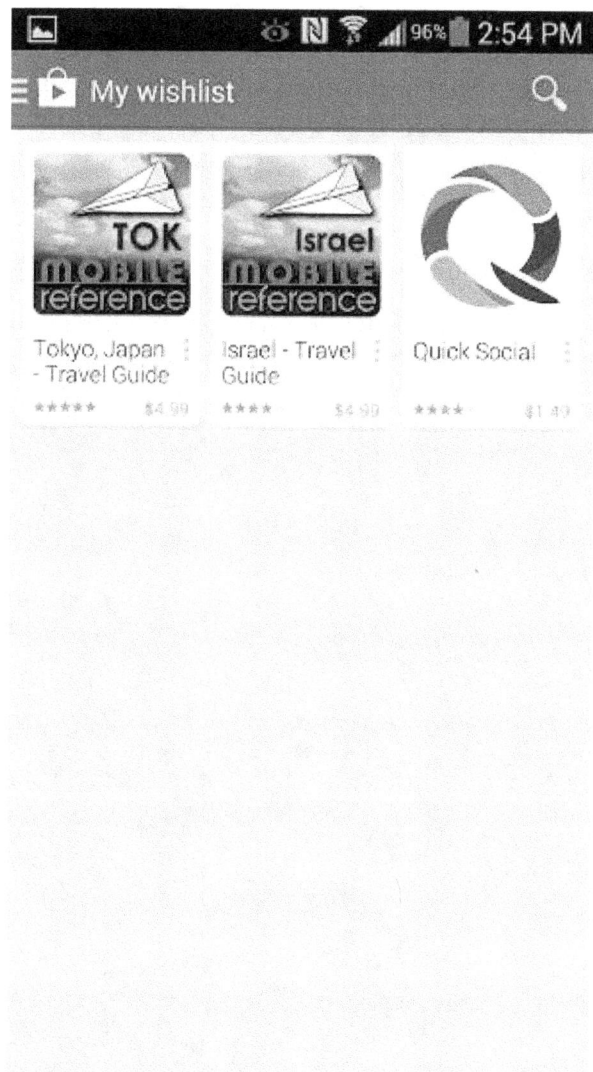

Figure 9: Wishlist

6. Changing the Look of the Application Screen

By default, the application screen is arranged as a grid of icons in alphabetical order. You can also view the applications as an alphabetical list, or as a grid that can be customized by moving icons around. To change the look of the application screen:

1. Touch the ⊞ icon in the lower right-hand corner of the Home screen. The Application screen appears, as shown in **Figure 10**.
2. Touch the ⊟ key. The Application Screen menu appears, as shown in **Figure 11**.
3. Touch **View type**. A list of arrangement options appears.
4. Touch an arrangement. The application icons are arranged accordingly. For instance, the alphabetical list can be quickly scrolled, as shown in **Figure 12**. You can also jump to the first letter of an application by using the alphabet on the right-hand side of the screen.

Figure 10: Application Screen

Figure 11: Application Screen Menu

Figure 12: Alphabetical List

7. Closing Applications Running in the Background

Most applications will keep running even after they are exited, and some take up a considerable amount of memory. To speed up the performance of the Galaxy Note 3, try closing some or all of these applications while they are not in use. To close an application running in the background, press and hold the **Home** button. A list of running applications appears, as shown in **Figure 13**. Touch an application and slide your finger to the left or right, if viewing the screen in portrait mode, or slide your finger up or down if viewing the screen in landscape mode. The application is closed and disappears from the list.

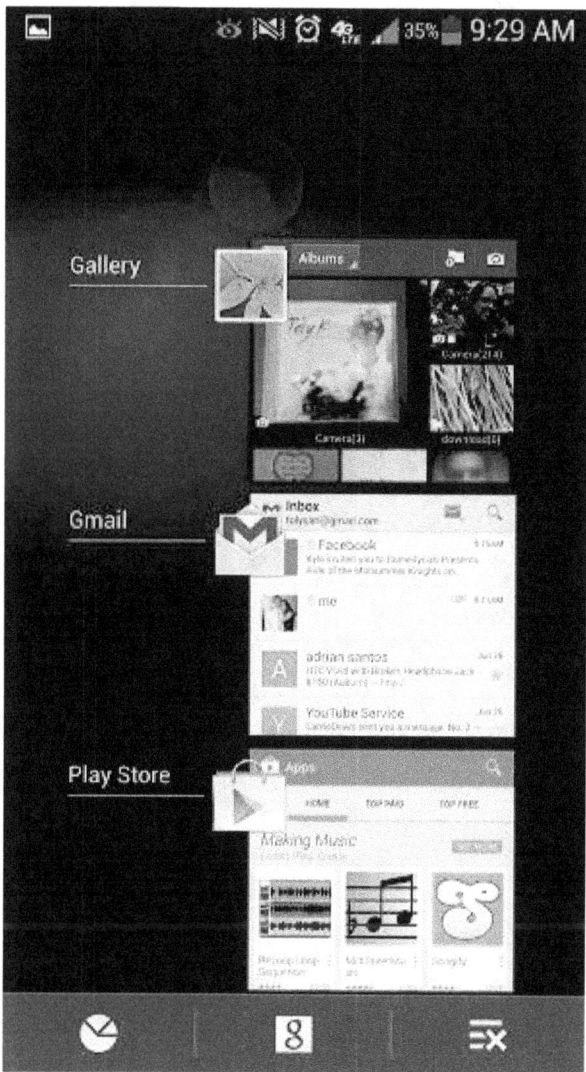

Figure 13: List of Running Applications

8. Organizing Applications into Folders

The Galaxy Note 3 can store applications in folders on the Home screens. This is especially useful to reduce clutter and find applications faster. To create a folder on the Home screen:

1. Touch and hold an application icon. The phone briefly vibrates and 'Create folder' appears at the top of the screen, as outlined in red in **Figure 14**.
2. Drag the application icon on top of 'Create folder' and release the screen. The Create Folder dialog appears.
3. Enter a name for the folder and touch **OK**. The folder is created, as outlined in **Figure 15**.

4. Touch the new folder. The folder opens and the contained applications appear, as shown in **Figure 16**.
5. Touch and hold an icon inside a folder and drag it anywhere outside of the folder. The application icon is removed from the folder.
6. Touch and hold any icon that is not in a folder and drag it on top of the new folder. The icon is added to the folder.

Note: A folder is not deleted when the last application icon is removed from it.

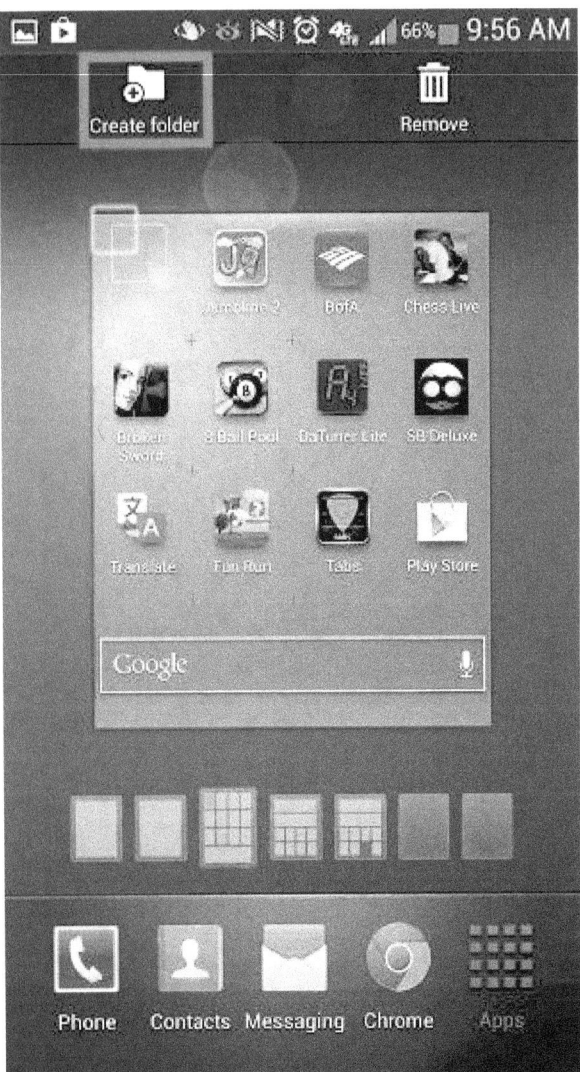

Figure 14: Creating a Folder

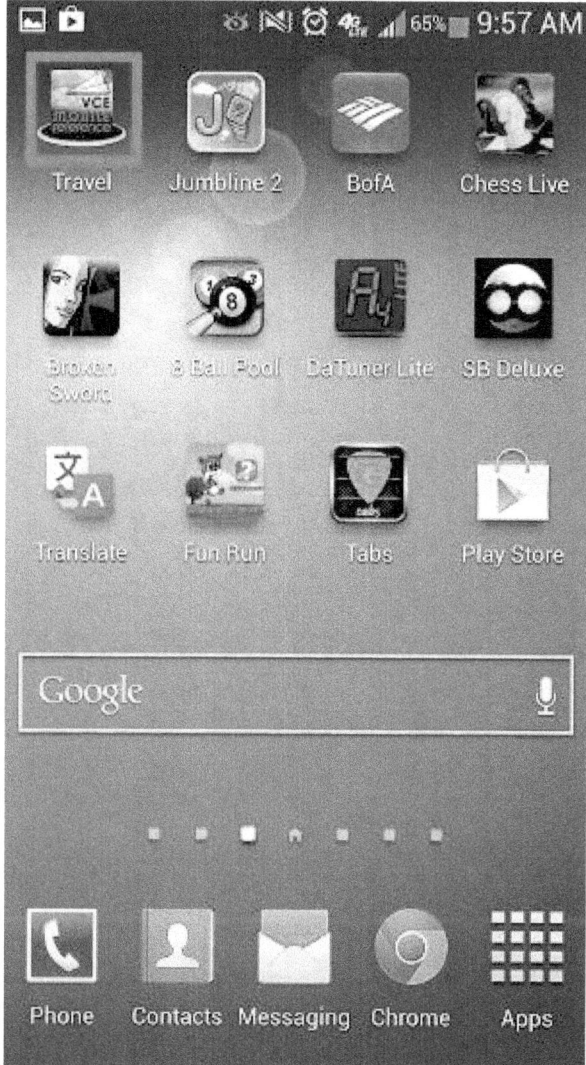

Figure 15: Folder Created

Figure 16: Applications in a Folder

9. Installing a Previously Purchased Application

After purchasing an application on an Android device registered to your account, you can download the same application for free on any Android device registered to the same account. To install previously purchased applications while using the Play Store:

1. Touch the left edge of the screen and slide your finger to the right. The Play Store menu appears.
2. Touch **My Apps**. The My Apps screen appears.

3. Touch **ALL** at the top of the screen. A list of all applications, both installed and uninstalled, appears.
4. Touch the name of an application. The Application description appears. If you cannot find the application, refer to *"Switching between Google Accounts"* below to learn how to view applications purchased under a different Google account registered to your phone.
5. Touch the `INSTALL` button. The Permissions screen appears.
6. Touch the `ACCEPT` button. The application is installed on your phone.

10. Updating Installed Applications

Application developers will sometimes release updates for their applications. To update your installed applications while using the Play Store:

1. Touch the left edge of the screen and slide your finger to the right. The Play Store menu appears.
2. Touch **My Apps**. The My Apps screen appears.
3. Touch **INSTALLED** at the top of the screen. A list of installed applications appears.
4. Touch an application under 'Updates'. The Application description appears. If there are no applications under 'Updates', then there are no updates available for your installed applications.
5. Touch **UPDATE**. The Permissions screen appears.
6. Touch the `ACCEPT` button. The application is updated.

Note: You can also touch **UPDATE ALL** *to the right of 'Updates' to update all of your out-of-date applications at once. There is no confirmation dialog when using this method.*

11. Switching between Google Accounts

If you use more than one Google account on your phone, you may wish to switch to another account to download and manage applications. To switch between Google Accounts while using the Play Store:

1. Touch the left edge of the screen and slide your finger to the right. The Play Store menu appears.
2. Touch the ⌄ icon next to your email address. A list of registered Google accounts appears, as shown in **Figure 17**. If you do not see the Google account, you may need to add it to your phone. Refer to *"Adding a Google Account to the Phone" on page 168* to learn how.

3. Touch an account. The selected account will now be used to purchase and manage applications.

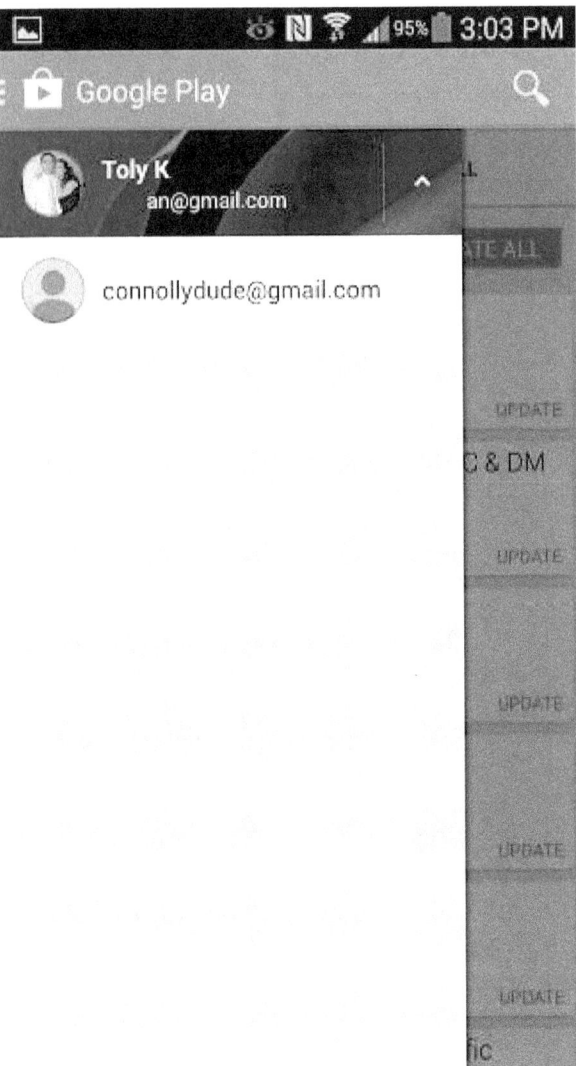

Figure 17: List of Google Accounts

List of Best Free Applications for the Note 3

Here is a list of FREE applications that are specifically recommended for the Note 3.

1. Swiftkey
2. Real Racing 3
3. MyScript Calculator
4. Flipaclip
5. SIGNificant
6. How to Draw
7. Picsart
8. Map Note
9. Maze Racer
10. News Ace

1. Swiftkey

Genre: Productivity

Description: This application is actually free to try for one month, but costs $3.99 to purchase. This predictive keyboard learns from your email, text messages, and social networks as you use it. It then suggests the next word in a sentence based on what you have already entered. This is probably the first application that you should download when you get your Note 3.

Screenshots:

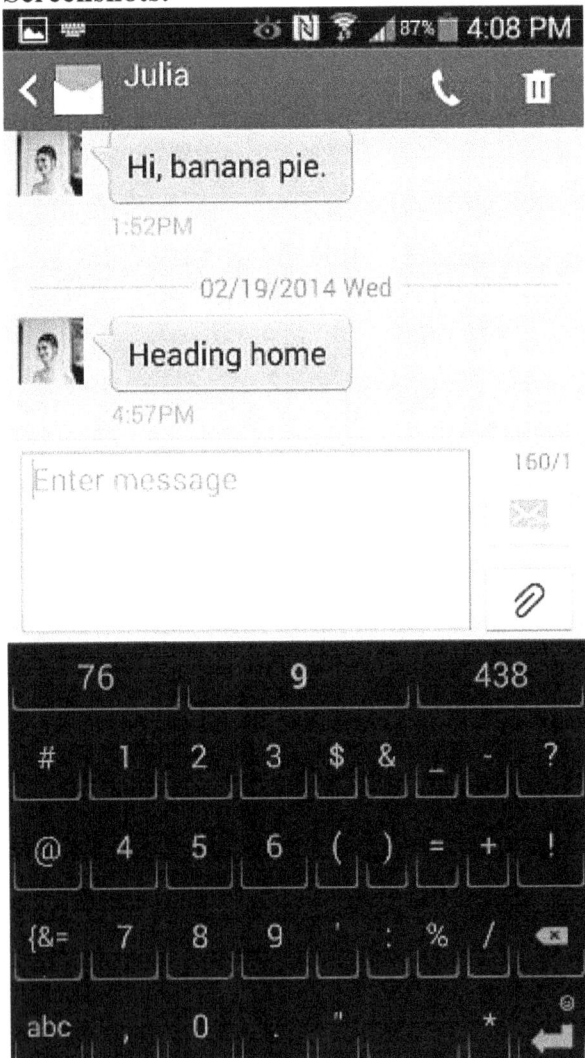

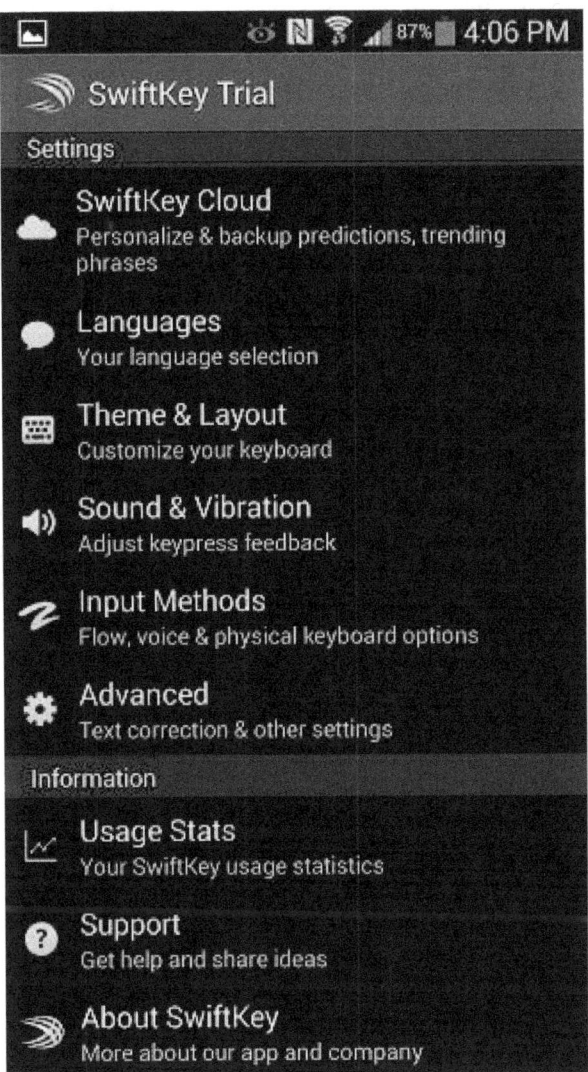

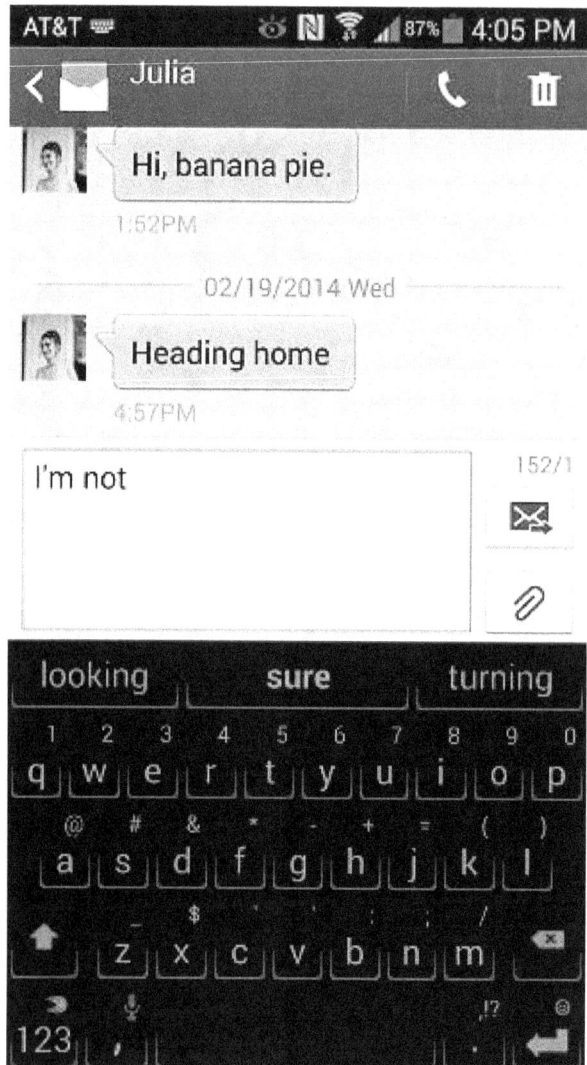

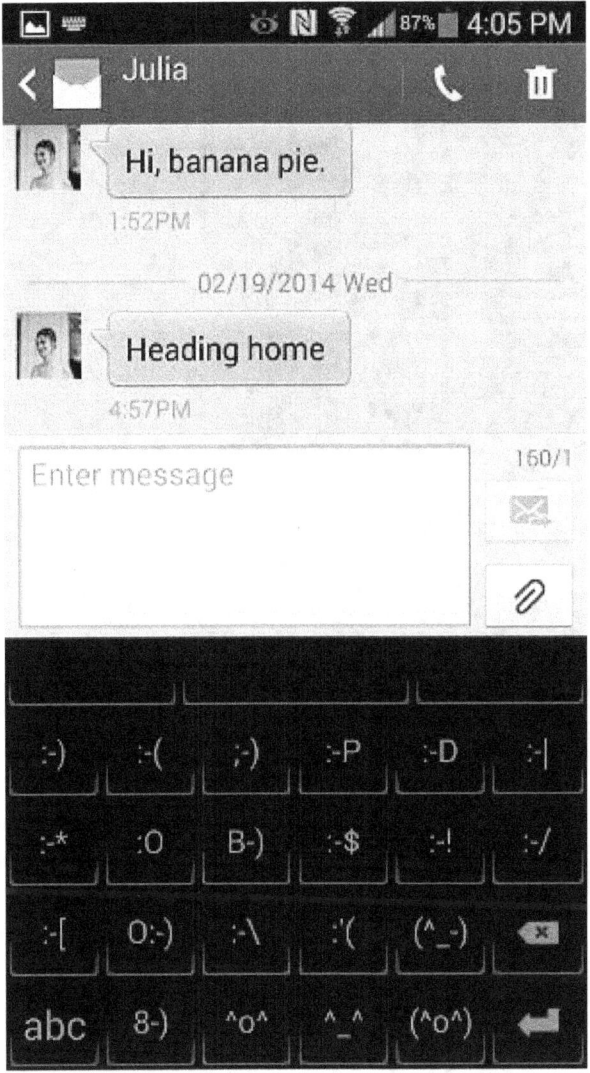

2. Real Racing 3

Genre: Games
Description: Racing game that uses the Note 3's enormous screen to its fullest potential. The graphics and gameplay are one of the best for mobile device racing games.

Screenshots:

3. MyScript Calculator

Genre: Productivity

Description: A calculator application optimized for the Note 3's stylus. MyScript recognizes your handwriting, converting it into a mathematical expression. Most of the features of standard scientific calculators are supported.

Screenshots:

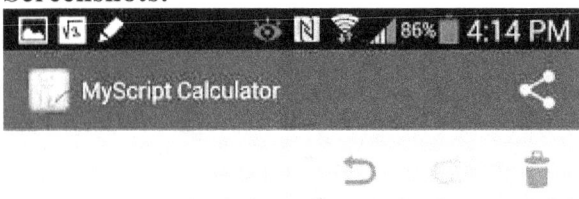

$$\frac{12\times22}{70}=3.771\ldots$$

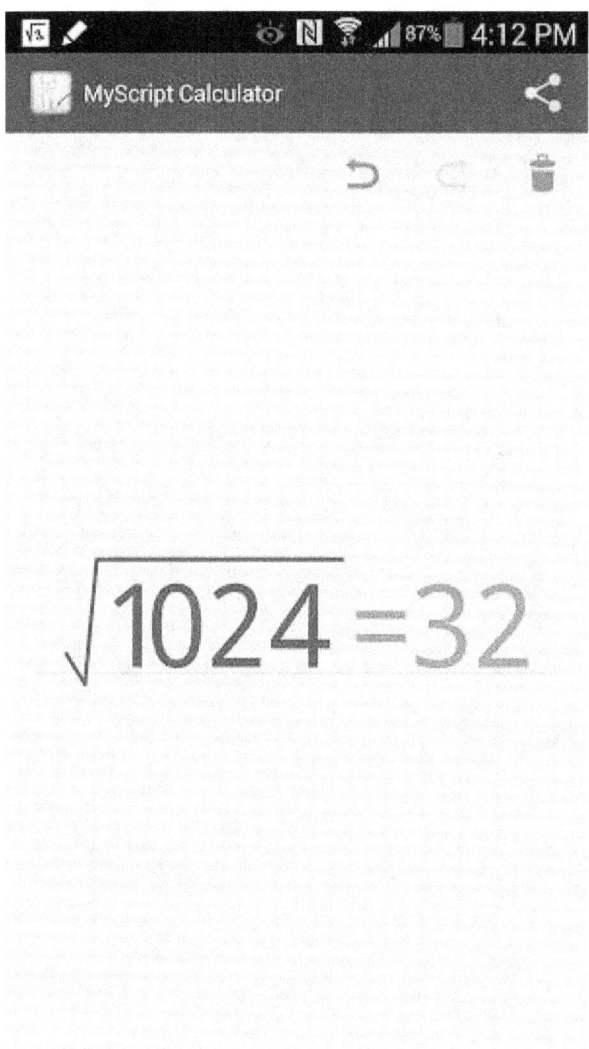

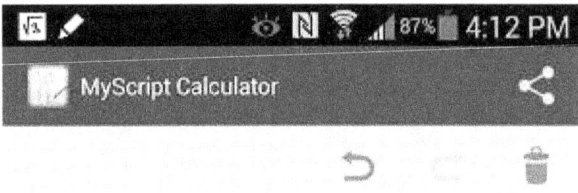

4. Flipaclip

Genre: Art/Media

Description: This neat drawing application allows you to create a flipbook cartoon by drawing one frame at a time. Once you are done drawing, you can choose the frame rate and other options, and even upload your cartoon to youTube, Facebook, Vine, or Instagram from within the application.

Screenshots:

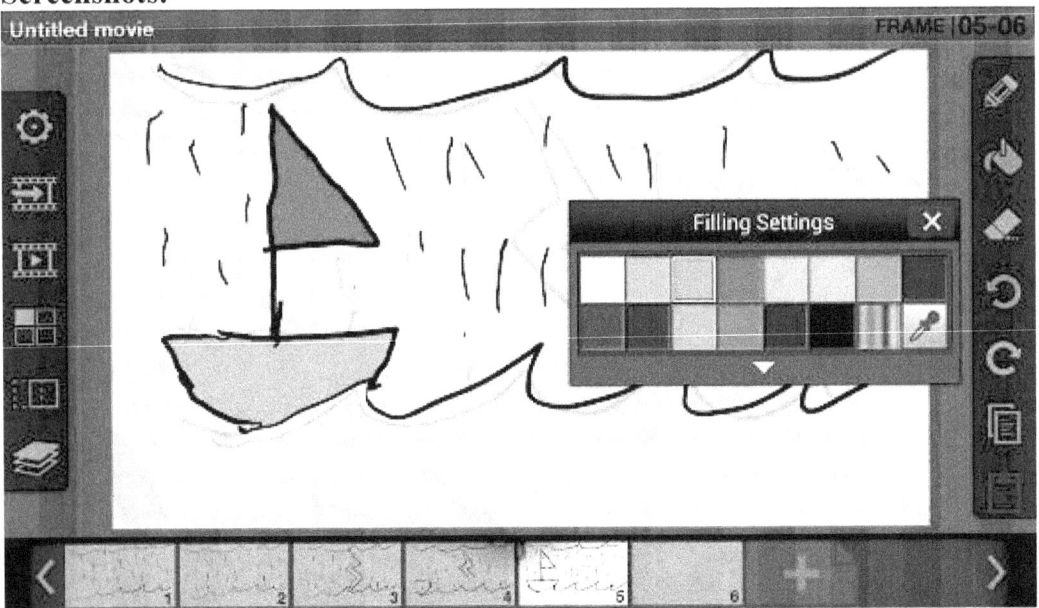

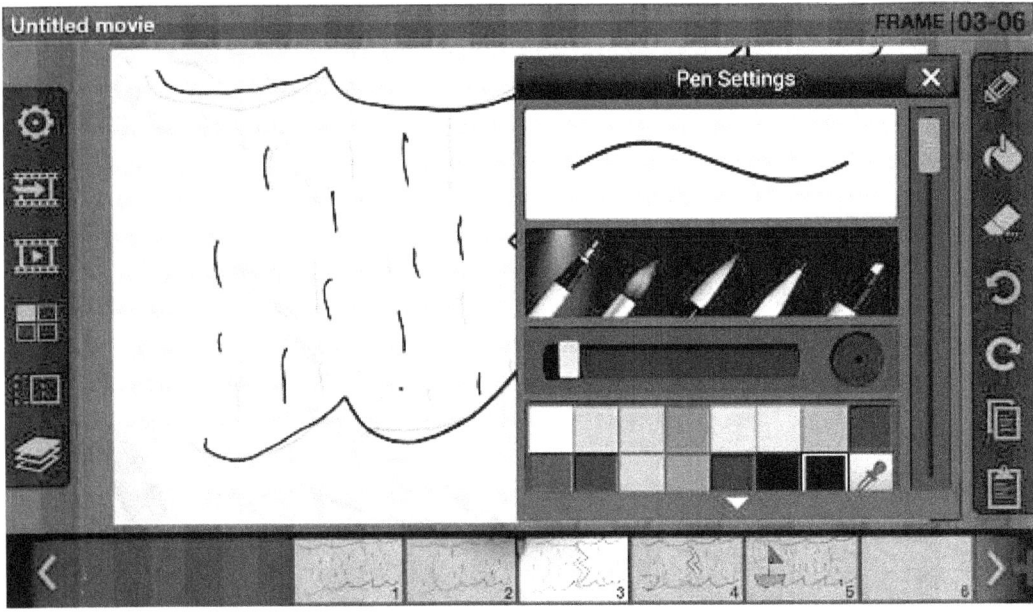

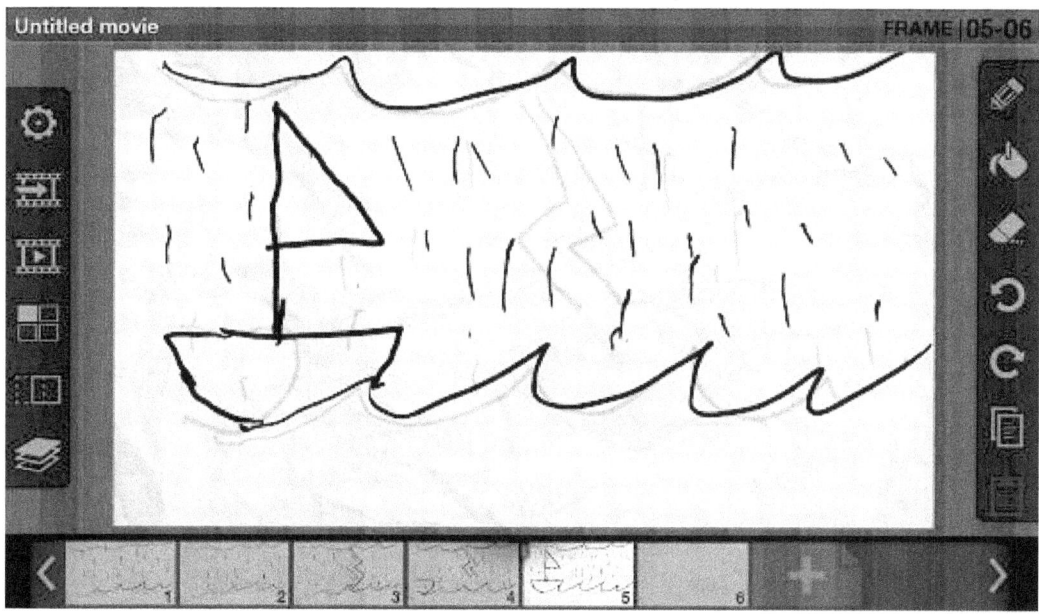

5. SIGNificant

Genre: Productivity
Description: This application allows you to fill out and sign PDF documents using the S Pen.

Screenshots:

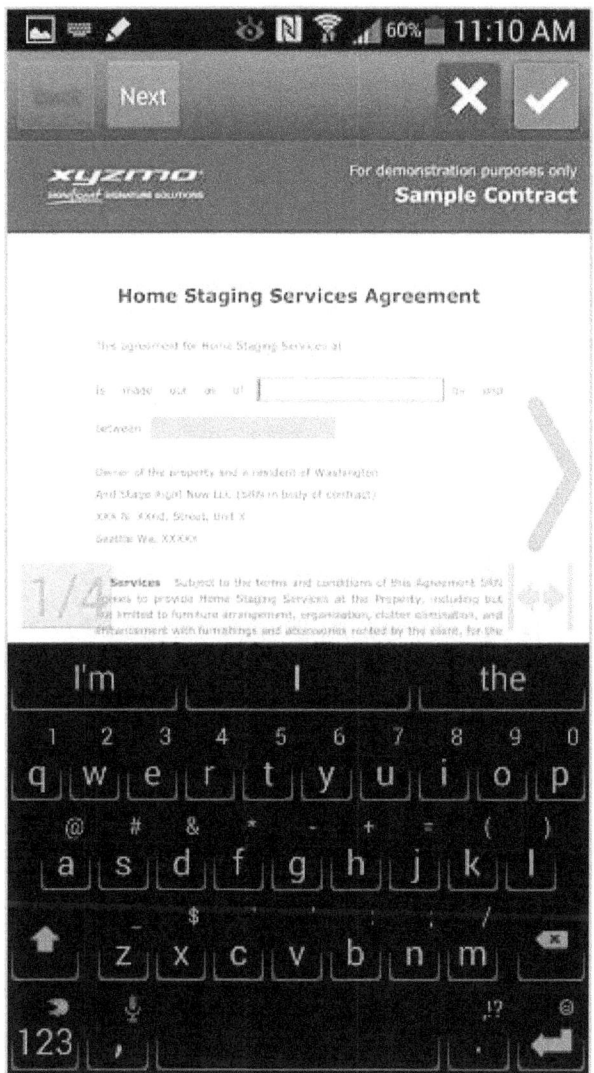

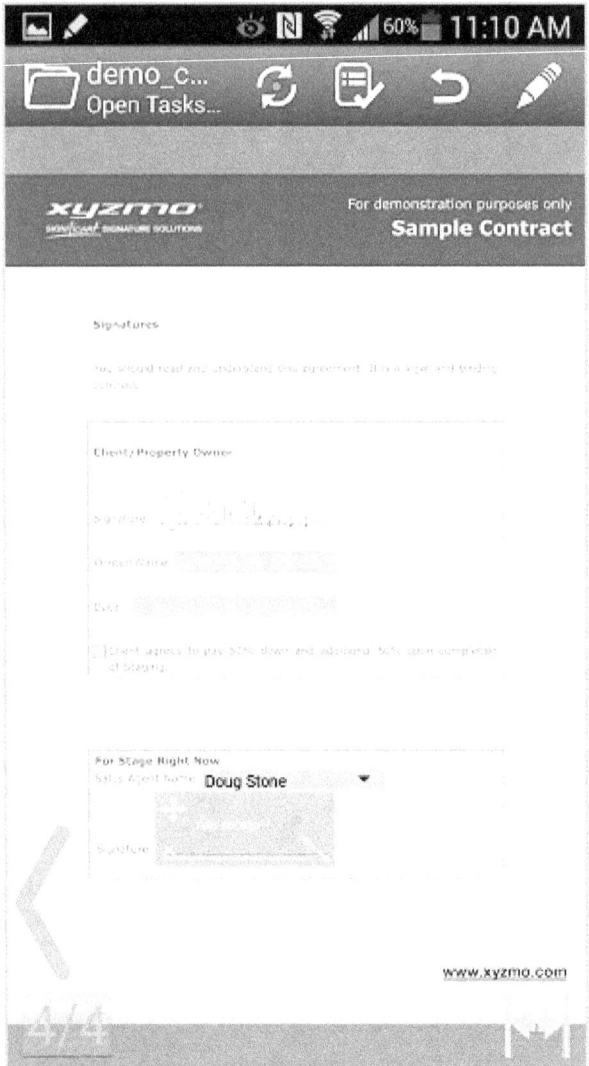

6. How to Draw

Genre: Art
Description: This application teaches you how to draw by providing guidelines for pre-loaded doodles. As you move through the steps tracing the lines, the drawing fills in.

Screenshots:

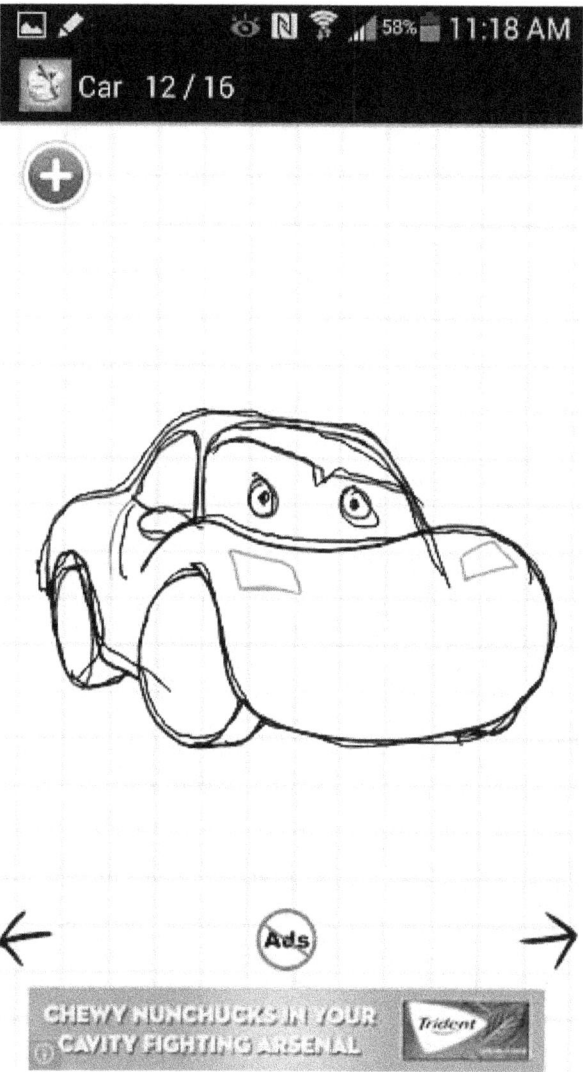

Frog
17 steps

Turtle
26 steps

Cup
16 steps

Elephant
23 steps

Kitty
10 steps

7. Picsart

Genre: Media
Description: This application allows you to add various effects and mark up photos in your gallery or to capture photos with pre-loaded effects right from the application.

Screenshots:

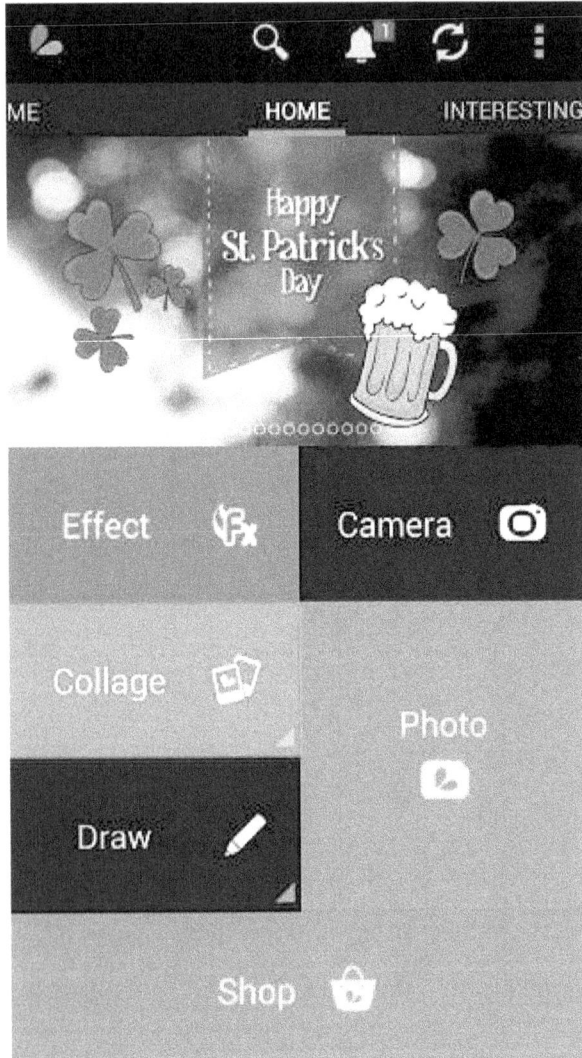

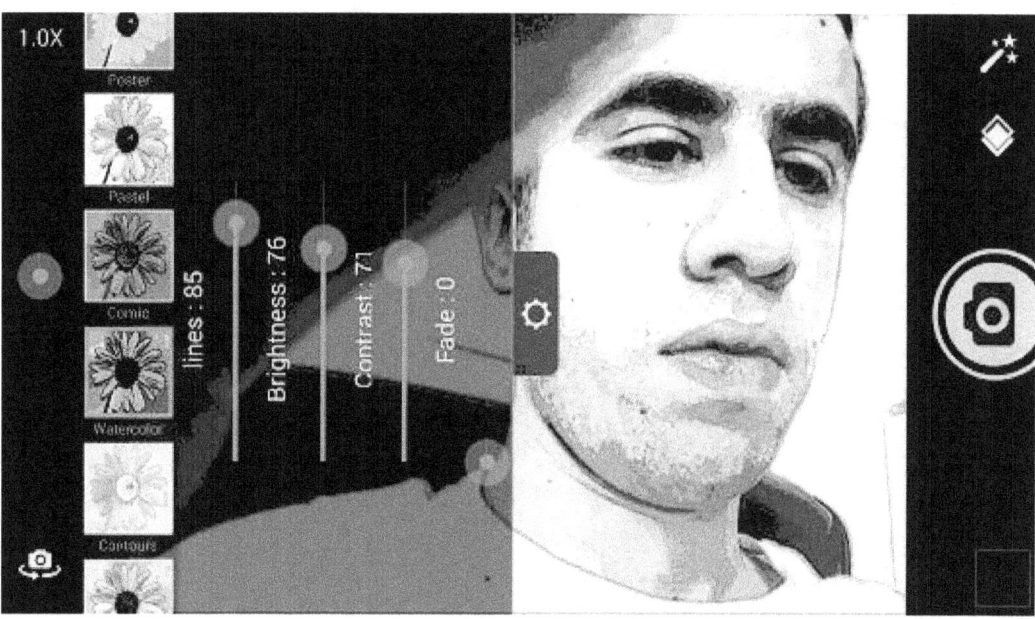

8. Map Note

Genre: Productivity
Description: This application allows you to mark up a map without needing to take a screenshot of it first. A GPS is built in to this application to help you to determine your current location.

Screenshots:

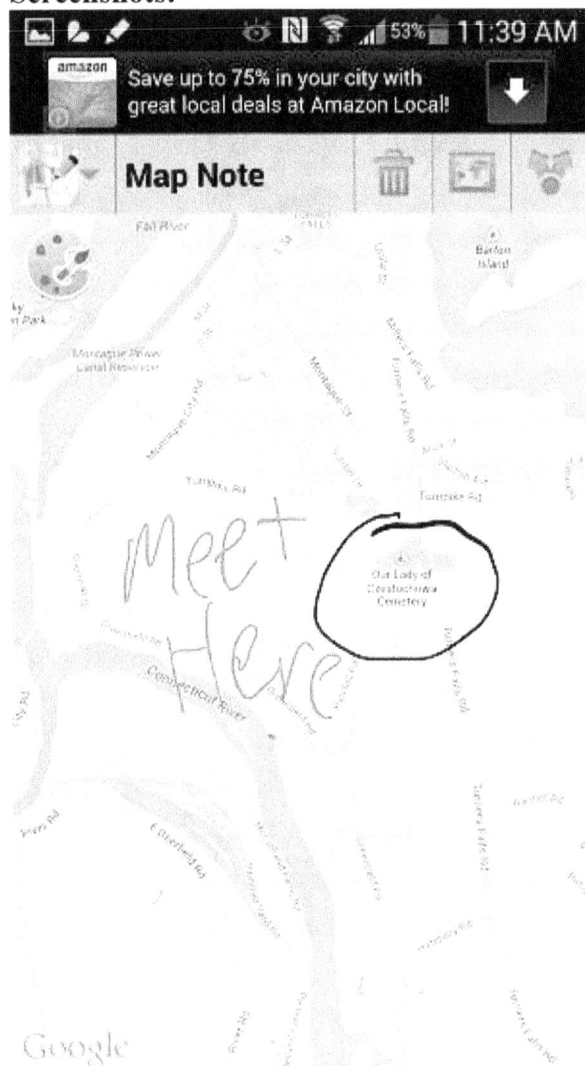

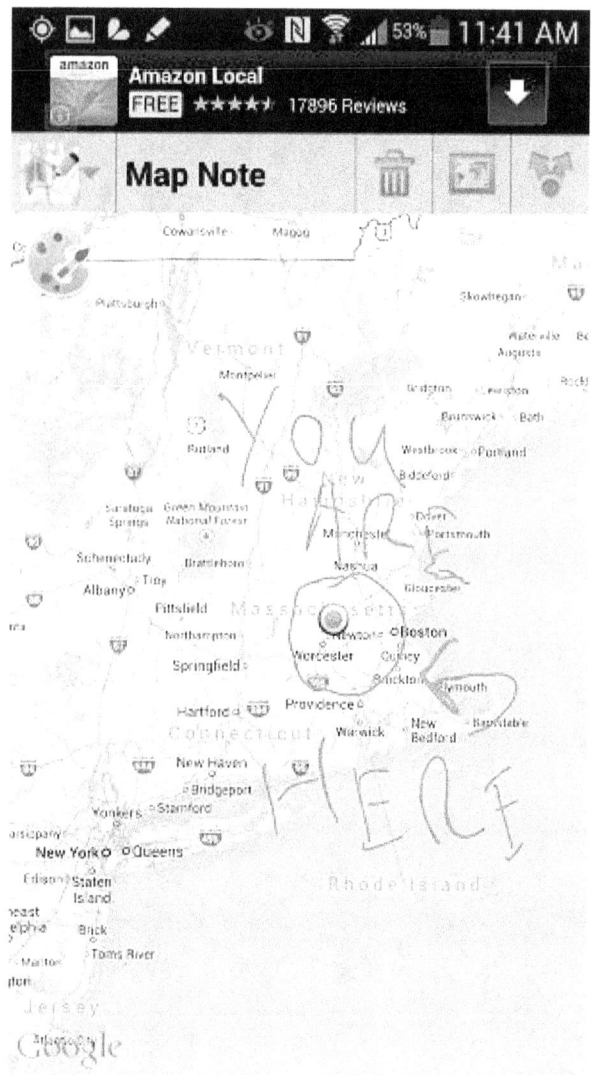

9. Maze Racer

Genre: Games
Description: Use the S Pen to reach the end of the maze in as little time as possible. Touching any of the walls will force you to start the maze from the beginning.

Screenshots:

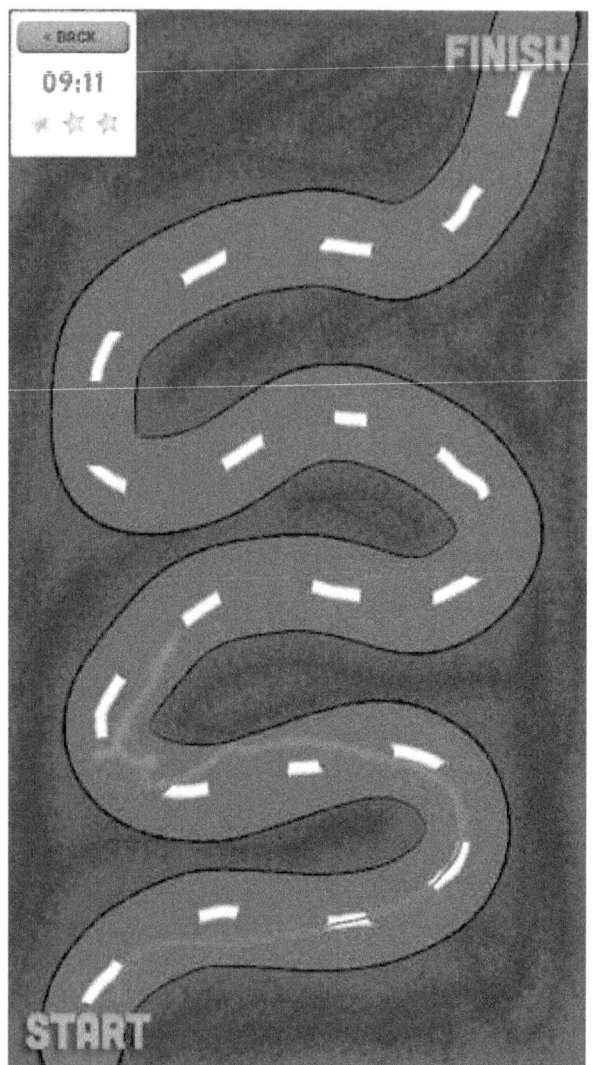

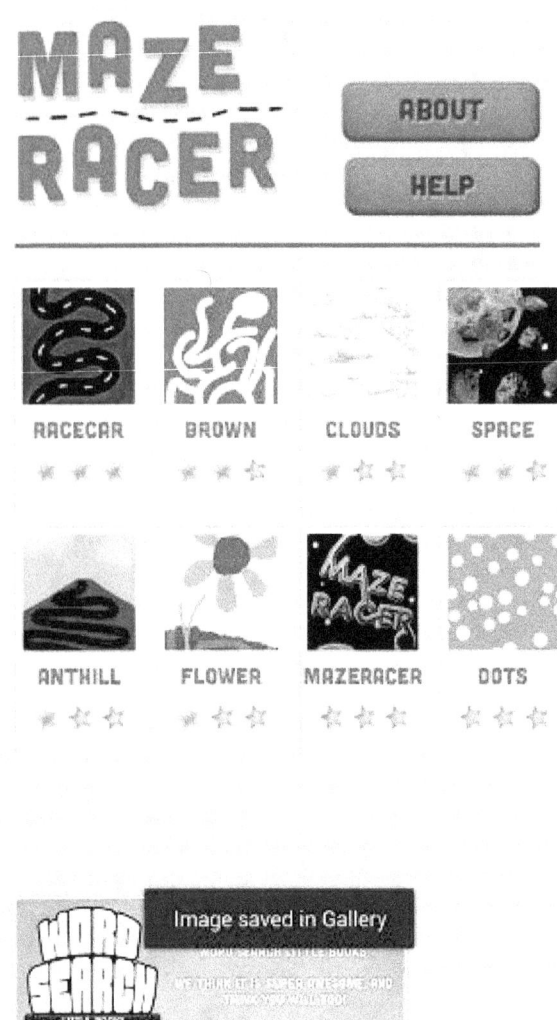

10. News Ace

Genre: Media
Description: Read, mark up, organize, and share news articles using this S Pen optimized newsstand application.

Screenshots:

engadget   5:18 AM (2 hours ago)

Google adds the 'Polar Bear capital of the worl...

 One of the more immediate effects of climate change is that the icy habitats of the

Xiaomi shipped over 15 million MI2 series phones, lowers MI2s t...

While Xiaomi's been pushing its budget Redmi Android phone into Singapore recently, it's also managed to

Google+ for Android learn

Game makers can now start their own Steam sales, to your wallet's...

If you're like many of the PC gamers we know, you wait eagerly for Valve's Steam sales, they're

Apple explai iPhone's fingerprint sensor keeps your info...

If you've ever wanted to know how the iPhone 5s Touch ID fingerprint security works

If you've ever wanted to know how the iPhone 5s Touch ID fingerprint security works beyond a basic overview, you'll be glad to hear Apple has just delivered a motherlode of new details. An updated version of its iOS Security white paper (PDF) explains much of what happens to your finger data after you touch the sensor. In short, your information may be more hack-resistant than it seems at first glance. Each A7 chip has a unique secure space that neither the A7 nor Apple can read, and every authentication session is encrypted end-to-end. The company is also offering a deeper explanation of what it does with your fingerprint image, noting that the print only lasts in memory until it's turned into a

Adjusting Wireless Settings

Table of Contents

1. Setting Up Wi-Fi

Use a nearby Wi-Fi hotspot or a home router to attain a much faster internet connection than 3G or 4G. Wi-Fi is required to download large applications. To turn on Wi-Fi:

1. Touch the ▦ key. The Home Screen menu appears, as shown in **Figure 1**.
2. Touch **Settings**. The Settings screen appears, as shown in **Figure 2**.
3. Touch **Wi-Fi**. The Wi-Fi settings screen appears.
4. Touch the OFF switch in the upper right-hand corner of the screen.

   The ON switch appears and Wi-Fi is turned on. A list of available Wi-Fi networks appears, as shown in **Figure 3**.
5. Touch a Wi-Fi network. The Wi-Fi Network Password prompt appears, if the network is password protected. Otherwise, the Galaxy Note 3 connects to the Wi-Fi network.
6. Enter the network password, if required, which is usually found on your wireless router.
7. Touch **Connect**. The Galaxy Note 3 connects to the Wi-Fi network.

Figure 1: Application Screen

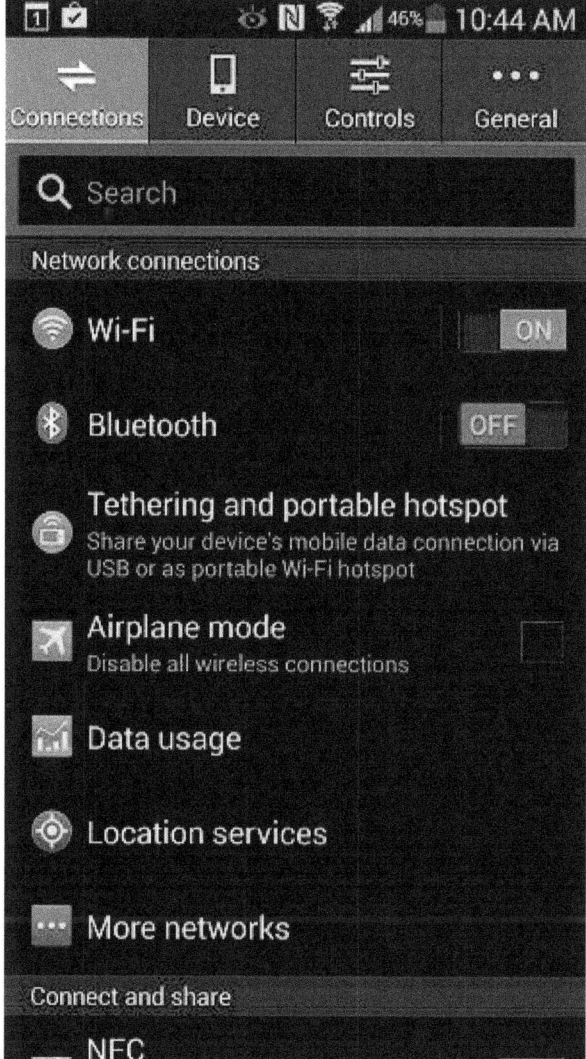

Figure 2: Settings Screen

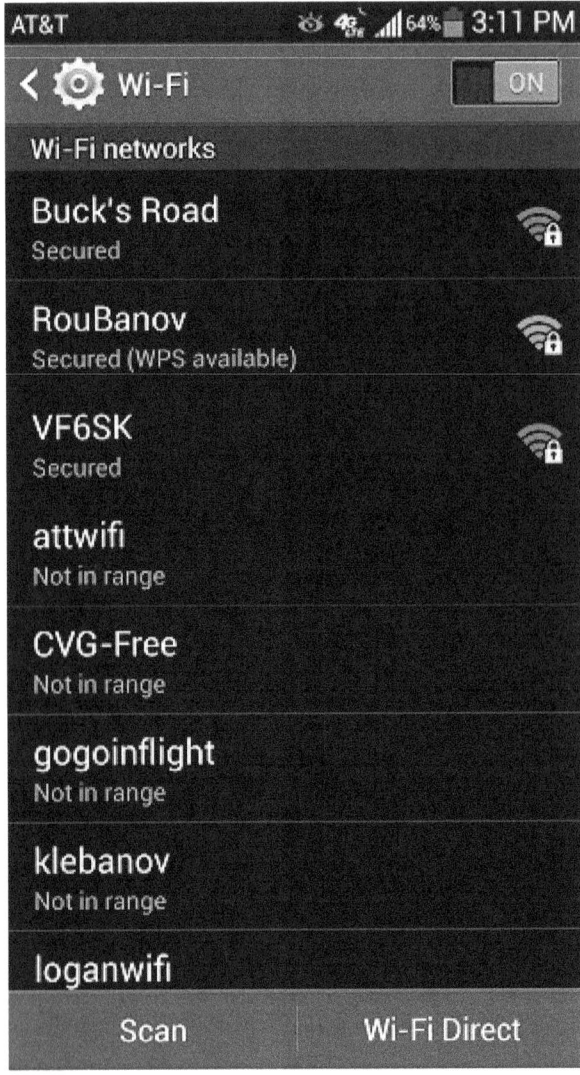

Figure 3: List of Available Wi-Fi Networks

2. Setting Up Bluetooth

To use a wireless Bluetooth headset, you will need to turn on Bluetooth. However, if you leave it on while your headset is not in use, it will significantly reduce the battery life of your phone. To turn Bluetooth on or off:

1. Touch the ⊟ key. The Home Screen menu appears.
2. Touch **Settings**. The Settings screen appears.
3. Touch **Bluetooth**. The Bluetooth Settings screen appears.

4. Touch the **OFF** switch in the upper right-hand corner of the screen.

The **ON** switch appears and Bluetooth is turned on. A list of Bluetooth devices that are within range and able to pair with the Galaxy Note 3 appears, as shown in **Figure 4**. To make the Galaxy Note 3 visible to other devices, touch **Galaxy Note 3** at the top of the Bluetooth Settings screen. The Galaxy Note 3 becomes visible for two minutes.

5. Touch a device in the list. The Pairing Request window appears, as shown in **Figure 5**.
6. Touch **Pair** on both devices. The devices are paired.

7. Touch the **ON** switch in the upper right-hand corner of the screen. Bluetooth is turned off and all paired devices are disconnected.

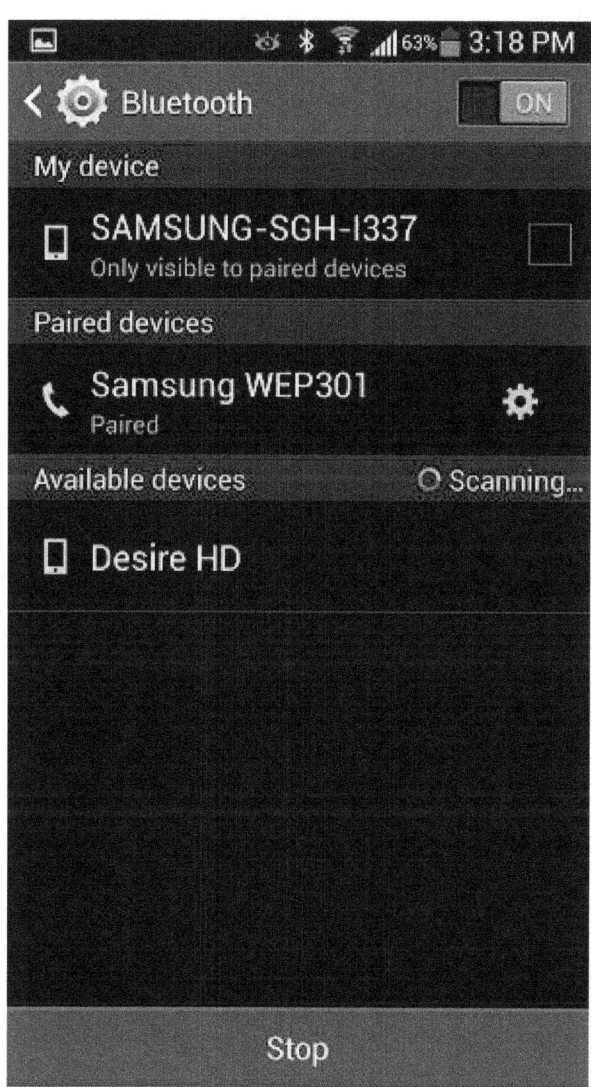

Figure 4: List of Available Bluetooth Devices

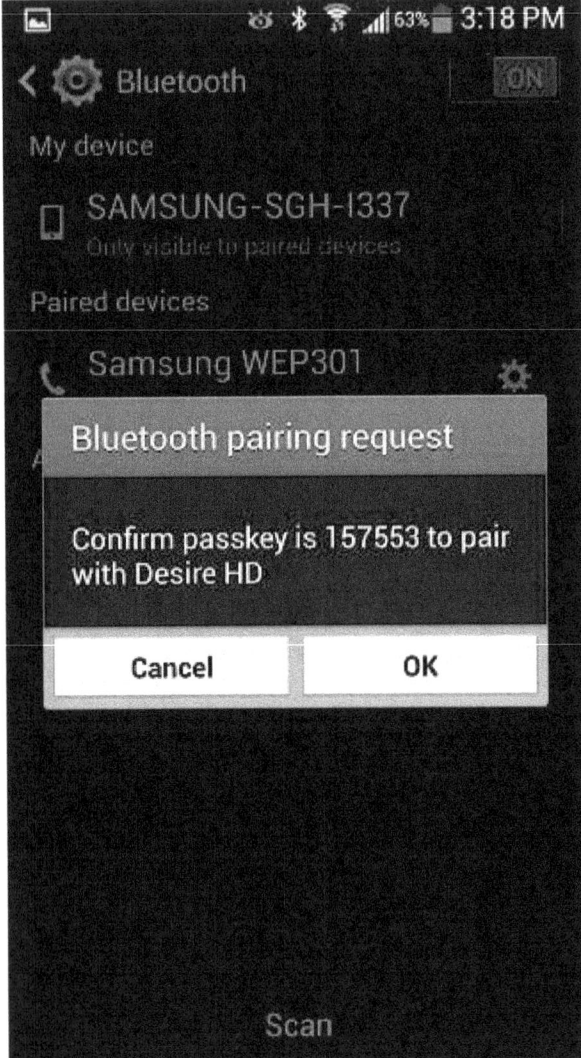

Figure 5: Pairing Request Window

3. Turning Airplane Mode On or Off

Airplanes do not allow wireless communications while in flight. Continue using your phone by enabling Airplane Mode before take-off. You may not place or receive calls, send or receive text messages or emails, or surf the Web while in airplane mode. Airplane Mode is also useful when traveling outside of your area of service to avoid any roaming charges and to preserve battery life. To turn Airplane Mode on or off:

1. Touch the ▦ key. The Home Screen menu appears.

2. Touch **Settings**. The Settings screen appears.

3. Touch **Airplane mode**. A ✓ mark appears next to 'Airplane mode' and the feature is turned on.

4. Touch **Airplane mode** again. The ✓ mark next to 'Airplane mode' disappears and the feature is turned off.

4. Enabling or Disabling the Mobile Network

Turning the mobile network on allows you to make calls, and also allows the Galaxy Note 3 to use data for email and internet. Disabling the mobile network is useful when you are in an area with little or no service, in order to conserve battery life. The mobile network is turned on by default. To enable or disable the mobile network:

1. Touch the ▤ key. The Home Screen menu appears.
2. Touch **Settings**. The Settings screen appears.
3. Touch **More networks**. The Additional Networks screen appears, as shown in **Figure 6**.
4. Touch **Mobile networks**. The Mobile Network Settings screen appears, as shown in **Figure 7**.
5. Touch **Data enabled**. The ✓ mark next to 'Data enabled' disappears and the Mobile Network is disabled.
6. Touch **Data enabled** again. The ✓ mark appears next to 'Data enabled' and the Mobile Network is enabled.

Note: Turning on Airplane Mode has the same effect as turning off the mobile network. Refer to "Turning Airplane Mode On or Off" on page 256 to learn how to turn on Airplane Mode. Only manually turn off the mobile network when diagnosing a problem with spotty service.

Figure 6: Additional Networks Screen

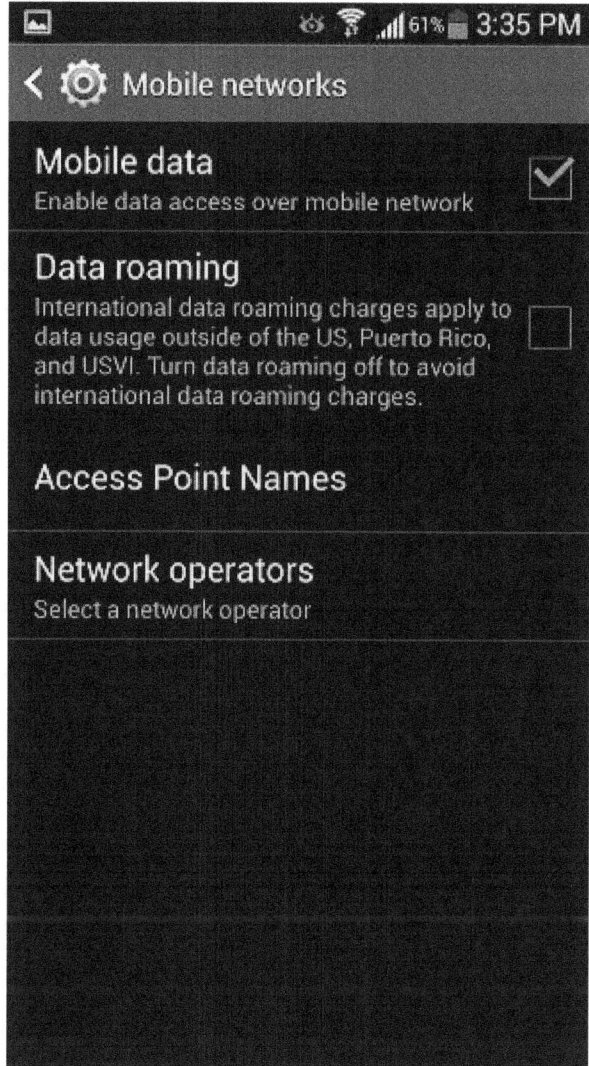

Figure 7: Mobile Network Settings Screen

5. Turning Data Roaming On or Off

When you are in an area with no wireless coverage, the Galaxy Note 3 can use the Data Roaming feature to acquire signal from other networks. Be aware that Data Roaming can be extremely costly. Contact your network provider for details. By default, Data Roaming is turned off. To turn Data Roaming on or off:

1. Touch the ▤ key. The Home Screen menu appears.
2. Touch **Settings**. The Settings screen appears.
3. Touch **More networks**. The Additional Networks screen appears.
4. Touch **Mobile networks**. The Mobile Network Settings screen appears.
5. Touch **Data roaming**. The ✓ mark appears next to 'Data roaming' and the feature is turned on.
6. Touch **Data roaming** again. The ✓ mark next to 'Data roaming' disappears and the feature is turned off.

Adjusting Sound Settings

Table of Contents

1. Setting the Vibration Intensity

The Galaxy Note 3 can vibrate during incoming calls, notifications, and when you touch either the ▣ or ↩ key. To set the intensity of the vibration:

1. Touch the ▣ key. The Home Screen menu appears, as shown in **Figure 1**.
2. Touch **Settings**. The Settings screen appears, as shown in **Figure 2**.
3. Touch **Device** at the top of the screen. The Personalization Settings screen appears, as shown in **Figure 3**.
4. Touch **Sound**. The Sound Settings screen appears, as shown in **Figure 4**.
5. Touch **Vibration intensity**. The Vibration Intensity window appears, as shown in **Figure 5**.
6. Touch the ◄ ◯ ► below the corresponding vibration type and drag it to the left to decrease the vibration intensity or to the right to increase it. Release the screen. The vibration is adjusted and the phone vibrates to preview the vibration intensity.
7. Touch **OK**. The vibration intensity is set.

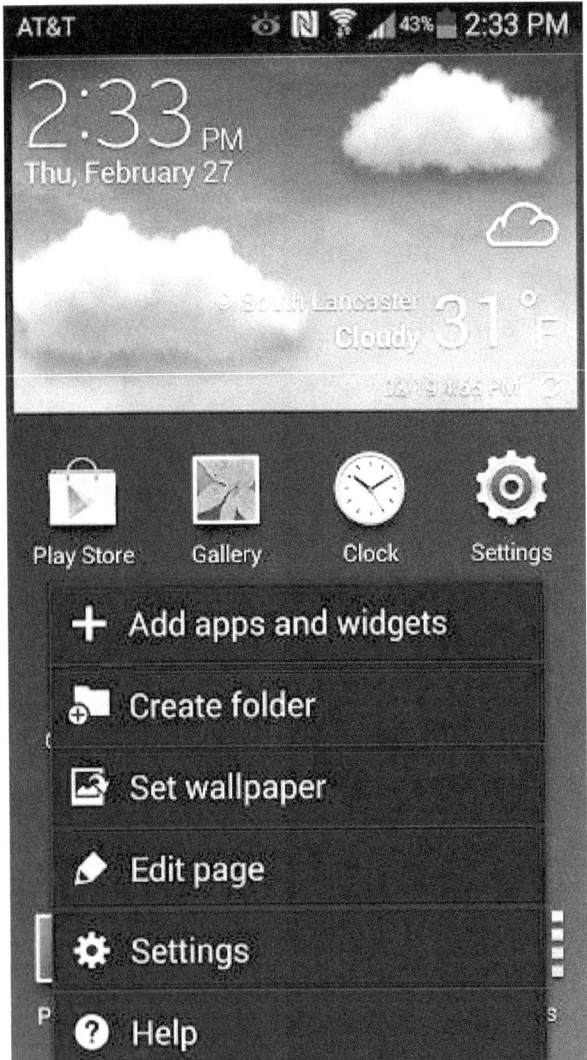

Figure 1: Home Menu

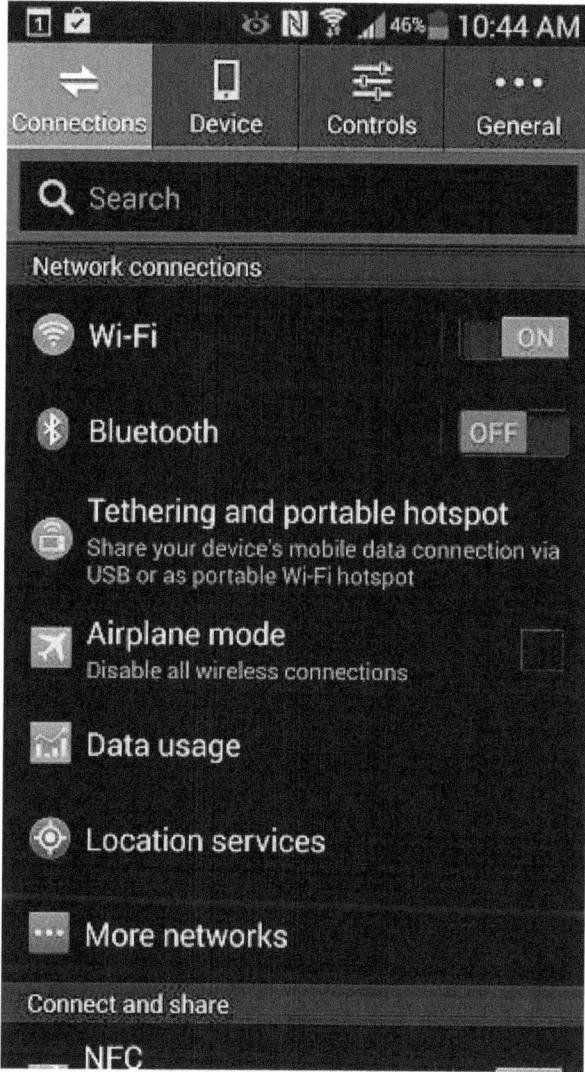

Figure 2: Settings Screen

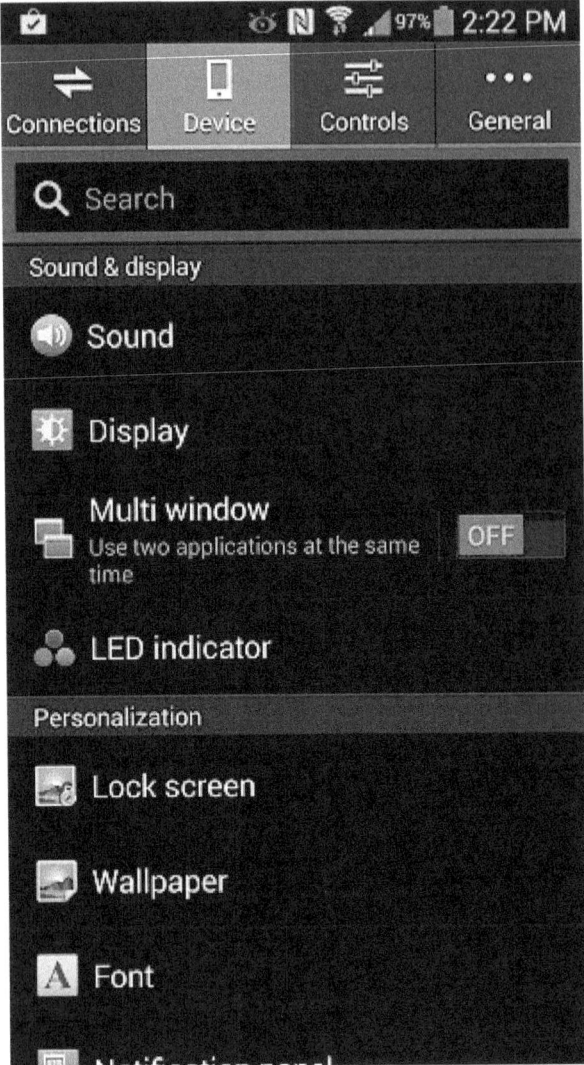

Figure 3: Personalization Settings Screen

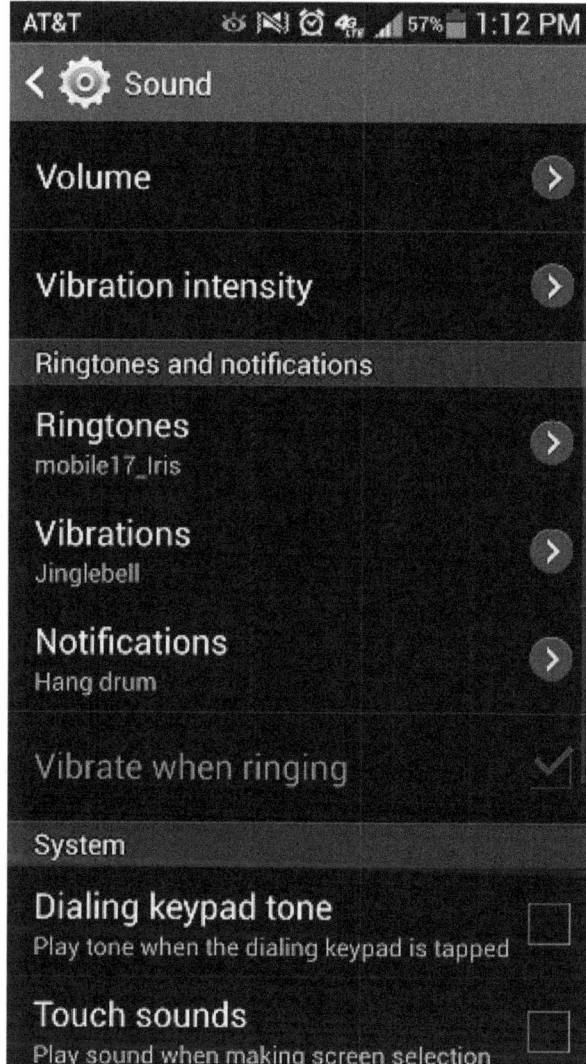

Figure 4: Sound Settings Screen

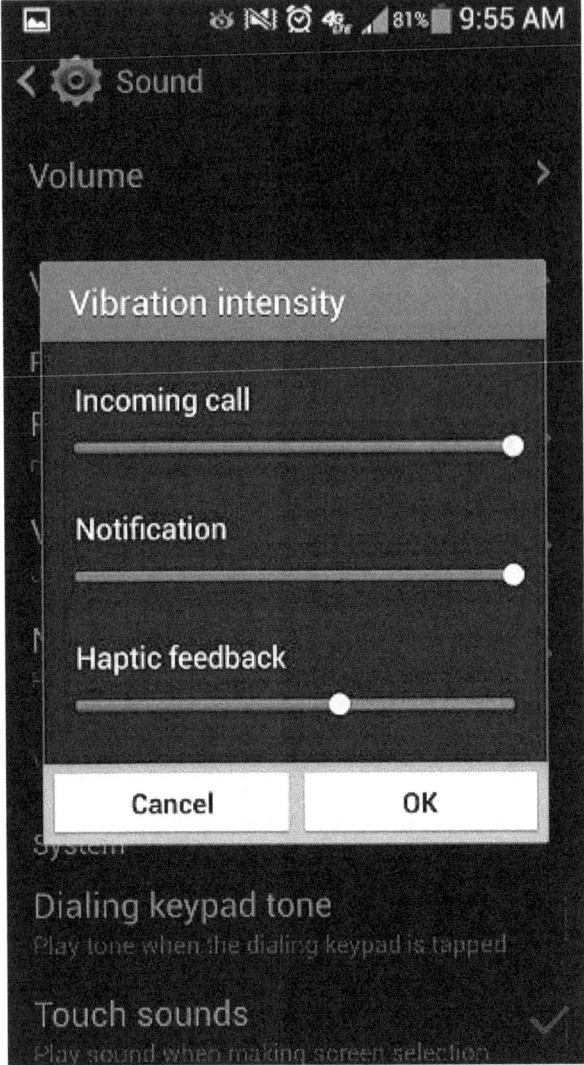

Figure 5: Vibration Intensity Window

2. Setting the Ringtone, Media, and Alarm Volume

The volume for various notifications can be set separately. To set the notification volumes:
1. Touch the ▤ key. The Home Screen menu appears.
2. Touch **Settings**. The Settings screen appears.
3. Touch **Device** at the top of the screen. The Personalization Settings screen appears.
4. Touch **Sound**. The Sound Settings screen appears.
5. Touch **Volume**. The Volume Settings window appears, as shown in **Figure 6**.

6. Touch the ◄ ► below the corresponding volume type and drag it to the left to decrease the volume or to the right to increase it. Release the screen. The volume is adjusted and a sound plays to preview the volume level.

7. Touch **OK**. The volume is set.

Note: The 'System' volume encompasses all system sounds, including the Alarm volume.

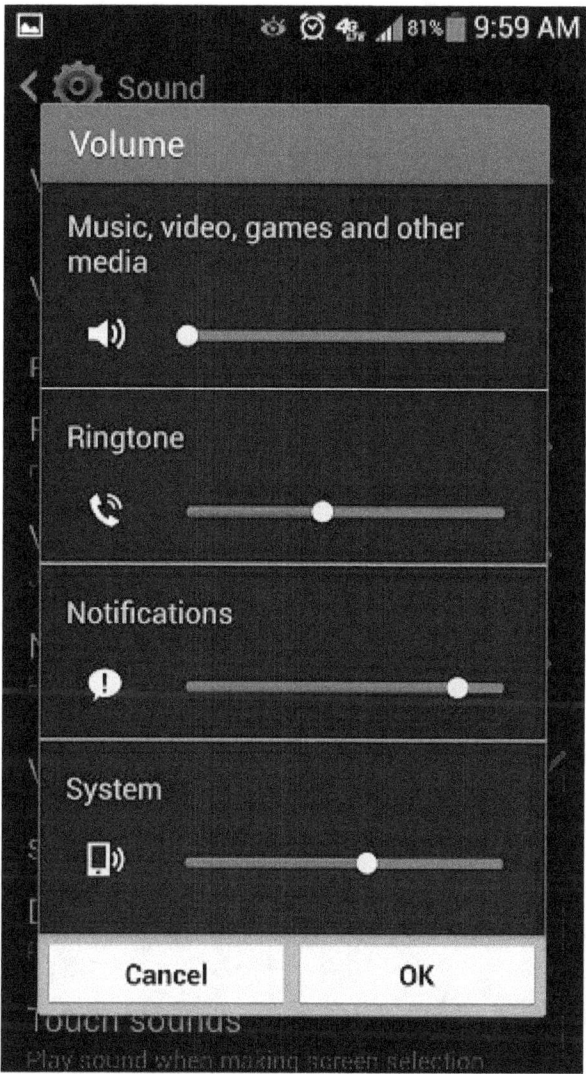

Figure 6: Volume Settings Window

3. Setting the Default Ringtone

You may change the ringtone that sounds every time somebody calls you. To set the default ringtone:

1. Touch the ▣ key. The Home Screen menu appears.
2. Touch **Settings**. The Settings screen appears.
3. Touch **Device** at the top of the screen. The Personalization Settings screen appears.
4. Touch **Sound**. The Sound Settings screen appears.
5. Touch **Ringtones**. A list of available ringtones appears, as shown in **Figure 7**. The ringtone that is currently in use has a ⬤ button next to it.
6. Touch a ringtone. A preview of the entire ringtone is played.
7. Touch **OK**. The default ringtone is set.

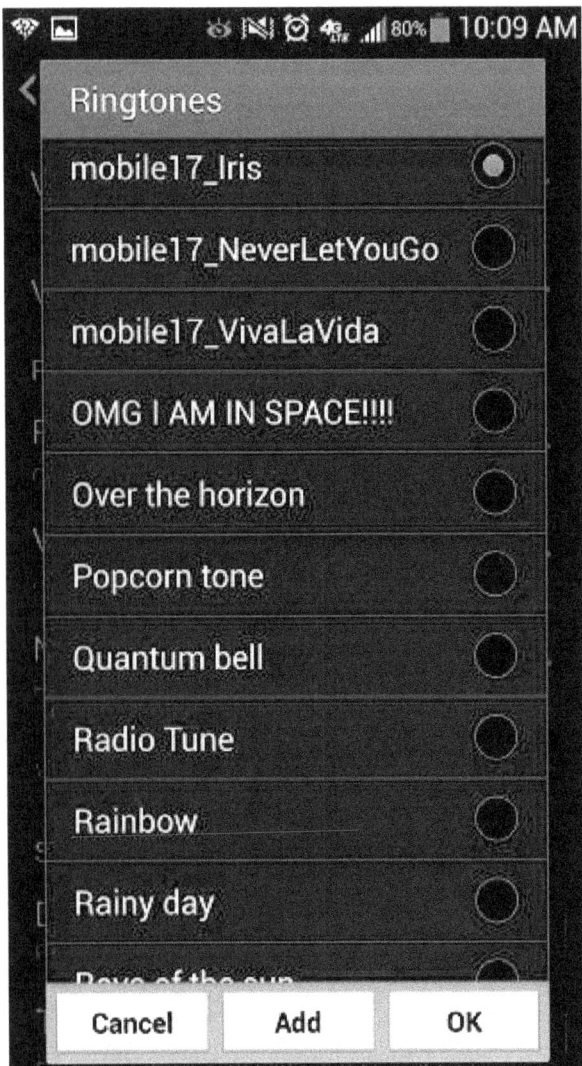

Figure 7: List of Available Ringtones

4. Setting the Default Vibration Pattern

The Galaxy Note 3 can use a series of vibrations, similar to Morse code, to create a custom pattern that allows you to determine the identity of a caller without looking at the phone. To set the default vibration pattern:

1. Touch the ▤ key. The Home Screen menu appears.
2. Touch **Settings**. The Settings screen appears.
3. Touch **Device** at the top of the screen. The Personalization Settings screen appears.
4. Touch **Sound**. The Sound Settings screen appears.
5. Touch **Vibrations** under 'Ringtones and notifications'. A list of vibration patterns appears, as shown in **Figure 8**. The pattern that is currently in use has a ⬤ button next to it.
6. Touch a vibration pattern. The phone vibrates to preview the pattern.
7. Touch **OK**. The default vibration pattern is set.

Figure 8: List of Vibration Patterns

5. Setting the Default Notification Sound

When an event occurs, such as an incoming text or voicemail, a sound is played, known as the notification sound. To change the default notification sound:

1. Touch the ▤ key. The Home Screen menu appears.
2. Touch **Settings**. The Settings screen appears.

3. Touch **Device** at the top of the screen. The Personalization Settings screen appears.

4. Touch **Sound**. The Sound Settings screen appears.

5. Touch **Default notification sound**. A list of available notification sounds appears, as

   shown in **Figure 9**. The notification sound that is currently in use has a ⬤ button next to
   it.
6. Touch a notification sound. A preview of the sound is played.
7. Touch **OK**. The default notification sound is set.

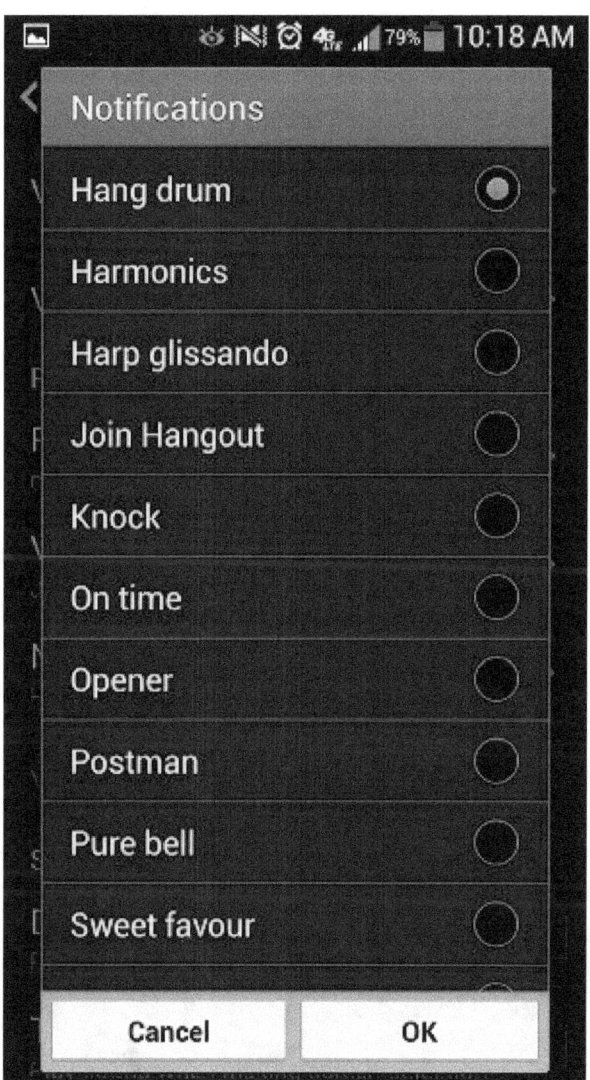

Figure 9: List of Available Notification Sounds

6. Turning Ringer Vibration On or Off

The Galaxy Note 3 can vibrate every time the ringtone sounds. Before you can adjust this setting, you must turn on the ringtone volume. You can do so by pressing the Volume Up button on the left side of the phone. To turn ringer vibration on or off:

1. Touch the ▤ key. The Home Screen menu appears.
2. Touch **Settings**. The Settings screen appears.
3. Touch **Device** at the top of the screen. The Personalization Settings screen appears.
4. Touch **Sound**. The Sound Settings screen appears.
5. Touch **Vibrate when ringing**. A ✓ mark appears next to 'Vibrate when ringing' and the feature is turned on.
6. Touch **Vibrate when ringing** again. The ✓ mark disappears and the feature is turned off.

7. Turning System Sounds On or Off

Some system sounds, such as dial pad touch tones and screen lock sounds, can be turned on or off. To turn system sounds on or off:

1. Touch the ▤ key. The Home Screen menu appears.
2. Touch **Settings**. The Settings screen appears.
3. Touch **Device** at the top of the screen. The Personalization Settings screen appears.
4. Touch **Sound**. The Sound Settings screen appears.
5. Touch one of the following options under 'System' to turn the corresponding sound on or off:

   - **Dialing keypad tone** - Turns the sounds made when touching a number on the dial pad on or off.
   - **Touch sounds** - Turns the sounds made when making a selection on the screen on or off.
   - **Screen lock sound** - Turns the sounds made when locking and unlocking the screen on or off.
   - **Haptic feedback** - Turns the vibration made when pressing the ▤ key or ⮌ key on or off.
   - **Pen attach/detach sound** - Allows you to select the sound that is made when you take out the S Pen, or put it back in its holster.

Adjusting Display Settings

Table of Contents

1. Adjusting the Brightness

The Galaxy Note 3 can be set to automatically detect lighting conditions by using a built-in light sensor. When Automatic Brightness is turned off, a single brightness setting is maintained in any lighting. To customize the brightness settings:

1. Touch the ▤ key. The Home Screen menu appears, as shown in **Figure 1**.
2. Touch **Settings**. The Settings screen appears, as shown in **Figure 2**.
3. Touch **Device** at the top of the screen. The Personalization Settings screen appears, as shown in **Figure 3**.
4. Touch **Display**. The Display Settings screen appears, as shown in **Figure 4**.
5. Touch **Brightness**. The Brightness window appears. By default, Automatic Brightness is turned on.
6. Touch **Automatic brightness**. The ✓ mark next to 'Automatic brightness' disappears and the feature is turned off. An adjustment bar appears.
7. Touch and drag the ▬ ▬ slider to the left to decrease the brightness or to the right to increase it. Touch **OK**. The brightness is adjusted. Alternatively, touch **Cancel** to continue using the Automatic Brightness feature.

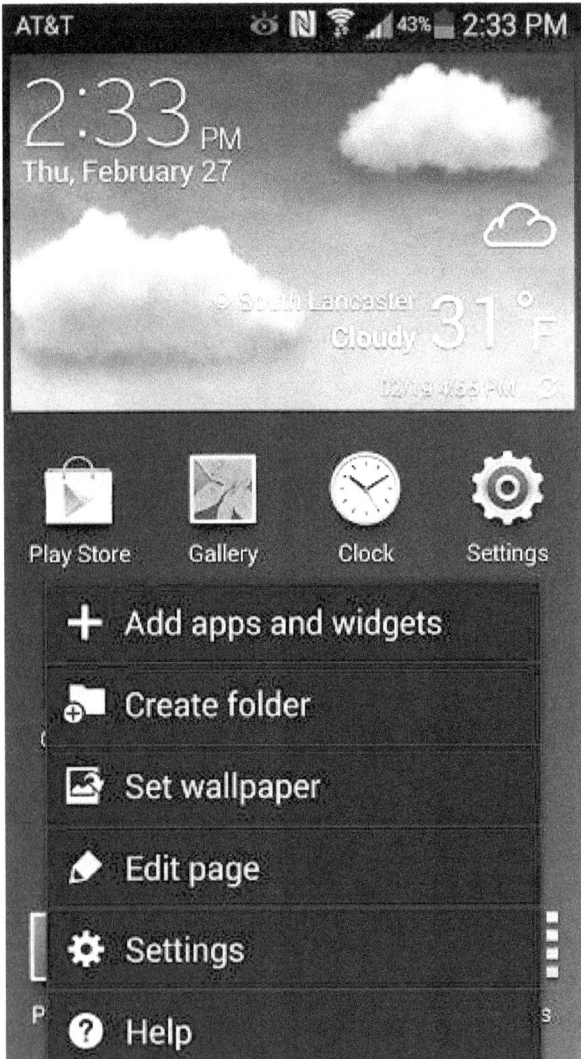

Figure 1: Home Screen Menu

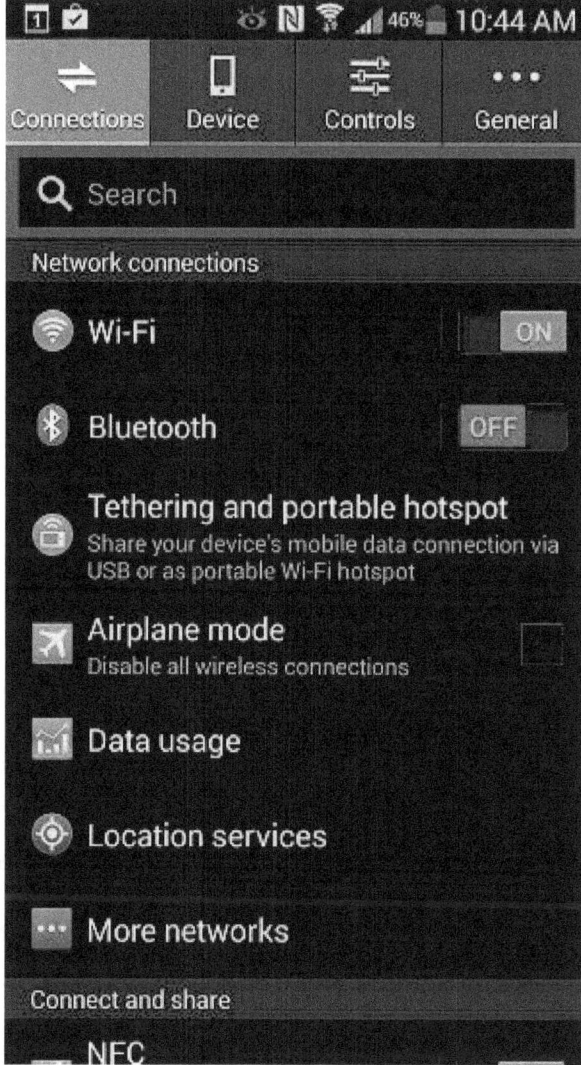

Figure 2: Settings Screen

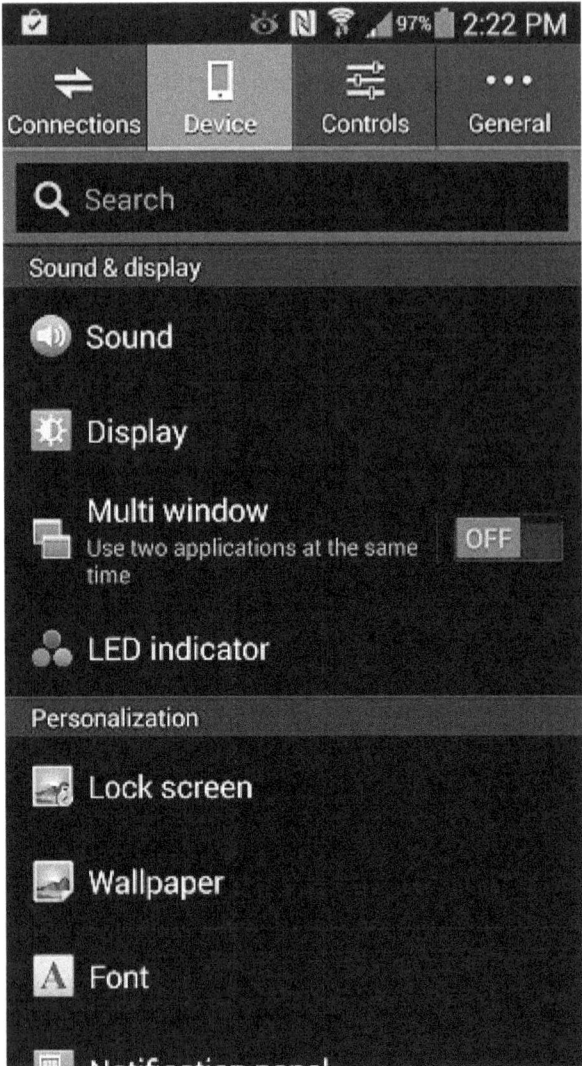

Figure 3: Personalization Settings Screen

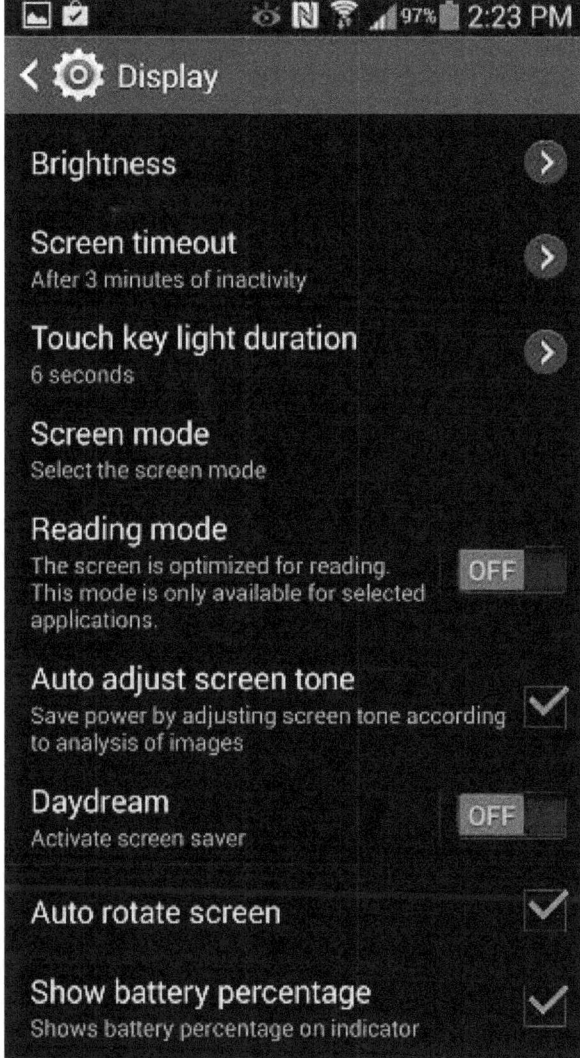

Figure 4: Display Settings Screen

2. Changing the Wallpaper

The wallpaper is the image that appears behind the application icons and widgets on the Home screens. To change the wallpaper:

1. Touch the ▭ key. The Home Screen menu appears.
2. Touch **Set wallpaper**. The Set Wallpaper menu appears, as shown in **Figure 5**.
3. Touch **Home screen**, **Lock screen**, or **Home and lock screens** to set the wallpaper for the corresponding screen(s). The Wallpaper Selection menu appears, as shown in **Figure 6**.

4. Touch **Live wallpapers** or **Wallpapers** to select a pre-loaded wallpaper. Alternatively, touch **Gallery** or **Photos** to select a wallpaper from your own pictures. The corresponding list of images appears.
5. Touch a picture and then touch **Done** to set the new wallpaper from the Gallery, or touch **Set Wallpaper** after selecting a pre-loaded wallpaper. The new wallpaper is set.

Note: When using an image from the Gallery, you may need to crop it. Refer to "Editing a Photo" on page 131 to learn how.

Figure 5: Set Wallpaper Menu

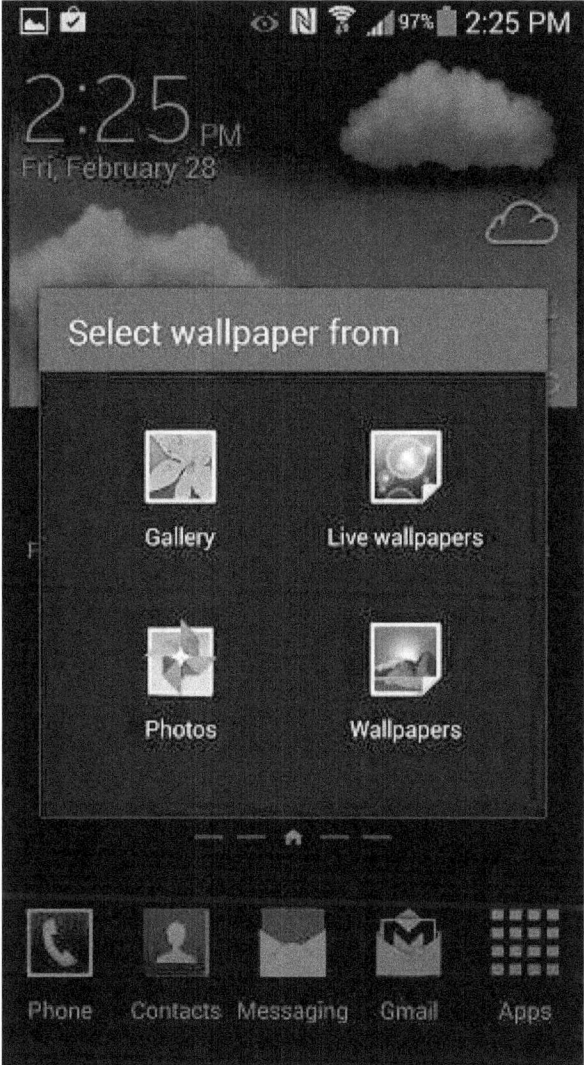

Figure 6: Wallpaper Selection Menu

3. Turning Multi Window On or Off

The Galaxy Note 3 can split the screen in two and display two applications at once using a feature known as Multi Window. To turn Multi Window on or off:

1. Touch the ▤ key. The Home Screen menu appears.
2. Touch **Settings**. The Settings screen appears.
3. Touch **Device** at the top of the screen. The Personalization Settings screen appears.

4. Touch **Multi window**. The ✓ mark next to 'Multi window' disappears and the feature is turned off.

5. Touch **Multi window** again. The ✓ mark appears and the feature is turned on.

Note: Refer to "Tips and Tricks" *on page 318 to learn how to use the Multi Window feature.*

4. Turning Auto Rotate On or Off

In most applications, the screen will automatically rotate when the phone is rotated. By default, Auto Rotate is turned on. To turn Auto-Rotate on or off:

1. Touch the ▨ key. The Home Screen menu appears.
2. Touch **Settings**. The Settings screen appears.
3. Touch **Device** at the top of the screen. The Personalization Settings screen appears.
4. Touch **Display**. The Display Settings screen appears.
5. Touch **Auto rotate screen**. The ✓ mark next to 'Auto rotate screen' disappears and the screen will no longer rotate automatically.
6. Touch **Auto rotate screen** again. Auto Rotate is turned on and the ✓ mark reappears.

5. Setting the Screen Timeout

The screen timeout can be adjusted to automatically lock the Galaxy Note 3 after it is idle for a set period of time. To change the screen timeout:

1. Touch the ▨ key. The Home Screen menu appears.
2. Touch **Settings**. The Settings screen appears.
3. Touch **Device** at the top of the screen. The Personalization Settings screen appears.
4. Touch **Display**. The Display Settings screen appears.
5. Touch **Screen timeout**. The Screen Timeout settings appear, as shown in **Figure 7**.
6. Touch an option in the menu, indicating how long the phone will be idle before it locks itself. The screen timeout is set.

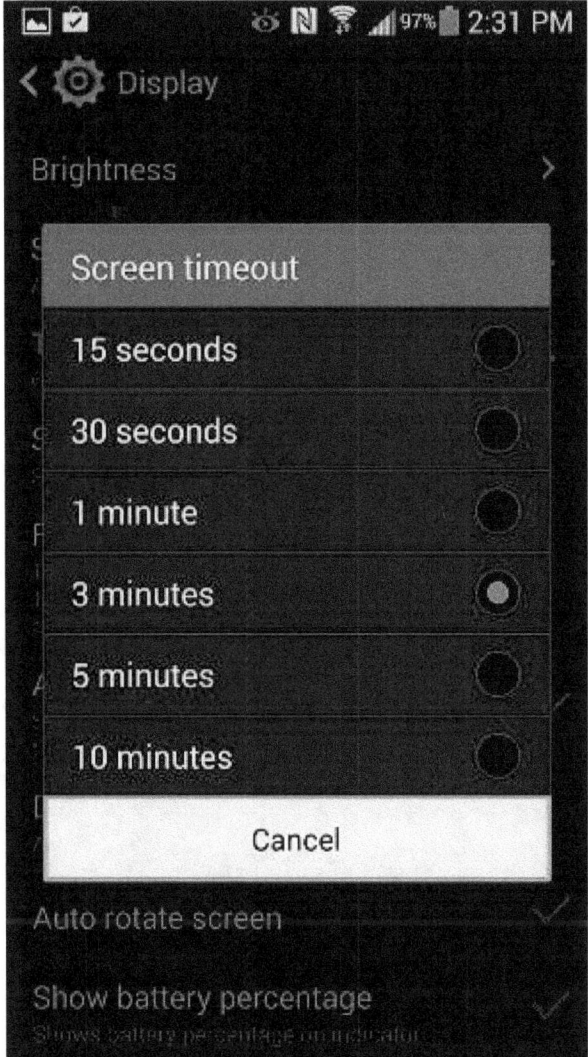

Figure 7: Screen Timeout Settings

6. Changing the Font

The Galaxy Note 3 allows you to customize the type of font that is used in menus, certain applications, and when entering text. You can also adjust the size of the font. To change the font:

1. Touch the ▤ key. The Home Screen menu appears.
2. Touch **Settings**. The Settings screen appears.
3. Touch the icon at the top of the screen. The Personalization Settings screen appears.
4. Touch **Font**. The Font menu appears, as shown in **Figure 8**.

5. Touch **Font style**. A list of font styles appears, as shown in **Figure 9**.
6. Touch a font in the list. A confirmation dialog appears.
7. Touch **Yes**. The new font style is applied.
8. Touch **Font size**. The Font Size menu appears, as shown in **Figure 10**.
9. Touch a font size in the list. The new font size is applied.

Figure 8: Font Menu

Figure 9: List of Font Styles

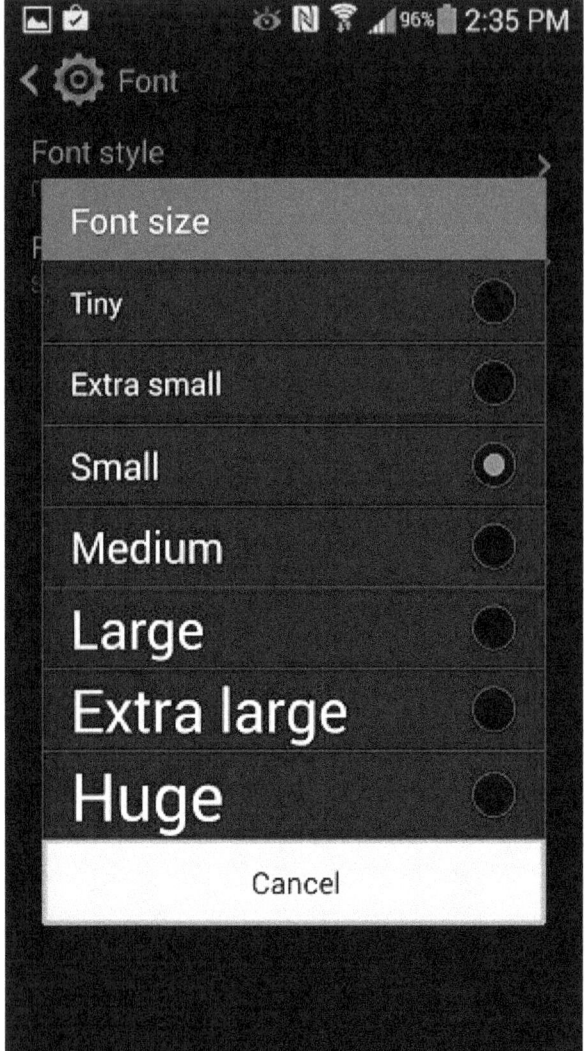

Figure 10: List of Font Sizes

7. Setting the Soft Key Light Duration

The ▭ and ◁ soft keys, also known as the touch keys, light up only when they are needed or when they are touched. The amount of time that they stay lit while not being touched can be customized. To set the soft key light duration:

1. Touch the ▭ key. The Home Screen menu appears.
2. Touch **Settings**. The Settings screen appears.
3. Touch **Device** at the top of the screen. The Personalization Settings screen appears.

4. Touch **Display**. The Display Settings screen appears.
5. Scroll down and touch **Touch key light duration**. The Touch Key Light Duration menu appears, as shown in **Figure 11**.
6. Touch one of the options in the menu. Selecting **Always off** will keep the soft key light off at all times. Selecting **Always on** will keep the soft key light on at all times. The soft key light duration is set.

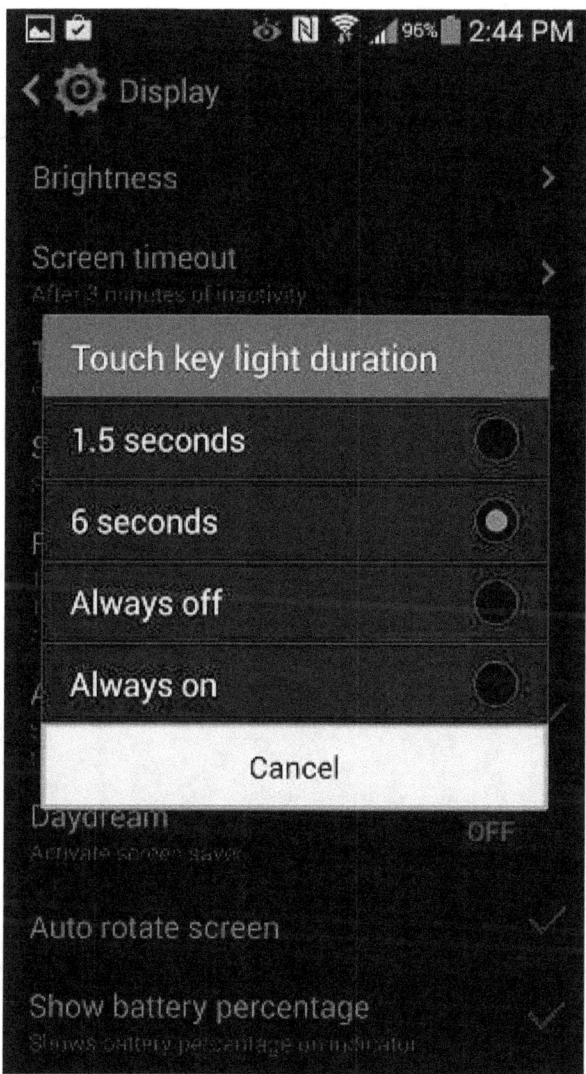

Figure 11: Touch Key Light Duration Menu

8. Turning the Battery Percentage On or Off

The Galaxy Note 3 can display the exact percentage of battery life remaining in the upper right-hand corner of the screen. By default, this feature is turned on. To turn the battery percentage on or off:

1. Touch the ▭ key. The Home Screen menu appears.
2. Touch **Settings**. The Settings screen appears.
3. Touch the 🖳 icon at the top of the screen. The Personalization Settings screen appears.
4. Touch **Display**. The Display Settings screen appears.
5. Touch **Show battery percentage** at the bottom of the screen. The ✔ mark next to 'Show battery percentage' disappears and the battery percentage is hidden.
6. Touch **Show battery percentage** again. The ✔ mark reappears and the battery percentage appears in the upper right-hand corner of the screen, as outlined in **Figure 12**.

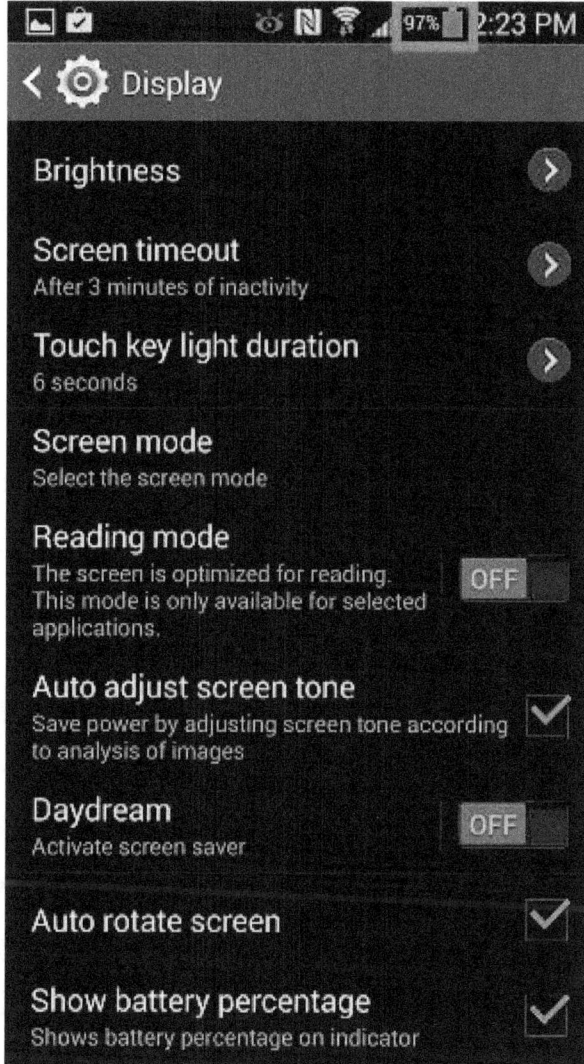

Figure 12: Battery Percentage

9. Turning High Touch Sensitivity On or Off

The touchscreen on most smartphones only responds when you touch it using bare skin. The touchscreen on the Galaxy Note 3 can be set to respond when you touch it while wearing gloves. To turn high touch sensitivity on or off:

1. Touch the ▤ key. The Home Screen menu appears.
2. Touch **Settings**. The Settings screen appears.
3. Touch **Controls** at the top of the screen. The Controls Settings screen appears, as shown in **Figure 13**.

4. Scroll down and touch **Increase touch sensitivity**. A ✓ mark appears and high touch sensitivity is turned on.

5. Touch **Increase touch sensitivity** again. The ✓ mark disappears and high touch sensitivity is turned off.

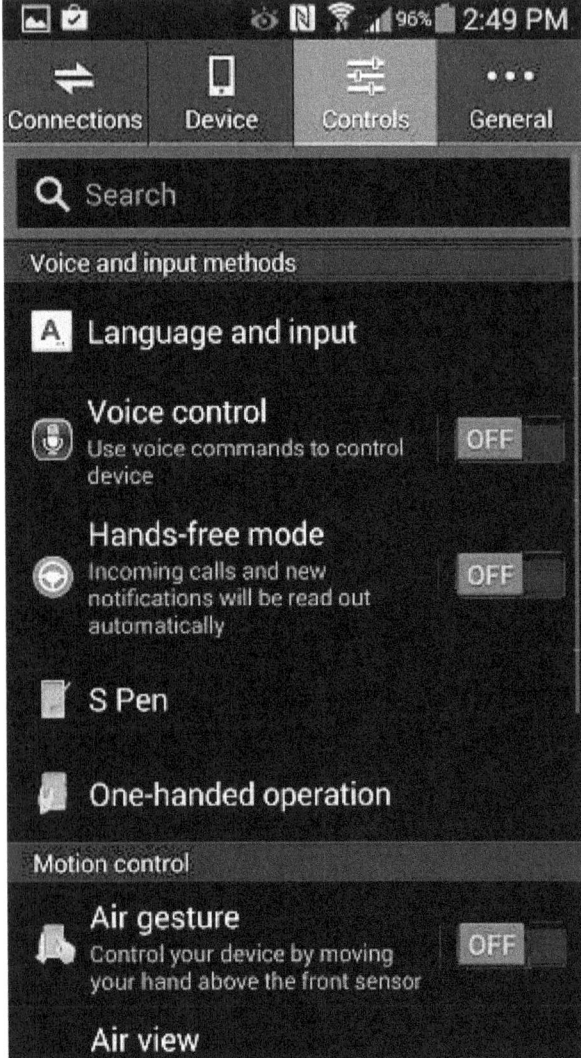

Figure 13: Controls Settings Screen

10. Setting the Home Screen Mode

Depending on the amount of experience you have with Android phones, you may wish to use a simpler Home screen in order to avoid being overwhelmed. To set the Home Screen mode:

1. Touch the ▣ key. The Home Screen menu appears.
2. Touch **Settings**. The Settings screen appears.
3. Touch **Device** at the top of the screen. The Personalization Settings screen appears.
4. Touch **Easy mode**. The Easy Mode screen appears, as shown in **Figure 14**.
5. Touch the OFF switch in the upper right-hand corner of the screen. The ON switch appears and a confirmation dialog is shown.
6. Touch **OK**. Easy Mode is turned on, as shown in **Figure 15**.

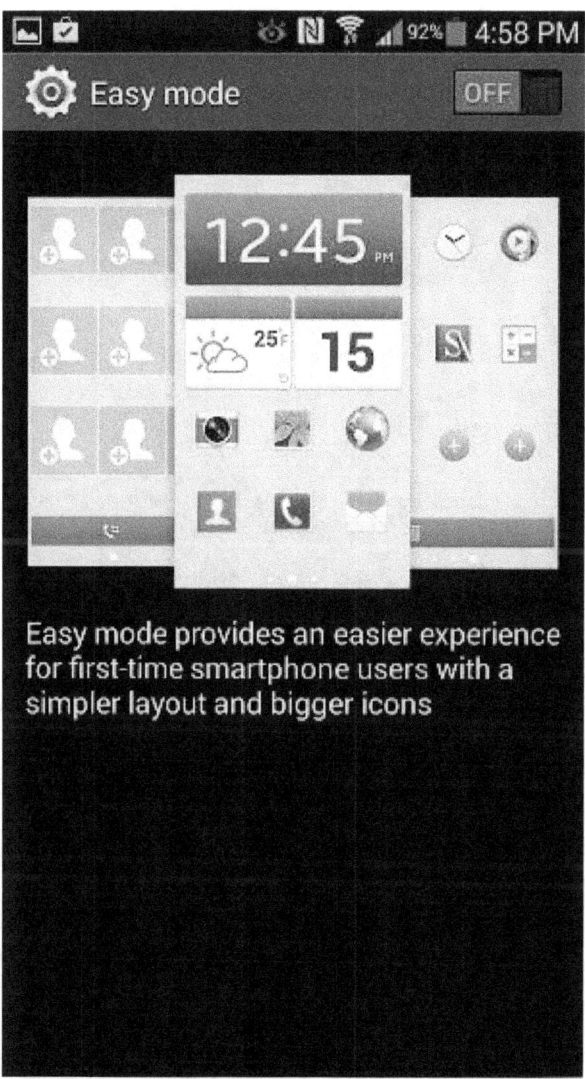

Figure 14: Easy Mode Screen

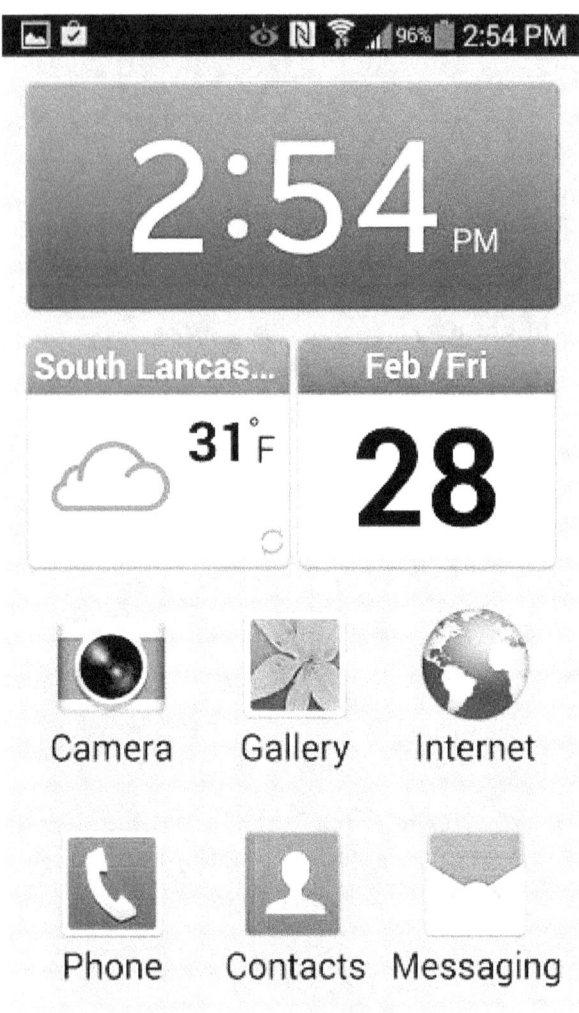

Figure 15: Easy Mode Turned On

11. Turning Motions and Gestures On or Off

The Galaxy Note 3 allows you to perform certain tasks without touching the screen by using its sensor, which is located near the earpiece. To turn motions and gestures on or off:

1. Touch the ▤ key. The Home Screen menu appears.
2. Touch **Settings**. The Settings screen appears.
3. Touch **Controls** at the top of the screen. The Controls Settings screen appears.
4. Scroll down and touch one of the following options under 'Motion control' to turn the corresponding motions or gestures on or off:

Air gesture

Touch the [OFF] switch next to one of the following options to turn it on, or touch the [ON] switch to turn it off:

- **Quick glance** - Allows you to quickly view the time, new message alerts, and the battery percentage when you wave your hand above the top of the phone while it is locked.
- **Air jump** - Allows you to quickly scroll through a web page by skipping one screen-sized page at a time when you wave the side of your hand in front of the phone.
- **Air browse** - Allows you to scroll through pictures in the gallery or songs in the Music application by waving your hand to the left or right.
- **Air move** - Allows you to move application icons, shortcuts, widgets, and calendar events to another page by waving your hand to the left or right.
- **Air call-accept** - Allows you to pick up an incoming call by waving your hand over the top of the phone.

Air View

- **Air view mode** - Allows you select whether you can use your finger or the S Pen to preview item information when you hover your finger or S Pen over it.
- **Air view pen options** - Allows you to select the information that is shown when you hover your finger or S Pen above an item on the screen. Choose from the following options:
    - o **Information preview** - Preview the text, information, or a full-size image, by hovering over it.
    - o **Progress preview** - Preview a scene in a video or show the amount of time elapsed by hovering over the progress bar.
    - o **Speed dial preview** - Preview the name of the contacts assigned to speed dial numbers by hovering over them.
    - o **Icon labels** - Identify the names of certain buttons that do not have labels, such as the 'Add Contact' button (+)
    - o **List scrolling** - - Allows you to scroll through a list by holding your finger or S Pen at the top or bottom edge of the list.
    - o **Sound and haptic feedback** - Plays a sound and briefly vibrates when you hover your finger or S Pen over an Air View-enabled item.

Motions

Touch the [OFF] switch next to one of the following options to turn it on, or touch the [ON] switch to turn it off:

- **Direct call** - Allows you to call the contact whose information is currently on the screen by putting the phone up to your ear.
- **Smart alert** - Causes the phone to vibrate when it is picked up if there is a missed call or a new text message.
- **Zoom** - Allows you to hold the phone with two fingers touching the screen and tilt it to zoom in to a photo.
- **Browse an image** - Allows you to tilt the phone while zoomed in to a photo to pan around the photo.
- **Mute/pause** - Allows you to mute incoming calls and pause music by turning the phone over and laying it on its screen while the screen is turned on.

Palm motion

Touch the [OFF] switch next to one of the following options to turn it on, or touch the [ON] switch to turn it off:

- **Capture screen** - Allows you to capture a screenshot by waving the side of your hand from left to right or right to left across the screen.
- **Mute/pause** - Allows you to pause music by covering the screen with the palm of your hand while the screen is turned on.

12. Turning Eye Recognition Features On or Off

The Galaxy Note 3 has eye recognition software which can be used to perform certain functions without touching the screen. To turn eye recognition features on or off:

1. Touch the ▢ key. The Home Screen menu appears.
2. Touch **Settings**. The Settings screen appears.
3. Touch **Controls** at the top of the screen. The Controls Settings screen appears.
4. Scroll down and touch **Smart screen**. The Smart Screen settings appear, as shown in **Figure 16**.
5. Touch one of the following features to turn it on or off:
    - **Smart stay** - Causes the screen to remain on while you are looking at it.

- **Smart rotation** - Causes the screen orientation to follow your eyes. This feature is especially useful for preventing unwanted screen rotation when you are lying down on your side with the phone.
- **Smart pause** - Causes a video that is playing to pause when you look away from the screen.
- **Smart scroll** - Causes text to automatically scroll up or down when you tilt your head accordingly.

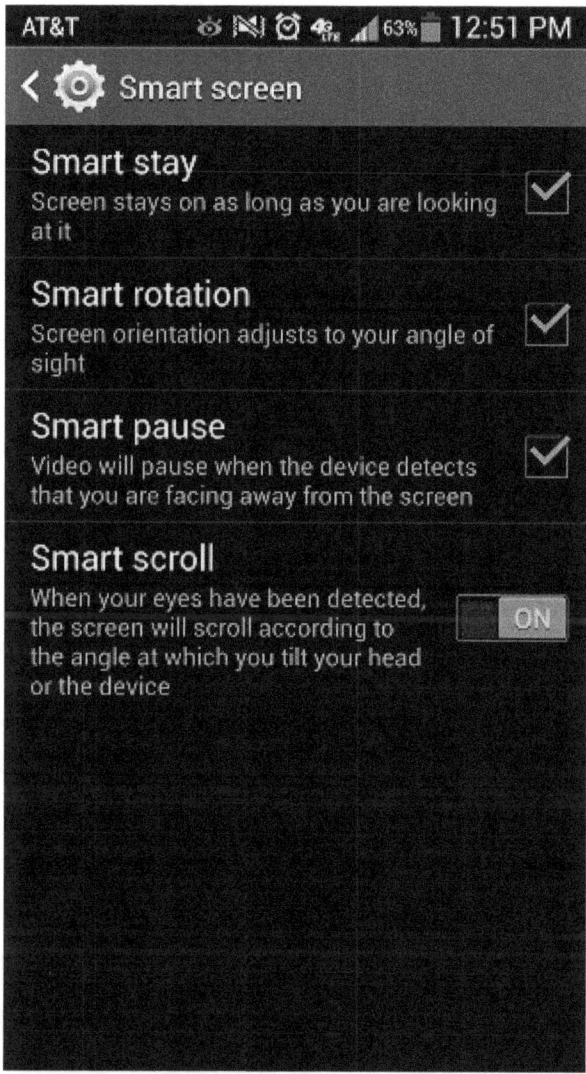

Figure 16: Smart Screen Settings

13. Customizing the LED Notification Light

The LED light to the right of the earpiece is used to notify you of certain events. To customize the LED notification light:

1. Touch the ▭ key. The Home Screen menu appears.
2. Touch **Settings**. The Settings screen appears.
3. Touch **Device** at the top of the screen. The Personalization Settings screen appears.
4. Touch **LED indicator**. The LED Indicator settings appear, as shown in **Figure 17**.
5. Touch one of the following options to turn it on or off:

   - **Charging** - Causes the red LED indicator to light up when the phone is charging and the screen is off.
   - **Low battery** - Causes the red LED to light up when the battery level is low and the screen is off.
   - **Notifications** - Causes the blue LED to light up when you have missed calls or messages and the screen is off.
   - **Voice recording** - Causes the blue LED to light up when you are recording voice with the screen turned off.

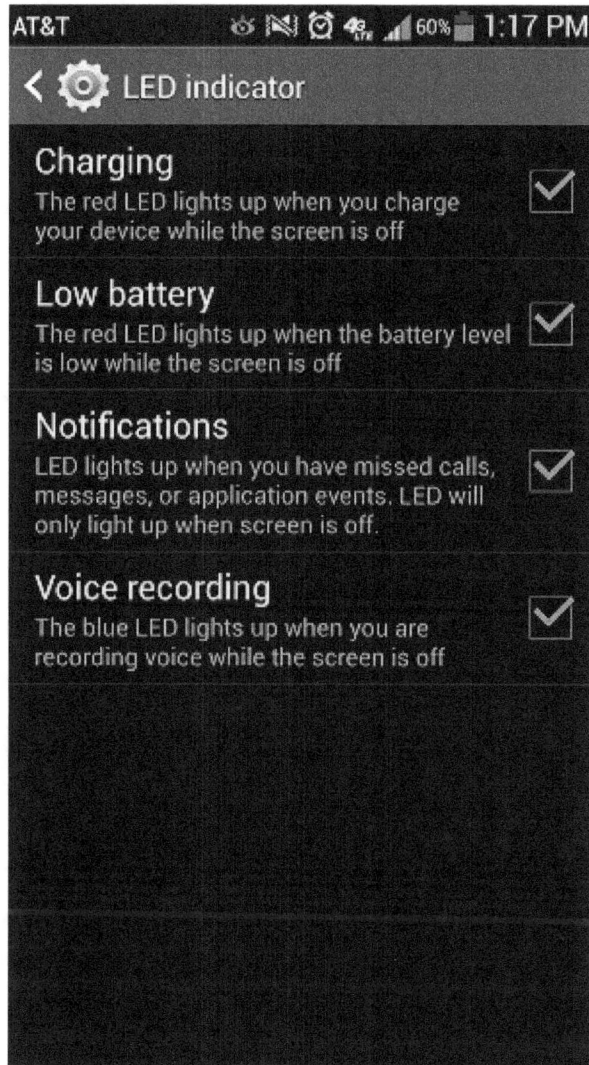

Figure 17: LED Indicator Settings

Adjusting Security Settings

Table of Contents

1. Setting up Screen Lock Protection

Setting a security lock can help to prevent unauthorized users from accessing your phone. There are six options for locking the screen: Swipe, Face Unlock, Face and voice, Pattern, Personal Identification Number (PIN), and Password. To set up Screen Lock Protection:

1. Touch the ▤ key. The Home Screen menu appears, as shown in **Figure 1**.
2. Touch **Settings**. The Settings screen appears, as shown in **Figure 2**.
3. Touch the 👤 icon at the top of the screen. The Personalization Settings screen appears, as shown in **Figure 3**.
4. Touch **Lock screen**. The Lock Screen menu appears, as shown in **Figure 4**.
5. Touch **Screen lock**. The Screen Lock Selection menu appears, as shown in **Figure 5**.
6. Touch one of the following options to set the corresponding Screen Lock:

   - **Swipe** - Touch anywhere on the lock screen and swipe in any direction to unlock the phone. No setup is required for this method. This method does not provide any security.
   - **Signature** - Write your signature to unlock the phone. This method provides the minimum amount of security.
   - **Pattern** - Draw a pattern on the screen. This method provides medium security.
   - **PIN**- Enter a series of numbers to use as a passcode. This method provides medium high security.
   - **Password** - Enter an alphanumeric code. This method provides the highest level of security.
   - **None** - The screen will turn off, but the phone will not lock. No setup is required for this method.

To set up a signature lock:

1. Touch **Signature**. The Signature Registration screen appears.
2. Write your signature in the gray box, and then touch **Continue**. Repeat this process two more times.
3. Touch **Confirm** after writing your signature for the third time. The backup PIN screen appears.
4. Enter the backup PIN twice, and touch **OK** after the second entry. The Signature lock is set.

To set up a pattern lock:

1. Touch **Pattern**. The Pattern screen appears.
2. Draw the desired pattern. The pattern is entered.
3. Touch **Continue**. A confirmation screen appears.
4. Draw the same pattern again. The pattern is stored.
5. Touch **Confirm**. The Pattern lock is set and the backup PIN screen appears. You will need to enter the PIN twice.
6. When you are done, touch **OK**. The pattern lock is set.

To set up a PIN lock:

1. Touch **PIN**. The PIN Lock screen appears.
2. Enter the desired PIN. The PIN is entered. A PIN must be between four and 16 digits in length.
3. Touch **Continue**. A confirmation screen appears.
4. Enter the same PIN again. The PIN is entered.
5. Touch **OK**. The PIN lock is set.

To set up a password lock:

1. Touch **Password**. The Password screen appears.
2. Enter the desired password. The password is entered. A password must be between four and 16 characters in length.
3. Touch **Continue**. A confirmation screen appears.
4. Enter the same password again. The password is entered.
5. Touch **OK**. The Password lock is set.

Note: Repeat this process to change the screen lock. You will need to enter the current screen lock to change it.

Figure 1: Home Screen Menu

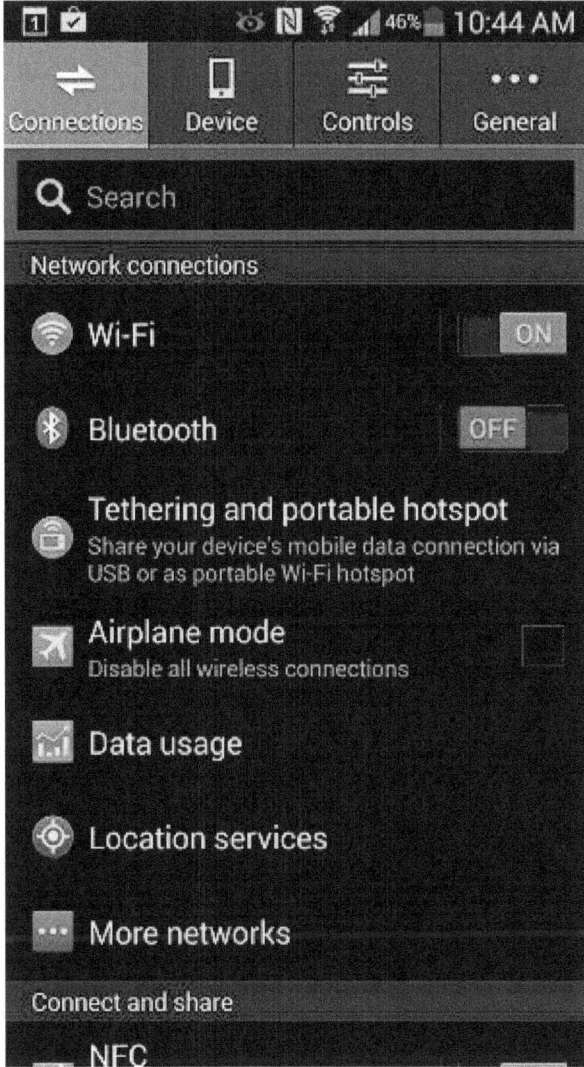

Figure 2: Settings Screen

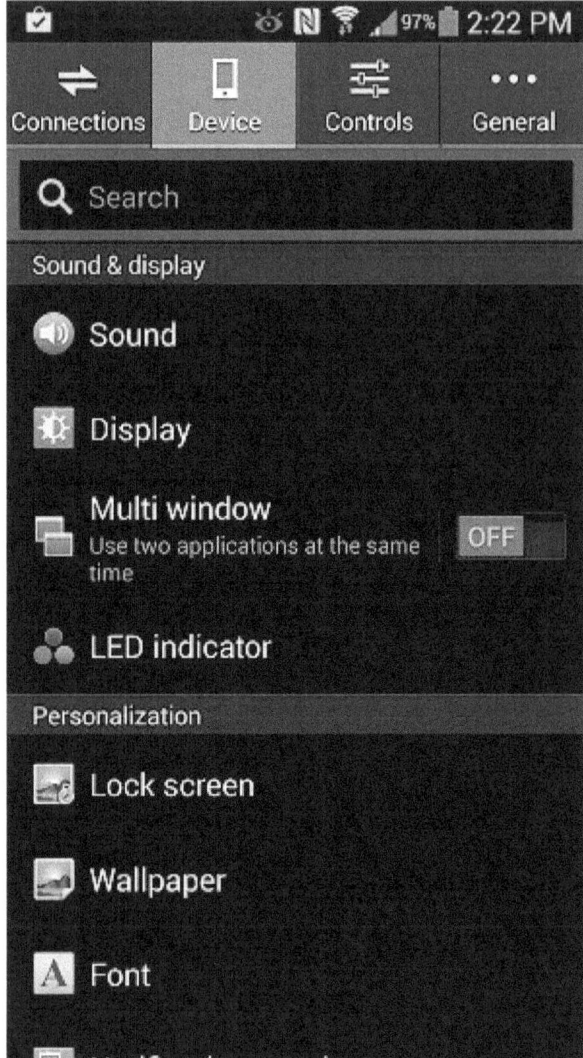

Figure 3: Personalization Settings Screen

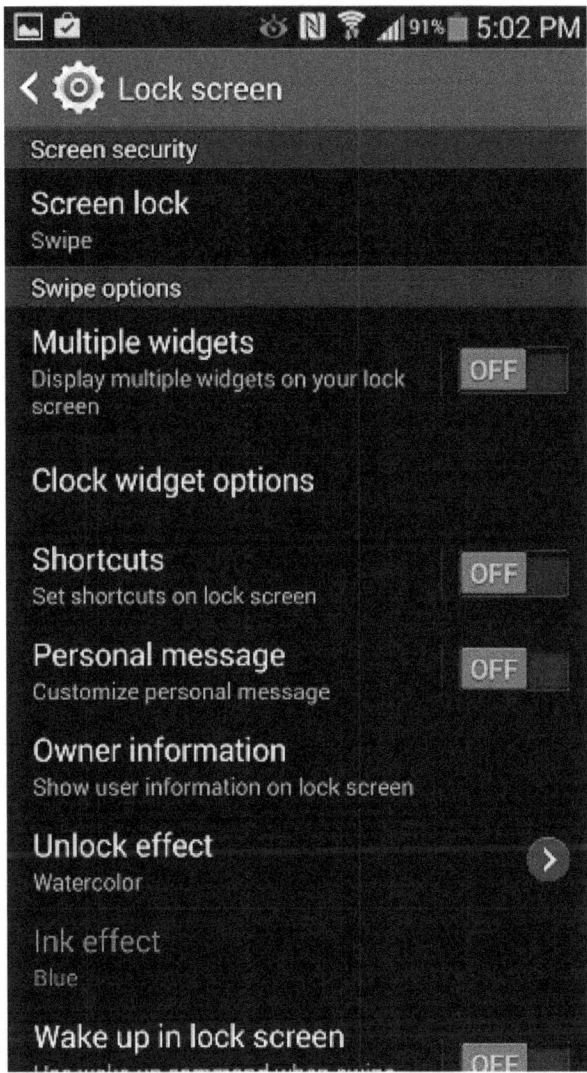

Figure 4: Lock Screen Menu

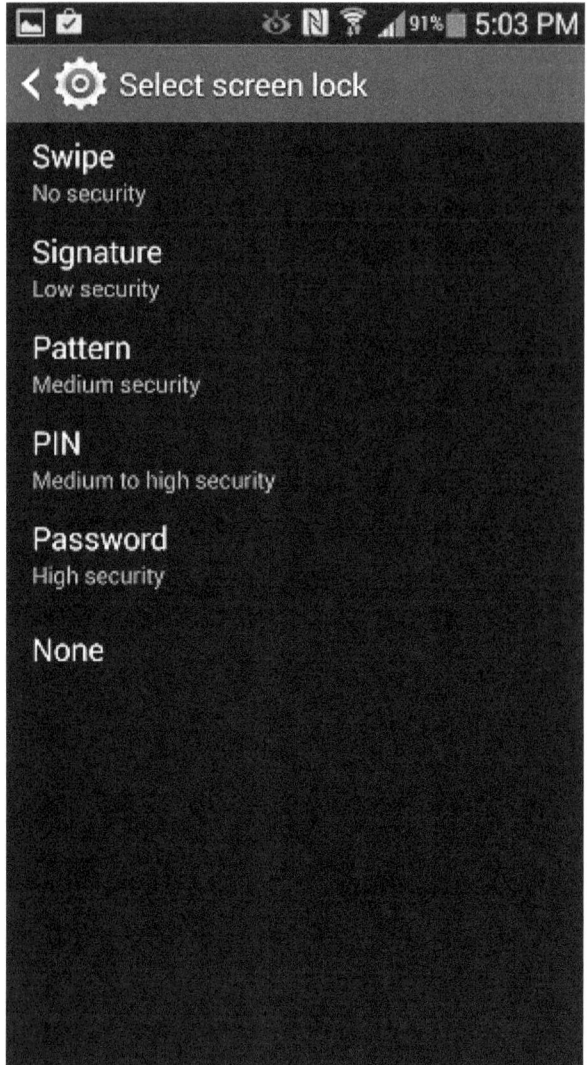

Figure 5: Screen Lock Selection Menu

2. Changing the Automatic Lock Time

After the Galaxy Note 3 is locked using the Power button, it will not require a password, pattern, or PIN to unlock it right away unless the lock time is set to 'Immediately'. The phone may be set to wait a certain amount of time before prompting for the screen lock. To change the Lock time:

Warning: Setting the Lock time to anything but 'Immediately' will leave your phone unprotected for the set period of time.

1. Touch the ▤ key. The Home Screen menu appears.
2. Touch **Settings**. The Settings screen appears.
3. Touch **Device** at the top of the screen. The Personalization Settings screen appears.
4. Touch **Lock screen**. The Lock Screen menu appears.
5. Touch **Secured lock time**. A list of lock time options appears, as shown in **Figure 6**.
6. Touch an option in the menu. The lock time is set. The phone will wait the selected interval before requesting a screen lock.

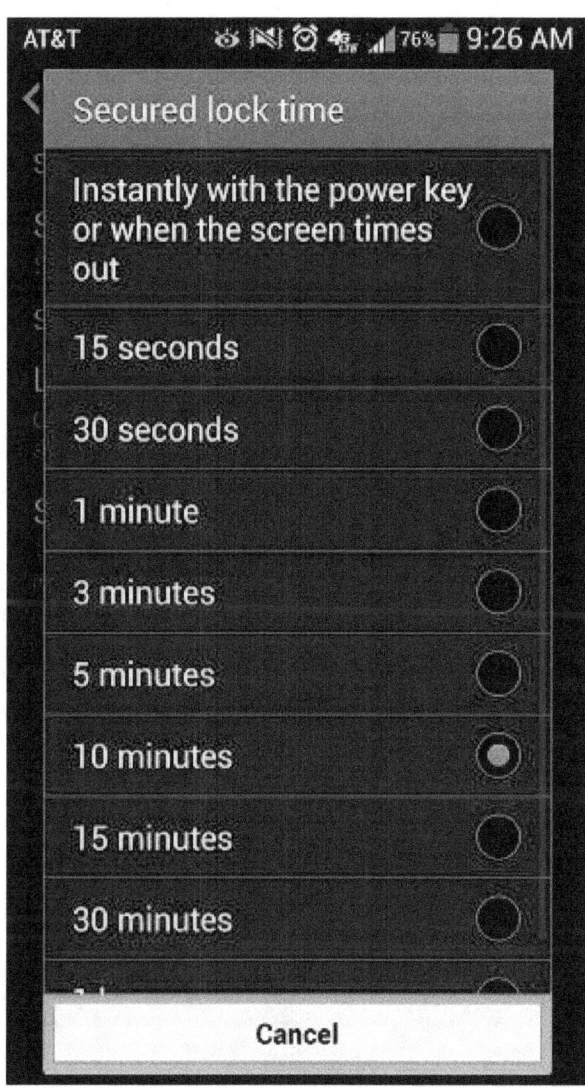

Figure 6: List of Lock Time Options

3. Making Passwords Visible

When entering a password, it can be concealed to prevent someone from viewing it over your shoulder. However, it may be more convenient to see what is being typed. To make passwords visible:

1. Touch the ▣ key. The Home Screen menu appears.
2. Touch **Settings**. The Settings screen appears.
3. Touch **General** at the top of the screen. The General Settings screen appears, as shown in **Figure 7**.
4. Scroll down and touch **Security**. The Security Settings screen appears, as shown in **Figure 8**.
5. Touch **Make passwords visible**. A ✓ mark appears next to 'Make passwords visible' and the feature is turned on.
6. Touch **Make passwords visible** again. The ✓ mark disappears and the feature is turned off.

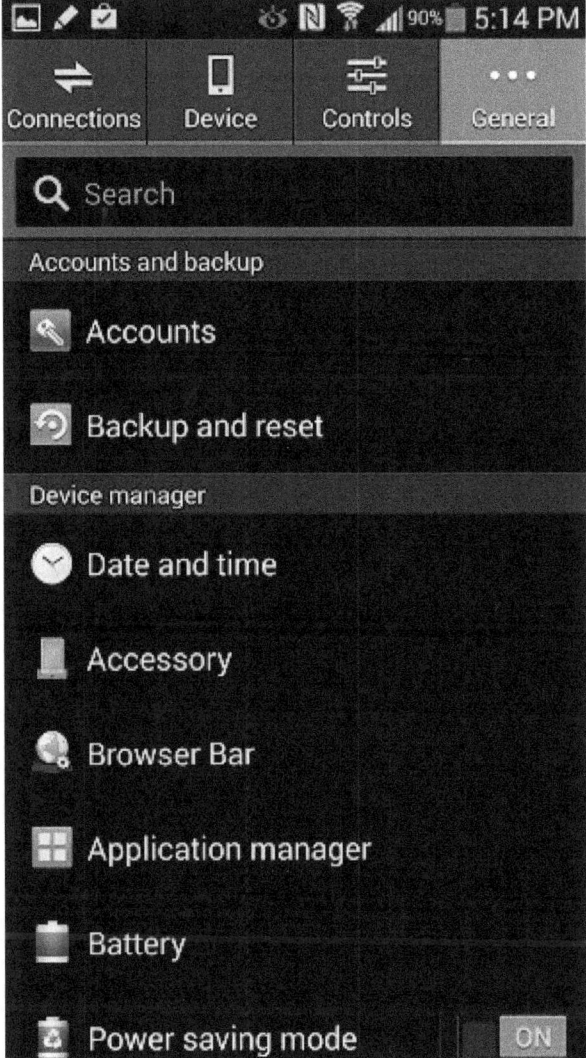

Figure 7: General Settings Screen

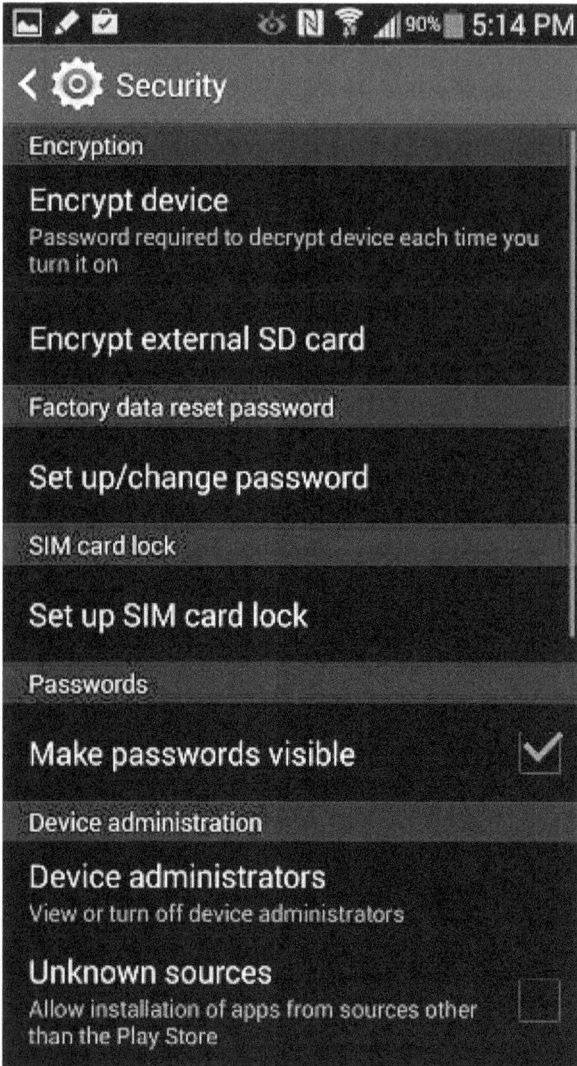

Figure 8: Security Settings Screen

4. Allowing the Installation of Applications from Unknown Sources

If you wish to install applications from sources other than the Play Store, you must first set the Galaxy Note 3 to allow such installations. To allow the installation of applications from unknown sources:

1. Touch the ▤ key. The Home Screen menu appears.
2. Touch **Settings**. The Settings screen appears.
3. Touch **General** at the top of the screen. The General Settings screen appears.
4. Scroll down and touch **Security**. The Security Settings screen appears.
5. Touch **Unknown sources**. A confirmation dialog appears.
6. Touch **OK**. A ✔ mark appears next to 'Unknown sources' and the feature is turned on.
7. Touch **Unknown sources** again. The ✔ mark disappears and the feature is turned off.

Adjusting Language and Input Settings

Table of Contents

1. Changing the Phone Language

The Galaxy Note 3 has six built-in languages from which to choose. Setting an alternate phone language will make all menu options and buttons appear in the selected language. Web pages and other content will still be displayed in the language in which they were originally written. To change the phone language:

1. Touch the ▤ key. The Home Screen menu appears, as shown in **Figure 1**.
2. Touch **Settings**. The Settings screen appears, as shown in **Figure 2**.
3. Touch **Controls** at the top of the screen. The Controls Settings screen appears, as shown in **Figure 3**.
4. Touch **Language and input**. The Language and Input Settings appear, as shown in **Figure 4**.
5. Touch **Language**. A list of available languages appears, as shown in **Figure 5**.
6. Touch a language. The phone's language is changed to the selected option.

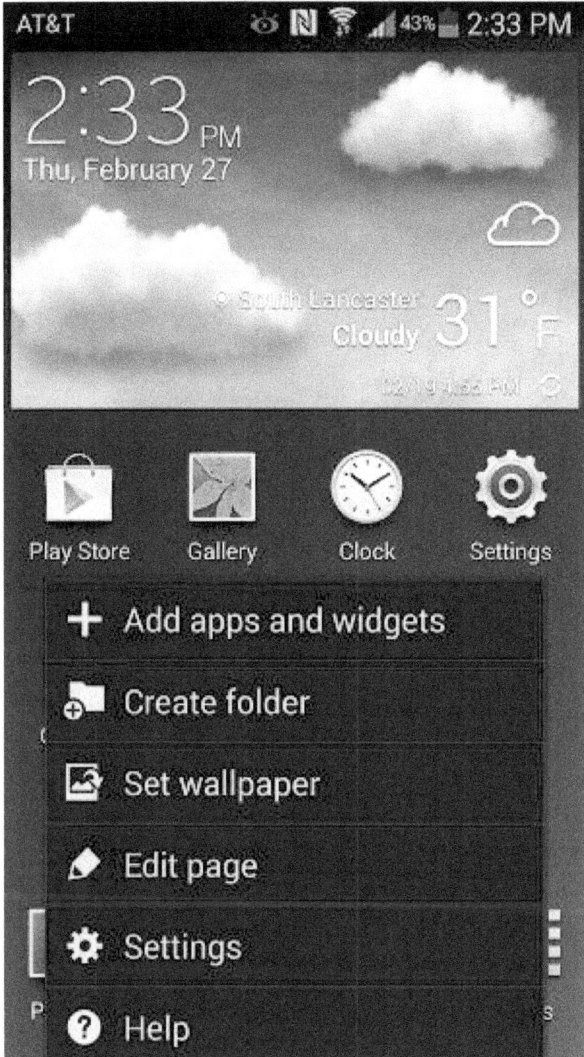

Figure 1: Home Screen Menu

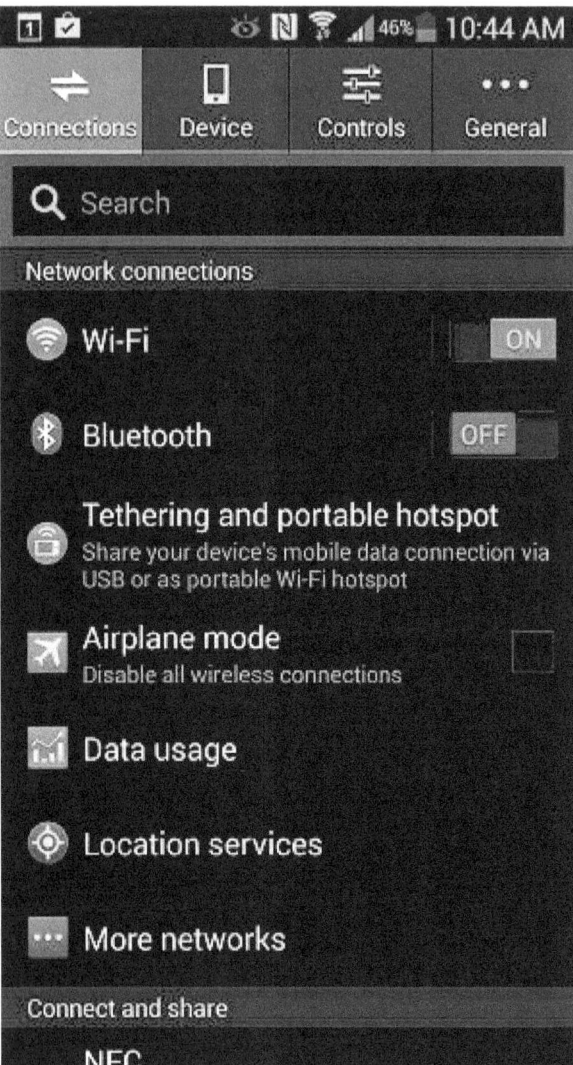

Figure 2: Settings Screen

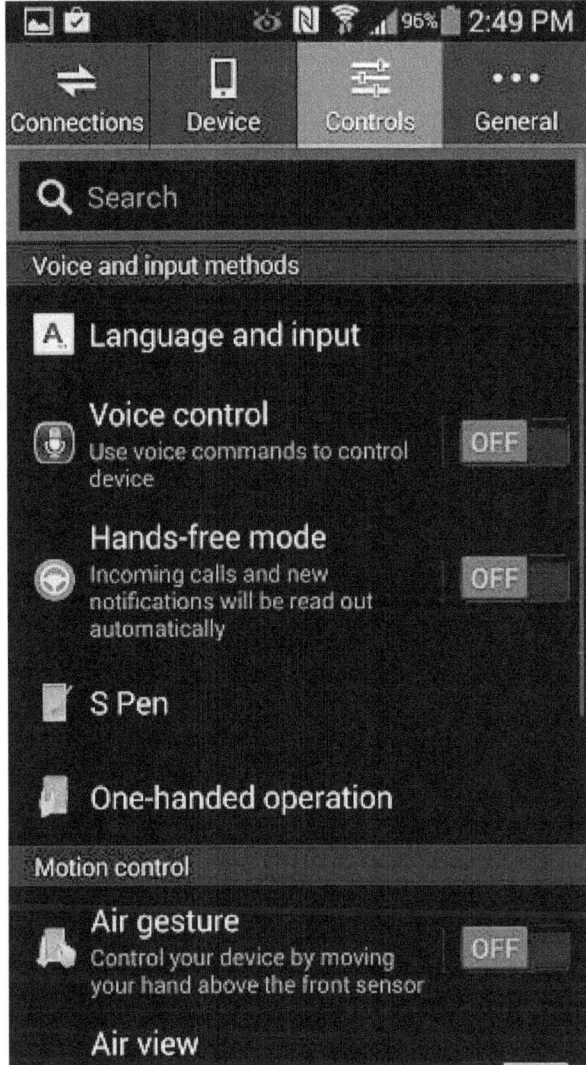

Figure 3: Controls Settings Screen

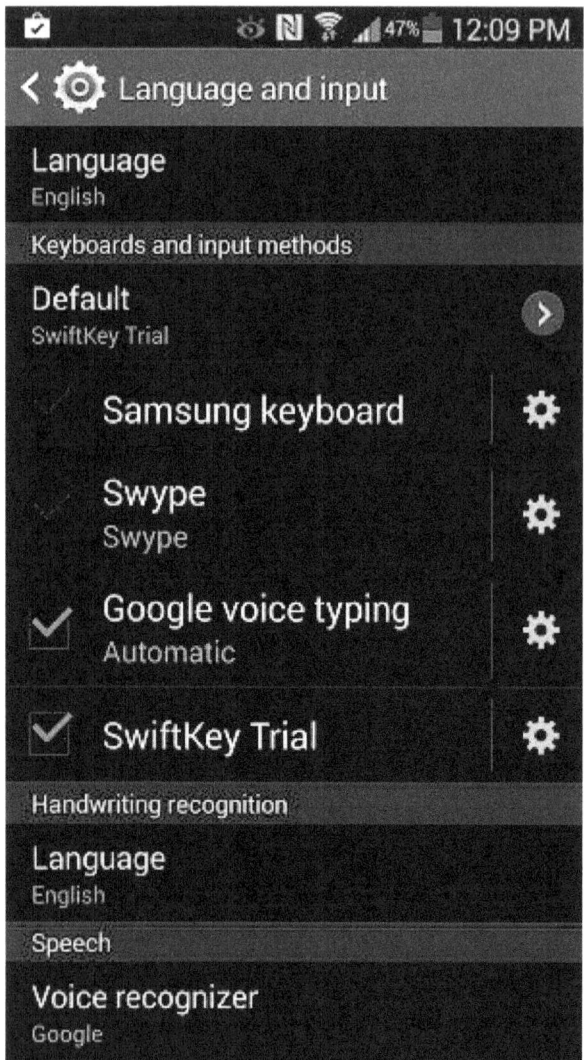

Figure 4: Language and Input Settings Screen

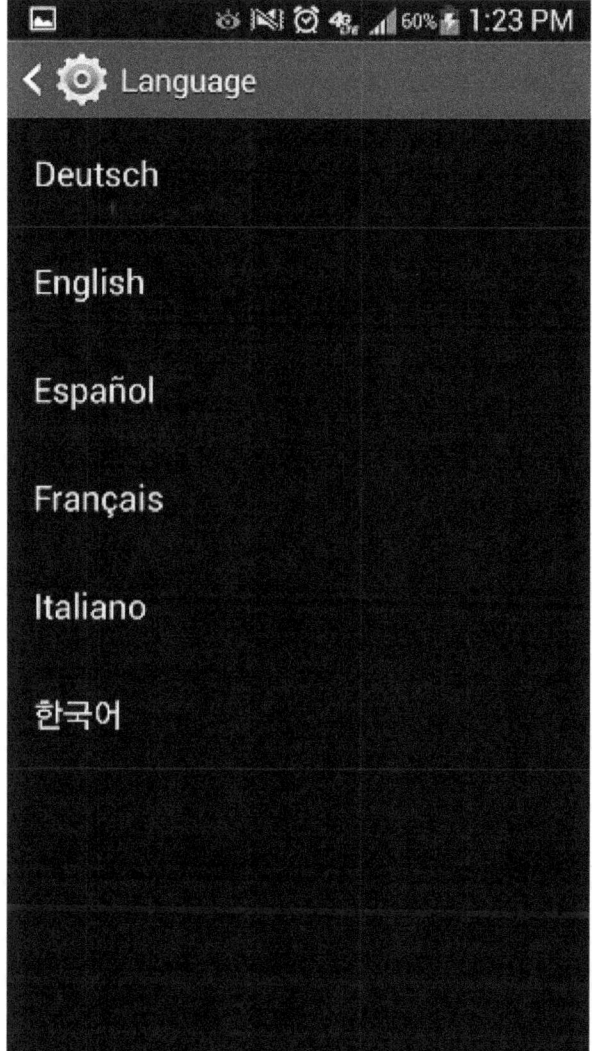

Figure 5: List of Available Languages

2. Adding an Input Language

The Galaxy Note 3 allows you to enter text in many different languages by using alternate keyboards. To change to an alternate keyboard at any time, touch the space bar and slide your finger to the left or right. To add an input language:

1. Touch the ▣ key. The Home Screen menu appears.
2. Touch **Settings**. The Settings screen appears.
3. Touch **Device** at the top of the screen. The Personalization Settings screen appears.
4. Touch **Controls** at the top of the screen. The Controls Settings screen appears.

5. Touch **Language and input**. The Language and Input Settings appear.

6. Touch the ⚙ icon next to 'Samsung Keyboard'. The Samsung Keyboard Settings appear, as shown in **Figure 6**.

7. Touch **Select input languages**. A list of available keyboards appears, as shown in **Figure 7**.

8. Touch a language. A ✓ mark appears next to the language, and the corresponding keyboard is now available when entering text. The phone may need to download the language, which will occur automatically. In this case, you will need to repeat this step, and touch the language under 'Downloaded languages' to add it.

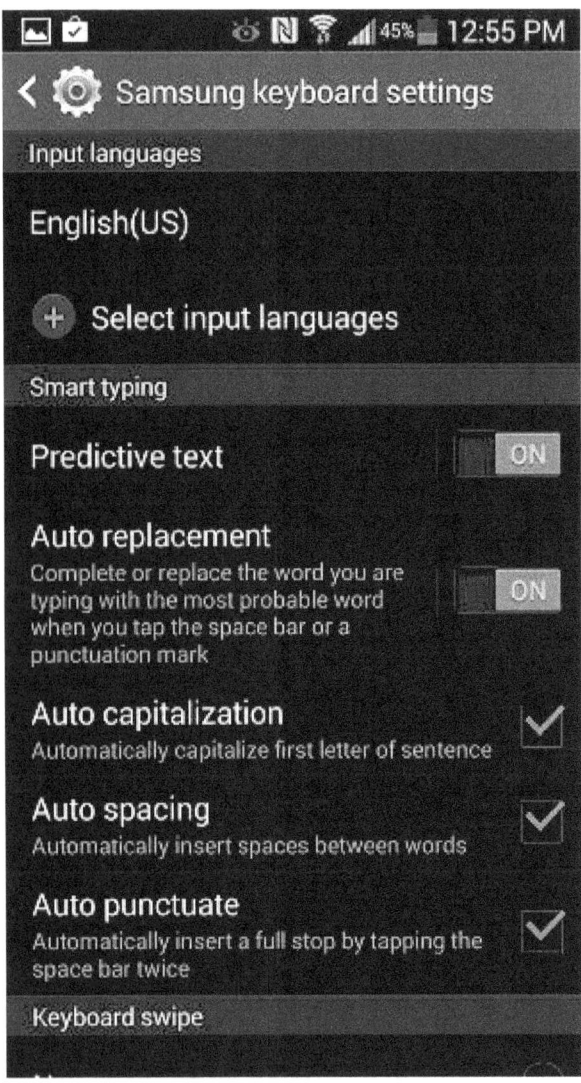

Figure 6: Samsung Keyboard Settings

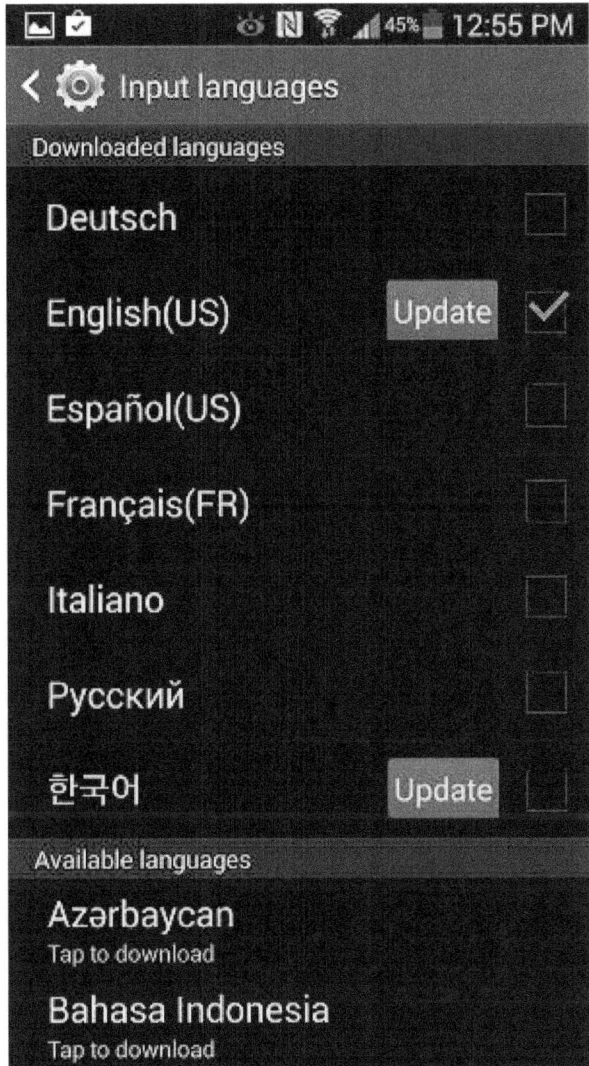

Figure 7: List of Available Keyboards

3. Personalizing Text Prediction

While entering text, the Galaxy Note 3 can guess the word that you are trying to enter, and guess the next word that you may wish to type. You will then receive suggestions based on what you have already typed. This feature allows you to enter text more quickly. In addition, the keyboard can learn from your text messages, emails, and social networks, making predictions more accurate. To turn predictive text on or off:

1. Touch the ▣ key. The Home Screen menu appears.
2. Touch **Settings**. The Settings screen appears.
3. Touch **Controls** at the top of the screen. The Controls Settings screen appears, as shown in **Figure 3**.
4. Touch **Language and input**. The Language and Input Settings appear.

5. Touch the ⚙ icon next to 'Samsung Keyboard'. The Samsung Keyboard Settings appear.

   By default, predictive text is turned on. You can always touch the �⬛ON switch next to 'Predictive text' to turn it off.
6. Touch **Predictive text**. The Predictive Text settings appear, as shown in **Figure 8**. By default, personalized data is turned on. You can always touch **Personalized data** to clear the ✓ mark and turn off the feature. This will not turn the predictive text feature off.
7. Touch one of the **Learn from** options in the menu. You may need to log in to your account in order to have the phone learn from your typing style. The keyboard is now customized based on your messages, emails, or social networks.

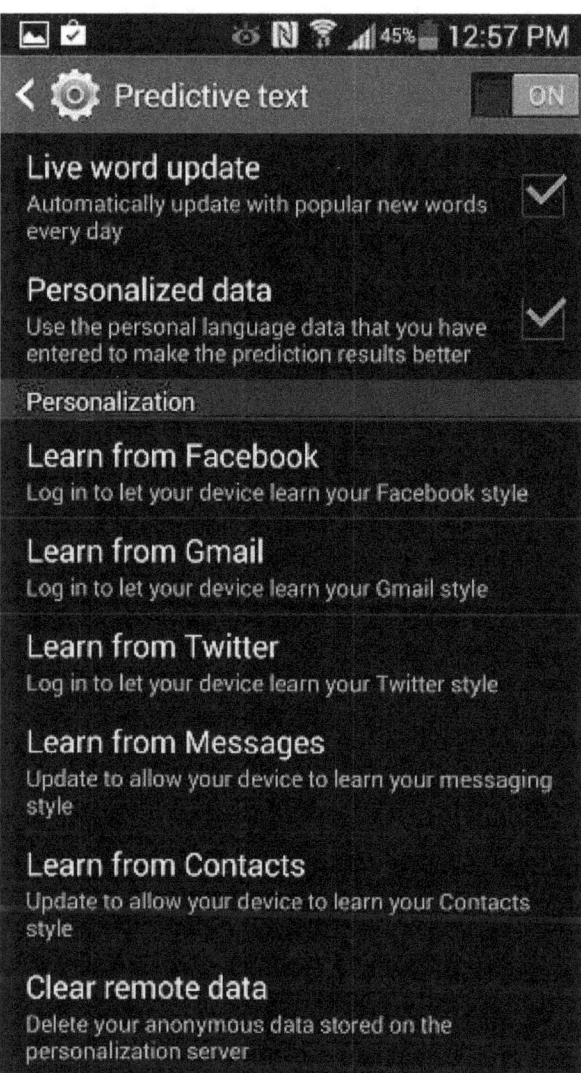

Figure 8: Predictive Text Settings

Tips and Tricks

Table of Contents

1. Maximizing Battery Life

There are several things you can do to increase the battery life of the Galaxy Note 3:

- Lock the phone whenever it is not in use. Because of its size and power, leaving the screen turned on will quickly kill the battery. To lock the phone, press the **Power** button once.
- Keep the Timeout Setting set to a small amount of time. This will dim and turn off the screen when the phone is idle. Refer to *"Setting the Screen Timeout"* on page 280 to learn how to adjust the Timeout setting.
- Turn down the brightness or turn on auto-brightness. To learn how to adjust the brightness, refer to *"Adjusting the Brightness"* on page 274.

- Turn off Wi-Fi, Bluetooth, and the mobile network when not in use. When Wi-Fi is turned on, the mobile network, which is responsible for data, is not in use. Refer to *"Setting Up Wi-Fi"* on page 251 to learn how to turn Wi-Fi off. Refer to *"Setting Up Bluetooth"* on page 254 to learn how to turn off Bluetooth. To learn how to turn off the mobile network, refer to *"Enabling or Disabling the Mobile Network"* on page 257.
- Minimize your use of the internet. Using data significantly decreases the battery life.
- Avoid using the camera and do not use the camera flash, if possible. Both need a lot of battery power to operate.

2. Adding an Extension to a Contact's Number

When entering a number for a stored contact, you may also add an extension that will be dialed once the number has been connected. To add an extension, add a Pause after the number. Touch the **Wait** key to do so. Add the extension following the semicolon that is added when pressing the 'Wait' key.

3. Checking the Amount of Available Memory

To check the amount of available memory at any time, press and hold the **Home** button. A list of open applications appear. Touch the icon at the bottom of the screen. Touch **Downloaded** at the top of the screen. The amount of available storage on the device and the SD card is shown under 'System storage' and 'SD card', respectively.

4. Calling a Number from a Website

A phone number can be dialed directly from a website. Most phone numbers that can be dialed are displayed in a blue box, although this also works for those that do not formally appear in blue. Touch the phone number. The keypad appears and the number is entered. Touch the button at the bottom of the screen. The phone dials the number.

5. Locking Text Messages

Text messages can be locked to prevent accidental deletion. When deleting an entire conversation, all of the unlocked text messages are deleted, unless "Delete locked messages" is checked. By default, "Delete locked messages" is unchecked. Refer to *"Deleting Text Messages"* on page 90 to learn more. To lock a message:

1. Touch the   icon. The Messaging screen appears.
2. Touch a conversation. The Conversation opens.
3. Touch and hold a text message. The Message options appear
4. Touch **Lock**. The text message is locked. To unlock the text message, follow steps 1-3, and then touch **Unlock message**.

6. Using MP3's as Ringtones

You can set any song in your personal music library as your phone's ringtone or a custom ringtone for a contact. To use an MP3 as a ringtone:

1. Touch the   icon at the bottom of the Home screen. The Application screen appears.

2. Touch the   icon. The Music application opens.
3. Find the song that you wish to set as a ringtone. You can browse music by touching one of the icons at the top of the screen, such as **Artists**.
4. Touch and hold a song. The Song menu appears.
5. Touch **Set as**. The Ringtone menu appears.
6. Touch **From the beginning** to use the entire song or touch **Auto recommendations** to use only part of the song, as recommended by other people.
7. Touch **Phone ringtone** to set the song as the default ringtone or touch **Caller ringtone** to set the song as a custom ringtone for the selected contact.
8. Touch **OK** in the upper right-hand corner of the screen. The song is set as the ringtone.

7. Capturing a Screenshot without Connecting the Phone to a Computer

To capture a screenshot, press the **Power** button and the **Home** button at exactly the same time. Hold the buttons for two seconds. A framed picture of the current screen briefly appears (a shutter sound can be heard, if your sound is turned on) and a screenshot is captured. Release the buttons. The screenshot can be found in the 'Screenshots' album in the Gallery.

8. Viewing All Quick Settings Icons in the Notification Bar

You do not have to go through the Application screen to adjust certain Phone settings. Touch the Notification bar at the top of the screen using two fingers and slide down. A list of all quick settings icons appears.

9. Clearing a Single Notification

While viewing notifications on the Notification screen (opened by touching the status bar and sliding your finger down), you can clear one notification at a time. Touch the notification and slide your finger to the left or right. The notification is cleared.

10. Adding Widgets to the Lock Screen

The Galaxy Note 3 allows you to access widgets, such as the calendar, without ever unlocking your phone. To add widgets to the lock screen:

1. Touch the ⊟ key. The Home Screen menu appears.
2. Touch **Settings**. The Settings screen appears.
3. Touch **Device** at the top of the screen. The Personalization Settings screen appears.
4. Touch **Lock screen**. The Lock Screen menu appears.
5. Touch **Multiple Widgets**. The Multiple Widgets screen appears.
6. Touch the OFF switch next to 'Multiple widgets'. A ✔ mark appears and the feature is turned on.

7. Touch **Favorite apps** or **Camera** to select which widget appears when you slide your finger from right to left on the lock screen.

8. Touch the clock and slide your finger from left to right while the phone is locked. An additional lock screen appears.

9. Touch the ✚ icon. A list of available widgets appears.

10. Touch a widget in the list. The widget is added to the lock screen.

11. Using the Google Now Voice Assistant

You can use Google's Voice Assistant to search for information, set reminders, send text messages, call contacts, and much more. To access the Voice Assistant, press the **Home** button twice quickly. Here are just a few of the commands that you can use:

1. **Search for**
2. **What is**
3. **Weather**
4. **Navigate to**
5. **Map of**
6. **Convert 36 degrees Celsius into Fahrenheit**
7. **Square root of 144**
8. **Listen to**
9. **Remind me to at**
10. **Set alarm for**
11. **Call**
12. **Send text to**
13. **Images of**
14. **Flight status of**

12. Blocking Calls, Notifications, Alarms, and the LED Indicator

If you do not wish to be disturbed during a certain time, you may turn on Blocking Mode to prevent the phone from receiving calls or notifying you of events. To turn on Blocking Mode:

1. Touch the ▦ key. The Home Screen menu appears.
2. Touch **Settings**. The Settings screen appears.
3. Touch **Device** at the top of the screen. The Personalization Settings screen appears.
4. Scroll down and touch **Blocking mode**. The Blocking Mode screen appears.
5. Touch the OFF switch next to 'Blocking mode'. Blocking mode is turned on and additional options become available.
6. Touch one of the options under 'Features' to customize the features that should be blocked.

7. Touch **Always** under 'Set time' to permanently turn on Blocking mode. You can always turn it off by touching the ON switch next to 'Blocking mode'.

8. Touch **Always** to clear the ✓ mark and set the times during which Blocking mode should automatically turn on. You can do this by touching the times next to 'From' and 'To'.

9. Touch **Allowed contacts** to customize the list of contacts that you wish to allow.

13. Viewing a Video while Using Another Application

The video player on the Galaxy Note 3 allows you to view a video in a movable window while viewing the Home screen or in another application. Only certain applications, such as Samsung's Internet application, are able to take advantage of this feature. To view a video while using another application, touch Video player when the phone asks you how you would like to play a video.

Then, touch the 🖼 icon. The video pops out and is displayed in a window. You can also move the window around by dragging it with your finger, or pause it by touching it once. When the video ends, the window automatically disappears.

14. Making the Phone Open Applications and Menus Faster (Advanced Tip)

You may notice that the Galaxy Note 3 can become a bit choppy when unlocking or switching from one screen to another. This effect is present because of the phone's animated transitions, which can be turned off under the developer settings. To turn off transition animations and speed up the phone:

Warning: This tip is for advanced users ONLY. Any attempt to edit any developer settings other than the ones mentioned in the steps below may bring harm to your phone.

1. Touch the 🖿 key. The Home Screen menu appears.

2. Touch **Settings**. The Settings screen appears.

3. Touch **General** at the top of the screen. The Permissions and Device Manager Settings appear.

4. Touch **About device**. The About screen appears.

5. Scroll down and touch **Build number** seven times. Developer options are now enabled.

6. Touch the 🖘 key and then touch **Developer options**. The Developer options appear.

7. Make sure all three of the following options are set to 'Off':

- **Windows animation scale**
- **Transition animation scale**
- **Animator duration scale**

Your phone will no longer lag when unlocking and opening applications.

15. Using Your Voice to Capture Photos

The camera on the Note 3 allows you to take a photo by saying either "Capture", "Shoot", "Smile", or "Cheese". To use your voice to capture photos:

1. Touch the ⬛ key. The Home Screen menu appears.
2. Touch **Settings**. The Settings screen appears.
3. Touch **Controls** at the top of the screen. The Controls Settings screen appears.
4. Touch **Voice control**. The Voice Control settings appear.
5. Touch the OFF switch next to 'Voice control'. The feature is turned on. Make sure that a ✓ mark appears next to 'Camera'. If it does not, touch **Camera** to enable the feature.

Note: The voice recognition in the Camera application is not always accurate, make sure that you speak clearly. For instance, dragging out the 'e' sound in the word 'Cheese' may cause the camera to misrecognize the word.

16. Turning the S Pen Pop-Up Window Off

The window that appears every time that you take the S Pen out of its holster may be turned off. To turn the S Pen pop-up window off:

1. Touch the ⬛ key. The Home Screen menu appears.
2. Touch **Settings**. The Settings screen appears.
3. Touch **Controls** at the top of the screen. The Controls Settings screen appears.
4. Touch **S Pen**. The S Pen settings appear.
5. Touch **Pen Detachment options**. The Pen Detachment options appear.
6. Touch **None**. The pop-up window will no longer appear.

17. Preventing S Pen Loss

The Note 3 can alert you with a sound if you take out your S Pen and then walk away from it while still holding your phone. To keep from losing your S Pen:

1. Touch the ▤ key. The Home Screen menu appears.
2. Touch **Settings**. The Settings screen appears.
3. Touch **Controls** at the top of the screen. The Controls Settings screen appears.
4. Touch **S Pen**. The S Pen settings appear.
5. Touch **S Pen keeper**. A confirmation dialog appears (the first time, and until you disable it).
6. Touch **OK**. The S Pen Keeper is turned on, and will alert you if you walk away from your stylus.

Note: This feature may not work if you are carrying your Note 3 in your hand when you walk away. When you put the Note 3 in your pocket, the notification will go off as soon as you take several steps.

Troubleshooting

Table of Contents

1. Galaxy Note 3 does not turn on

If the Galaxy Note 3 does not turn on:

- **Recharge the phone** - Use the included wall charger to charge the battery. If the battery power is extremely low, the screen will not turn on for several minutes. Do NOT attempt to use the USB port on your computer to charge the phone, as it will not work.
- **Replace the battery** - If you purchased the phone a long time ago, you may need to replace the battery.
- **Perform a Soft Reset** - If you have done one or both of the above and the phone still does not start, try performing a soft reset. To perform a soft reset:

  1. Press and hold the **Power** button and touch **Power off**. The phone turns off.
  2. Take out the battery and wait ten seconds. The phone resets.
  3. Re-insert the battery. Press and hold the **Power** button for three seconds. The phone turns on.

2. Galaxy Note 3 is not responding

If the phone is frozen or is not responding, try one or more of the following. These steps typically solve most problems on the phone:

- **Restart the phone** - If the phone freezes while running an application, try holding down the **Power** button. If this does not work, the best course of action is to perform a soft reset. Refer to *"Perform a Soft Reset"* on page 325 to learn how.
- **Remove Media** - Some downloaded applications or music may freeze up the phone. After restarting the phone, try deleting some of the media. To learn how to delete an application, refer to *"Uninstalling an Application"* on page 202. You may also erase all data at once and reset your phone to factory defaults by doing the following:

Warning: Any erased data is not recoverable.

1. Touch the ▣ key. The Home Screen menu appears.
2. Touch **Settings**. The Settings screen appears.
3. Touch **General** at the top of the screen. The General Settings screen appears.
4. Touch **Backup and reset**. The Backup and Reset screen appears.
5. Touch **Factory Data Reset**. The Reset screen appears.
6. Touch **Reset device**. A confirmation dialog appears.
7. Touch **Delete all**. All data is erased and the phone resets.

3. Can't make a call

If you cannot make a call using the phone, check the following:

- **Service** - If there are no bars shown at the top right of the screen, then the network does not cover you in your location. Try walking to a different location or even to a different part of a building.
- **Airplane Mode** - Make sure Airplane mode is turned off. If it is already off, try turning Airplane mode on for 15 seconds and then turning it back off. Refer to *"Turning Airplane Mode On or Off"* on page 256 to learn how to turn Airplane mode off.
- **Area code** - Make sure you dialed an area code with the phone number.
- **Restart** - Turn the phone off and back on, as this sometimes solves the problem.

4. Can't surf the web

Make sure the mobile network or Wi-Fi is turned on. Refer to *"Enabling or Disabling the Mobile Network"* on page 256 or refer to *"Setting Up Wi-Fi"* on page 251 to learn more.

5. Screen or keyboard does not rotate

If the screen does not turn or the full, horizontal keyboard is not showing when the phone is turned on its side, the problem may be one of the following issues:

- It is very likely that the application does not support the horizontal view.
- Make sure that the phone is not lying flat while rotating. Hold the phone upright to change the orientation in applications that support it.
- Make sure auto-rotate is turned on. Refer to *"Turning Auto Rotate On and Off"* on page 280 to learn more.

6. Low Microphone Volume, Caller can't hear you

If you are talking to someone who can't hear you, try removing any cases or other accessories, as these may cover up the microphone. If the caller cannot hear you at all, you may have accidentally muted the conversation. To learn how to turn mute on or off while on a call, refer to *"Using the Mute Function During a Voice Call"* on page 52.

If you find yourself accidentally muting the conversation often, there may be something covering up the light sensor, preventing the screen from dimming and locking the mute button. Taking off any accessories may also correct this problem, as some cases cover up the sensor completely.

7. Display does not adjust brightness automatically

If the phone does not dim in dark conditions or does not become brighter in bright conditions, try taking any cases or accessories off. Cases may block the light sensor at the top of the phone, located near the earpiece. Also, Auto Brightness may be turned off. To learn how to turn Auto Brightness on or off, refer to *"Adjusting the Brightness"* on page 273.

8. Application does not install correctly

Sometimes applications may not download or install correctly. If this happens, try canceling the download and re-downloading the application. If the application is already installed, try uninstalling an application and re-installing it. Refer to *"Uninstalling an Application"* on page 202 to learn more.

9. Touchscreen does not respond as expected

If there is a problem with the touchscreen, try the following in the order in which the steps appear:

1. Remove any cases or screen protectors from the touchscreen.
2. Clean the screen with a soft, damp cloth.
3. Wash and dry your hands thoroughly. Grease and other residue on your skin may cause the touchscreen to function improperly.
4. Restart your device to clear any temporary software bugs.

10. Phone becomes very hot

Some applications require a lot of power and may cause the phone to become hot to the touch. This is normal and should not affect your device's or battery's life span or performance.

11. Camera does not turn on

If the camera does not turn on, try one of the following:

- Make sure the phone's battery is charged and above 15%. The camera will not turn on if the battery level is too low.
- Free up some memory by transferring files to a PC or deleting files from your device, as there may not be enough remaining memory to store new pictures. The camera may not turn on if the memory is too low.
- Restart the phone and try turning on the camera again.

Index

Trademarks

www.ingramcontent.com/pod-product-compliance
Lightning Source LLC
Chambersburg PA
CBHW080407290526
45791CB00008BA/2175